MW01195324

Student Development and Social Justice

Tessa Hicks Peterson

Student Development and Social Justice

Critical Learning, Radical Healing, and Community
Engagement

Tessa Hicks Peterson
Pitzer College
Claremont, CA, USA

ISBN 978-3-319-57456-1   ISBN 978-3-319-57457-8   (eBook)
https://doi.org/10.1007/978-3-319-57457-8

Library of Congress Control Number: 2017943469

Cover illustration: © Image Source/Getty

Printed on acid-free paper

This Palgrave Macmillan imprint is published by Springer Nature
The registered company is Springer International Publishing AG
The registered company address is: Gewerbestrasse 11, 6330 Cham, Switzerland

FOREWORD

What are the causes of the traumas of injustice that are suffered by more and more in our increasingly troubled world? How can we mitigate these painful and damaging experiences? More specifically, how can each of us engage with our own pain and that of others so that we can begin to heal and positively transform our suffering? As the negative effects of modernity and globalization continue to intensify and social and political institutions seem unable or unwilling to respond effectively to multiple calls for justice, these questions have come to deeply concern many scholars and activists.

The book you are holding in your hands presents one of the most imaginative and practical sets of responses to the above questions to appear in the twenty-first century century. Tessa Hicks Peterson takes major steps in unearthing methods for understanding trauma-inducing structures and behaviors and suggests how to begin healing the web of life that has been so deeply damaged. One of the great strengths displayed by the author is her ability to combine and make accessible the healing and liberating techniques of a Buddhist peace activist, the largely unknown regenerative work of Latin American grassroots intellectuals, and the bold thinking of a new crop of contemplative and socially engaged Western academics. She does so in such a way that the concepts jump off the page with relevance. The book deftly spans the divide between social activism and cutting-edge social justice scholarship to advance important conversations about cultivating peace in remarkably new ways through higher education, pedagogy, and research.

With lucid expositions and careful scholarship, Hicks Peterson invites readers to reconsider and reconfigure the university in relation to surrounding and distant communities. Her vibrant writing and the action toolkits she offers make a persuasive case for anchoring university–community relations in a variety of critical and contemplative pedagogies, transpersonal inquiries, holistic mind–body practices, and non-exploitive community engagement models. She argues convincingly that providing an education that draws deeply from earth-centered living traditions and grassroots struggles for peace and justice can challenge stale belief systems, strengthen physical, emotional, and spiritual wellbeing, and foster and expand a much needed social justice consciousness amongst faculty and students alike. Such community-rooted education ensures that colleges and universities will remain accountable and responsible to the communities with which they engage. Investigating this profoundly thoughtful book can help us offset the generalized self-absorption and unbridled pessimism of our era.

Whether scholar or activist, professional or layperson, everyone will find valuable resources and pragmatic tools in this book. Crafted by a rigorous scholar, creative educator, and seasoned social activist, I believe this book will better prepare us to honestly and skillfully face our responsibilities to the many communities that are desperately fighting for economic survival and ethno-racial and cultural affirmation, locally and throughout the world. By the time one closes this book, one is left with a sense of the interbeing of all life that is the heart of all wisdom traditions. It puts the struggles we have in common into a new perspective and bolsters the hope and possibility of mitigating and transforming the pain and suffering of these challenging times.

Lourdes Arguelles, Ph.D., LMFT
Professor Emerita of Education and Cultural Studies
Claremont Graduate University
Claremont, CA, USA

Lopon (Senior Dharma Teacher)
Drikung Kyobpa Choling, Escondido, CA, USA

and

Senior Staff Therapist, The Clinebell Institute of Pastoral
Counseling and Psychotherapy, Claremont, CA, USA

ACKNOWLEDGEMENTS

Fundamental concepts presented in this book are inspired by great thinkers and movement leaders such as Paolo Freire, Mahatma Gandhi, Thich Nhat Hanh, bell hooks, and Martin Luther King Jr., as well as their lesser known comrades who worked arduously for social change by their sides. Additionally, there are a number of contemporary scholar-activists who have deeply informed this work, most of whom I've had the pleasure of knowing and learning from directly, and to whom I am most grateful. These include Lourdes Arguelles, Jeannette Armstrong, Beth Berila, Jose Calderon, Nadinne Cruz, Alane Daugherty, Leela Fernandes, Shawn Ginwright, Donald Harward, Tom Hayden, bell hooks, Jorge Ishizawa, Robin D.G. Kelley, Hala Khouri, Joanna Macy, John McKnight, Tania Mitchell, Margo Okazawa-Rey, Parker Palmer, Grimaldo Rengifo-Vasquez, Estela Roman, Daniel Siegal, Bryan Stevenson, Susan Phillips, Valorie Thomas, Larry Ward, and Kathleen Yep. I would like to offer specific and tremendous gratitude to the many students, faculty, community partners, and activist scholars who read versions or portions of this book and provided critical and valuable feedback, including Lourdes Arguelles, Oswaldo Armas, Hannah Bowman, Caroline Bourscheid, Rex Campbell, Jessica Chairez, Jim Conn, Nadinne Cruz, Ylen Chantal Esteves, Halford Fairchild, Ashley Finley, Nick Flores, Donald Harward, Barbara Holland, Barbara Junisbai, Hala Khouri, Cade Maldonado, Melinda Herrold-Menzies, Tricia Morgan, Sandy Mayo, Estela Roman, Alison Rollman, Omar Sefi, Andrea Smith, Erich Steinman, Christine Victorino, Kathleen Yep, and students in my Fall, 2016 and Spring, 2017 Research Methods for Community Change class. Special thanks are also due to my tireless editor, Jaida Samudra, who made me realize how immensely challenging it is to write clearly, concisely, and beautifully (but still I try). My gratitude also extends to my past students and community partners (here and in Mexico and Peru) who have taught me a great deal about community engagement and also much in matters of the mind, spirit, and heart. I also thank the many wise teachers and healers who have welcomed me into different cultural and healing traditions over the years (most especially, Julia Bogany, Tony Cerda, Cecelia Garcia, Hala Khouri, RobertJohn Knapp, Vicki Peterson, Sylvia Poareo, Estela Roman, Amen Santo, Vida Vierra, Luhui Isha, and Mati Waiya).

I deeply honor my ancestors for their sacrifices and traditions, as well as my nuclear family (my sister, Jessica, and my parents, Dennis and Stephanie), who were my first and continue to be my foremost teachers in all things love, community, and social change. Last but certainly not least, I have profound gratitude for my husband, John (whose dedication to justice, spirit, and family keeps me grounded as well as soaring), and our sons, Isaiah and Jonah (who remind me why I do this work every day, and also why I need to put it down to play ball, tell stories, and snuggle every night). This book is for them.

While my work is deeply informed by the knowledge I've received from other scholars, as well as insight from students, engagement with colleagues, teachings from elders, and lessons from community partners, all errors, erroneous assumptions, and instances of ignorance or arrogance are purely my own.

CONTENTS

LIST OF TABLES

PART I

Theories of Engagement

CHAPTER 1

Introduction: Know Peace, Know Justice

"No Justice! No Peace!" This rallying cry has been a mainstay in movements for social change since the 1965 civil rights march in Selma, Alabama to the 2017 women's march on Washington. As the message clearly indicates, without justice in the world, we cannot have peace—the two are intertwined. The message also suggests a threat of public disruption of peace in the streets unless the systems which have failed to recognize the plight of the oppressed are dismantled. It raises the power of the people to fight against the ideologies and structures that restrict the rights and access to opportunity of those they allege to serve. It mobilizes dissent as a democratic right and civic obligation to ensure that "liberty and justice for all" is not a slogan, but a lived virtue of the nation.

People mobilize around such concepts when they no longer find it tenable to live under the constraints of policies and social norms that denigrate their humanity, wellbeing, and political and economic opportunities (Palmer 2009). Such fights for peace and justice are usually led by those directly affected by oppression, with the support of allies and accomplices who see themselves as intricately bound to the fate of their neighbors. When changemakers convey their rage, hope, and demands with a force that is politically unstoppable and socially uncontainable, seemingly immovable social contracts (such as slavery, Jim Crow, suffrage, marriage inequality) either internally combust or are deliberately dismantled. Laws and norms are not ceded without struggle; sometimes that struggle is armed though it is often achieved through peaceful resistance

© The Author(s) 2018
T. Hicks Peterson, *Student Development and Social Justice*,
https://doi.org/10.1007/978-3-319-57457-8_1

informed by non-violent communication, civil disobedience, and a relentless faith that we *shall* overcome.

I propose that direct means for resisting fatalism, hopelessness, or complacency in the face of injustice today will also include a shift to *know peace and know justice*. This may be a subtle distinction but it involves a sense of peace and justice that is both political and affective, critically minded and heart centered, involving direct action as well as mindful contemplation. The move to *know peace* involves being willing to take care of ourselves and each other as part of *the struggle*. Cultivating a sufficiently peaceful inner world enables us to respond more mindfully and effectively to the enraging injustices around us. Practicing a love ethic that encourages the wellbeing of our minds, bodies, and spirits and that of our communities and planet enables us to deeply know peace in these places. The move to *know justice* involves understanding the root conditions that have led to instances of injustice, the people affected by it (even those who may seem culturally, politically, or geographically different and distant from oneself), and ways to shift the policies and practices that perpetuate it. It also involves knowing and sitting with the discomfort that arises from this understanding and cultivating the relationships, tools, and hope necessary to mobilize against injustice. It entails critically engaging with community and collectively envisioning a just society. To know peace and justice is to know that, at a fundamental level, our liberations are bound together.

Knowing peace and justice, intimately and politically, seems more important today than ever before. Granted, rampant instances of injustice and xenophobia are emblematic of the lack of recognition, and at times blatant exploitation, of the intellectual and cultural experiences of marginalized peoples that have long been a part of our nation's history. Such injustices are as common as the movements that arise to overturn them. Yet, strides made in recent decades in the realms of civil rights, social welfare, and economic equality are being destroyed at a rapidly increasing rate. In the United States, transnational connections are being challenged by ascendant ethno-nationalism and populist movements from the political right. The specific problems faced in the United States today are manifestations of global issues of disintegrating treaties, alliances, borders, social policies, and political processes. The polarization of our political parties is reflected in similar divisions and tensions among families and neighbors. Instead of building coalitions across differences to work to transform a system that benefits only the few to one that attends to the needs for justice and wellbeing of the many, we have seen an age-old trend re-emerge wherein those at the bottom are pitted against each other to fight for the crumbs.

Today's political climate is suffused with anger, fear, suspicion, and hopelessness. A great many people are walking around with a mix of political heartbreak and spiritual disillusionment compounded by the lack of basic rights and protection for the most vulnerable among us. The political has become more personal than ever. Entire communities suffer politically as well as emotionally and physically from a society that does not tend to the fullness of their humanity. These traumas of injustice leave our communities both disconnected and disempowered. "Trauma has been defined as anything that overwhelms our capacity to cope and respond and leaves us feeling helpless, hopeless and out of control" (Levine 1997). This indeed applies to many who are affected by interlocking forms of domination and injustice.[1] The trauma of injustice has become a collective inheritance with structural, psychological, social, physical, and spiritual repercussions.

Instead of perpetuating the blame-game or seeking quick fixes to get us out of our current predicament, we might consider looking to change it through the reinvigoration of our core values: equality, equity, democracy, freedom, justice, and love. Yet, reclaiming Dr. King's dream of the "beloved community" cannot be wished into being. We must each create it intimately and consistently within our own families, communities, schools, and workplaces. The effect of targeted groups being discriminated against or undervalued does not end with the unveiling of a new law, new multicultural center, or new promises by our elected officials. It requires that people on all sides of the political spectrum critically reflect on the biases and unwillingness that prevent them from becoming proximate to those who are different. It requires individuals to critically ponder if they resist working with sensitivity at the grassroots level and confront their own discomfort in order to convene across differences, practice deep listening, and mobilize collective agency for change. This necessitates that we bring together diverse segments of communities to engage in difficult dialogues with "the other" and together build the strategies that will help us bridge our many divides. It is also time to sharpen the tools of our economic–political analysis to understand and effectively challenge the new political climate that perpetuates such divides. Rather than being swept into separatist rhetoric and tactics, our only way forward is to adopt approaches that directly confront the pain of exclusion through social change strategies and alternative structures that make all communities feel heard, included, protected, and valued. Through critical reflection around how we treat ourselves, our families, our communities, and our planet, we can begin to thoughtfully link individual wellbeing and transformation to community wellbeing and social change.

When the pillars of a functioning democracy—equality, justice, and opportunity—seem more symbolic than achievable, our national community operates in a diminished state. We can no longer afford to ignore the necessity to care for and heal the self and others involved in social change. Unfortunately, the necessity to take care of personal and social wellbeing as part of the paradigm of changemaking has often been ignored or undervalued. This, despite the fact that almost every major social movement of the twentieth century included core strategies based on principles of peace, love, and faith. This, despite the fact that leading scholar activists broke the silence on this topic decades ago, calling ardently for healing spaces to be respected as part of the work for peace and justice.[2] The paucity of policies and practices that emphasize individual and collective wellbeing, healing, and empowerment, as they relate to community-building and social justice, is increasingly evident. As youth look to the future of the world they will soon inherit, they are demanding that we change this. They are demanding transparent dialogues about how to create respect for differences and opportunities for connection. They are demanding concerted efforts to disrupt the dominant narrative that our country is safe and inclusive for all people. They are demanding better role models and new movements to guide them. They are also demanding that our schools and our streets include spaces for healing.

BOOK OVERVIEW

This book responds to these demands by linking personal transformation with social change and threading together the wellbeing of individuals and communities. It recognizes that oppressive systems that diminish physical, mental, emotional, or spiritual wellbeing correlate with experiences of depression, anxiety, hopelessness, or complacency, which collectively threaten individuals' abilities to learn, connect, and thrive. This book suggests that institutions of higher educations can address these issues by recognizing that caring for students' wellbeing, distinct cultural identities, and sense of belonging nurtures academic success (Valenzuela 1999). Studies show that students who are supported in these areas demonstrate greater capacity for flourishing and self-realization, which in turn positively impacts academic achievement (Finley 2012a, b; Keyes and Haidt 2003; Schreiner 2010). For students to thrive in school and in life, they not only need the determination to succeed at their academic studies, but opportunities for engaged learning, diverse citizenship, and intra- and interpersonal development (Schreiner 2010).[3] They need schools that encourage them to take social responsibility for knowing peace and justice in themselves, their classrooms, and the communities around them.

Research indicates that integrating high-impact practices such as community engagement into the college experience supports not only students' civic and academic growth but also their sense of purpose, belonging, and wellbeing (Association of American Colleges and Universities 2013). Community engagement also increases individual and political awareness, bolsters a sense of social responsibility and civic duty, and creates opportunities for intercultural understanding. Connecting students, faculty, and classroom studies to social change movements, justice organizations, and grassroots efforts in local communities is thus one of the most effective and powerful tools for engaged learning and change making.

This book will demonstrate that with concerted efforts, institutions of higher education can guide young people into critical, contemplative community engagement for their own benefit and that of society. Providing guidance and support for young people to strengthen their skills for artful and non-violent communication, active listening, mindful awareness, critical consciousness, self-reflexivity, self-care, and strategies for social change provides a foundation for realizing these concepts in our world at large. This book is intended as a resource for anyone interested in connecting social change efforts with radical healing of self and community, including students interested in community change work, faculty involved with community-based teaching, service, or research, administrators attempting to link student wellbeing and development with community engagement, and community activists looking for justice-oriented partnerships with institutions of higher education.

The following concepts are central to the arguments and practices developed in this book:

- cultivating interconnection between self and "other" (including people within our own communities as well as those we do not yet know or understand) to harness the power that comes from *becoming proximate*;

- awakening political, cultural, and spiritual critical consciousness through mindful self-reflection and a willingness to *get uncomfortable*;
- disrupting oppression and injustice by *shifting dominant narratives* and addressing problems with a clear understanding of root conditions as well as a clear vision of the world we want to create instead;
- nurturing individual wellbeing and collective wellbeing of the community, thus *cultivating hope* that together we can heal our personal and shared traumas of injustice (Stevenson 2016); and
- facilitating *critical, contemplative, community engagement* partnerships and taking practical steps to integrate them into our academic institutions.

One of the primary tenets of this book is that community engagement enables us to become proximate to one another, which is a fundamental first step in making social change. "Community engagement" involves creating respectful, ethical and reciprocal partnerships among students, staff, and faculty of colleges and universities with community members, organizations and institutions. Community engagement is an umbrella term that collects together many forms of community-building, service provision, political organizing, civic engagement, participatory action research, advocacy, and accompaniment. Although there are multiple approaches to engagement, I am most interested here in exploring ones that explicitly work towards social justice. "Social justice" work involves confronting and transforming bias, exclusion, discrimination, and inequality in the individual and socio-political realms through changing relationships, perspectives, policies, structures, and systems to secure equitable and just treatment and access to human and civil rights for all individuals and groups. "The interlocking forces that create and sustain injustice" constitute what is known as "oppression," which itself is "restrictive, pervasive, and cumulative; socially constructed, categorizing, and group-based; hierarchical, normalized, and hegemonic; intersectional and internalized; and durable and mutable" (Bell 2016, pp. 5–6).

Not all forms of community engagement take a social justice approach, however. Some programs use the community as a kind of "living laboratory" for students to better understand how textbook theory plays out in "real life." Some community engagement models are apolitical; they aim to increase civic engagement without having students interrogate the factors that result in social injustice. Many community engagement programs are based in distinct disciplines that do not have a justice orientation. Feminist community engagement scholars have addressed this directly by encouraging "critical discourses" in community engagement programs that "challenge dominant conceptualizations of citizenship, offering transformative ways for students to practice citizenship that 'rely heavily' on the values and skills associated with social justice activism" (Iverson and James 2014, p. 20). In this vein, the focus of this book is to move beyond models that focus exclusively on student or disciplinary gains over social justice-oriented aims toward a model of critical, contemplative community engagement. Such a model values holistic learning, growth, and wellbeing across constituents and social change efforts amongst all participating communities. In order to resist, disrupt, and overturn injustice and oppression, we must be committed to learning critically about the systems we are a part of collectively and the attitudes we hold individually that perpetuate them. "Critical learning" involves cultivating socio-political awareness and consciousness about such systems, our roles in them, and means for their dismantling.

Political understanding and action must not be separated from emotional, physical, and spiritual wellbeing, however. Integrating self-awareness and radical healing with efforts to disrupt injustice is absolutely critical, lest attempts at change end up mirroring the violence, fragmentation, and inequality that already exist in our world today. This book therefore explores the entanglements of individual wellbeing with community wellbeing and the ways they connect to community engagement and social justice. It specifically concentrates on the "eudaimonic wellbeing" that results from finding purpose, realizing potential, and engaging with self and the world in a meaningful way. Eudaimonic wellbeing is distinct from "hedonic wellbeing," which centers on being in a positive affective state, that is, being happy and satisfied with life, without necessarily linking to self-realization or social engagement.[4] It necessitates moving towards the sense of fulfillment and belonging that comes as a result of an investment in both the realization and purposefulness of self *in conjunction with others.*

Interests of this book include both cultivating eudaimonic wellbeing as well as advocating for the societal conditions that support it, such as "sound infrastructure, opportunities for a good education, jobs and healthcare, and ensuring that people feel safe and secure" (Roumi qtd in Simons 2017, p. 4). The "pursuit of happiness" as a collective goal of our nation is as old as the nation itself, as noted in our own Declaration of Independence. This "fundamental human goal" is recognized as a pillar of a functioning society and draws on "psychological wellbeing, ecology, health, education, culture, living standards, time use, community vitality and good governance" (Simons 2017, p. 4). Wellbeing is thus intrinsically an individual and collective experience intricately joined to issues of peace and justice.[5]

This book presents diverse theoretical frameworks for social change and wellbeing as well as provides hands-on activities for those interested in more intentionally connecting theory to practice. The book is divided into two parts. Part I, *Theories of Engagement*, consists of Chaps. 1–4, which introduce key concepts, provide theoretical analyses of the main issues, offer critical reflection activities, and present models for community engagement. Part II, *Praxis of Engagement*,[6] consists of Chaps. 5–7, which bring community engagement models to life by presenting practical activities to be used in community partnerships or the community engagement classroom, listing possible student learning and community impact outcomes, discussing program assessment design, and providing examples of changes that can be made at the institutional level. These chapters (as well as the community engagement policies and syllabus samples available in the appendices) are intended to be of particular use for teachers and administrators attempting to integrate critical, contemplative critical engagement into institutions of higher education.

Following this introductory Chap. 1, Chap. 2, "Disrupting injustice and mobilizing social change," examines tangible steps towards making meaningful social change around issues of injustice in our communities. Educating and mobilizing students to take social responsibility for disrupting injustice requires that we provide them with relevant social knowledge and political strategies to become effective agents of change. The unique theoretical frameworks in this chapter speak across a broad range of disciplines, values, and methods, including indigenous knowledge systems (Apffel-Marglin and PRATEC 1998), theories of critical pedagogy (Freire 1970; Shor 1992), healing justice (Ginwright 2015; Macy and Brown 1998), and asset-based community development (Kretzmann and McKnight 1993). Collectively, they offer strategies for challenging oppression and creating an interconnected, beloved community. The chapter explores a four-part process that involves becoming proximate to communities and issues of injustice, shifting the historical and political narratives that exist about these injustices, getting uncomfortable with our own ignorance, arrogance, apathy, or pain, and, finally, cultivating hope as a collective act to drive social change efforts (Stevenson 2016).

Chapter 3, "Self-awareness and radical healing," examines the development of the mind, body, spirit, and social consciousness so that students are more equipped to grapple with understandings of self, other, and purpose in the world. This necessarily includes student awareness of values, identity, positionality, and personal wounds. This chapter explores positionality (how one sees the world and is seen in the world according to race, class, culture, gender, ability, citizenship, sexual identity and orientation, etc.) (Anzaldua 1987; Simons et al. 2011; McIntosh 1988, 2009), valuing interconnectedness and a love ethic (hooks 2000; King qtd in Washington 1986), mindfulness and self-realization practices (Berila 2015; Daughtery 2014; Hahn 2003), personal trauma and the traumas of injustice (Levine 2010), and the role of radical healing for individuals and communities (Lorde 1988; Watkins and Shulman 2008). These various components of self-awareness and healing collectively support students to become engaged and effective members of their communities.

Chapter 4, "Critical, contemplative community engagement," explores how to enact community engagement efforts so that student learning and community impacts embody a critical examination and interruption of the root causes and conditions of injustice, while promoting contemplative practices that fortify the wellbeing of individuals and collectives. This chapter discusses social justice-oriented frameworks for developing reciprocal social change partnerships that recognize the assets of the community while also addressing what the community has identified as problems and injustices (Calderon 2007; Keith 1995; Kezar and Rhoads 2001; Kivel 2007; Lewis 2004; Mitchell 2008; Vaccaro 2009; Ward and Wolf-Wendel 2000). This form of engagement requires a deep level of critical self-reflection that links the development of self and other through community engagement. This chapter examines the teaching and learning theories, partnership development factors, and social justice aims of the Critical, Contemplative, Community Engagement model.

Part II, *Praxis of Engagement* begins with Chap. 5, "Community Engagement Outcomes and Activities," which is organized around the four key processes of the Critical, Contemplative, Community Engagement model: becoming proximate, shifting narratives, getting uncomfortable, and cultivating hope (Stevenson 2016). Tangible tools presented include experiential activities for use in community partnerships and classrooms; possible student learning and community impact outcomes; community partnership considerations; and student reflections. Readers are encouraged to consider how the arguments presented in Part I, *Theories of Engagement*, come to life through the tangible and practical toolbox for community engagement that is offered throughout Part II, *Praxis of Engagement*.

Chapter 6 is an evaluation case study of "Healing ourselves, healing our communities," a paired course, local–global community engagement program conducted through Pitzer College in 2010. The program enacted the frameworks and strategies discussed in previous chapters through the study and practice of native healing traditions for personal and social change with local indigenous elders and youth in both the USA and Mexico. A direct assessment project focusing on these two courses provides an evaluation of the holistic academic and personal development of students, measuring learning across multiple objectives, including self-knowledge, community knowledge, and local–global connections. This chapter incorporates excerpts from student papers reflecting on the impact of developing raised consciousness, self-awareness, and self-care practices as well as an understanding of the global conditions impacting local indigenous knowledge traditions. This chapter provides concrete tools (student learning outcomes, assessment rubrics, and evaluation designs) to assist teachers and community partners interested in crafting similar programs and assessments.

The concluding Chap. 7, "Transforming Our Ourselves, Transforming Institutions," incorporates strategies for creating organizational change in colleges and universities. While individual change is critical, it will not transform institutions alone. For critical, contemplative community engagement to be sustained in these spaces, it needs to be better recognized, valued, and promoted in policy, such as in faculty appointments, promotion, and tenure reviews and in student graduation requirements. Readers are directed to sample syllabi and policies that may be used as transferable models. Using a social movement and organizing model to make such changes links the aspirations of participatory democracy both on and off campus. Finally, this chapter reflects on the limitations and opportunities connected to the research, theoretical models, and praxis components presented in this book, and suggests some next steps.

POSITIONALITY OF THE AUTHOR

Given that much of the work in this book derives from research I have conducted around intercultural understanding and community engagement, professional experiences I have had in civil rights and anti-bias education organizations, and my experiences teaching and directing community engagement programs, it seems vital to locate myself and my institution in this conversation. Acknowledging and reflecting on my own positionality stems from a commitment to an anti-racist and feminist methodology. Sharing the identities, experiences, and perspectives that filter my work is intended to disrupt positivist notions of scientific research as value free or objective.

My positionality is grounded in a family history which greatly informs who I am and how I see the world. My family story is one that traverses lines of both privilege and oppression based on religion, class, race, and political beliefs. Some of my family members have been persecuted and discriminated against because of their Jewish identity. Others in my family have been afforded considerable resources based on the confluence of their white race, upper-middle class status, and Christian religion, which helped pave the path towards their economic success and landholding across generations. While one set of grandparents was being blacklisted in the 1950s for their radical political engagement, another set was building their "American dream"—two separate, successful businesses—which were undeniably built on the land and backs of Mexicans and Native Americans as a result of the Homesteading Act. My parents responded to both sets of privileges and instances of oppression by becoming ardent Marxist organizers, artists, and teachers. Their all-encompassing social justice activism instilled in me from a young age the sacred notion that "activism is my rent for living on the planet" (Walker 2014).

I became involved with social justice work at the age of 16 through a number of very intensive trainings with the National Conference for Community and Justice. In the 25 years since, I have alternated between roles as participant, facilitator, trainer, director, and consultant of anti-bias/social justice education programs. As an upper-middle class, straight, cis-gendered, white woman doing this work, I have had ample opportunity to explore how my own privileges not only afford me multiple advantages and safety nets in my personal and professional life but also how vastly different my lived experiences are from many of the students, colleagues, and community members I work with who negotiate multiple forms of oppression. Yet, even with this heightened consciousness, I know that growing up and living within a society that is founded upon and carried out on an uneven and unjust playing field, I am a product of a societal conditioning that clouds my vision of true equality and justice. My work to disrupt personal and structural acts of bias and oppression, while nurturing social change and wellbeing, is a lifelong commitment.

My professional move from work within civil rights and human relations organizations to the academy began in 2006 when I first started teaching at Pitzer College. Pitzer is a small, private, liberal arts college located on original Californian native territory in the eastern edge of Los Angeles County, surrounded by a diverse region in the midst of major demographic shifts, environmental devastation, regional inequity, and a burgeoning of grassroots activism. Pitzer was founded in 1963, greatly influenced by the social movements of those times, and undergirded by a commitment to bridge activism and academia. The College's mission is to "produce engaged, socially responsible citizens of the world through academically rigorous, interdisciplinary liberal arts education emphasizing social justice, intercultural understanding, and environmental sensitivity" (Pitzer College 2017). My work as both an administrator and a professor at Pitzer focuses primarily around advancing community engagement policies and structures within the College and teaching interdisciplinary community engagement courses in partnership with prisons, day labor centers, urban farms, tribal nations, and other local community organizations.

Major portions of this book are informed by findings from an action research evaluation I conducted at Pitzer (Hicks 2009). It utilized the college as a case study in which to examine the benefits and limitations of community engagement for students, faculty, staff, community organizations, and community members. Of primary interest to the study was the role of community-campus partnerships in expanding traditional realms of knowledge construction, ownership, and distribution as well as in moving from short-term, transactional service programs to longitudinal, transformational social justice endeavors. This research, a subsequent assessment of a specific academic program that wove together radical healing and community engagement (see Chap. 6), and general reflections from my own experiences teaching and directing community engagement and anti-bias education programs inform the foundations of this book.

I am extremely conscious of the privilege, access, and accountability that I have as a white academic writing a book about social justice issues. My understanding of the issues presented in this book has been gleaned from social justice scholars and activists whose work has profoundly shifted my understandings of identity, healing, wellbeing, and community building. The majority of these antecedents are people of color who speak, write, and teach about justice issues from critical personal perspectives and rigorous socio-political analysis. I have tremendous gratitude for the generosity of the teachings I have received from Black feminist thought, Latinx epistemology, Indigenous knowledge, Buddhist philosophy, and ancient wisdom traditions. This book attempts to honor the work of these great thinkers, healers, and movement leaders that have come before me and to add to this chorus of voices a renewed commitment to weaving together critical learning, radical healing, and community engagement.

Notes

1. As scholar activist Shawn Ginwright has pointed out, "most cases of post-traumatic stress disorder (PTSD) among youth of color are actually ongoing, and persistent. Trauma for these young people, therefore, needs to be diagnosed within a Persistent Traumatic Stress Environment (PTSE), which more accurately focuses on both the individual and the environmental context in which trauma occurs [...] Over time, chronic stress also erodes hope, sense of agency, and the ability to see a brighter future" (2015, pp. 3 and 6).
2. See, for example, Alexander (2003), Anzaldúa (1987), Anzaldúa and Moraga (1981), hooks (1994), Lorde (1988), and West (1999).
3. "This sense of community and level of psychosocial well-being contributes to their persistence to graduation and allows them to gain maximum benefit from being in college" (Schreiner 2010).
4. "Be it flourishing (Keyes), well-being (Diener), wholeness (Long), thriving (Schreiner), identity (Magolda) or a myriad of other terms we use on our campuses, a common thread in this effort, as Don Harward has so persistently argued, is our conceptual reach back to the Aristotelian concept of eudaemonia. It is not about some superficial or even transient experience of being happy or even about feeling happy, but rather it turns to that more important, sustainable quality of purpose that underlies our sense of self, our motivation to persist, our trust in agency, and our responsibility to act for the common good" (Reich 2013, p. 2).
5. Happiness and collective wellbeing are increasingly being seen as connected to "the duty and the role of the government to create the right conditions for people to choose to be happy." A recent Los Angeles Times article highlighted manifestations of this in governments across the globe: "in 2013, Venezuela created a Vice Ministry of Supreme Social Happiness and Ecuador named a state secretary of *buen vivir,* or good living ... The United Nations has called on member states to place more emphasis on happiness as a measure for social and economic development. The organization now publishes a "World Happiness Report" (Simons 2017, p. 4). In addition, we can point to the Himalayan

kingdom of Bhutan's institution of a Gross National Happiness Index (in the early 1970s), and the United Arab Emirates' creation of a minister of happiness position in its cabinet in 2016 (ibid).

6. Praxis can be understood as theory + action + reflection. As the Freire Institute (2015) explains, "It is not enough for people to come together in dialogue in order to gain knowledge of their social reality. They must act together upon their environment in order critically to reflect upon their reality and so transform it through further action and critical reflection."

REFERENCES

Alexander, M. J. (Ed.). (2003). Sing, whisper, shout, pray. *Feminist visions for a just world*. Edgework Books.

Anzaldúa, G. (1987). *Borderlands: La frontera* (Vol. 3). San Francisco: Aunt Lute.

Anzaldúa, G. & Moraga, C. (Eds.). (1981). *This Bridge Called My Back: Writings by Radical Women of Color*. London: Persephone Press.

Apffel-Marglin, F., & PRATEC. (1998). *The spirit of regeneration: Andean culture confronting western notions of development*. New York: Zed Books.

Association of American Colleges and Universities. (2013). *It takes more than a major: Employer priorities for college learning and student success*. Washington, DC: Hart Research Associates. Retrieved March 3, 2017, from https://www.aacu.org/sites/default/files/files/LEAP/2013_EmployerSurvey.pdf.

Bell, L. A. (2016). *Teaching for diversity and social justice*. New York, NY: Routledge.

Berila, B. (2015). *Integration mindfulness into anti-oppression pedagogy*. New York, NY: Routledge.

Calderon, J. Z. (Ed.). (2007). *Race, poverty, and social justice: Multidisciplinary perspectives through service learning*. Sterling, VA: Stylus Publishing.

Daugherty, A. (2014). *From mindfulness to heartfulness: A journey of transformation through the science of embodiment*. Bloomington, IN: Balboa Press.

Finley, A. (2012a). *Making progress? What we know about the achievement of liberal education outcomes*. Washington, DC: AA&U.

Finley, A. (2012b). The joy of learning: The impact of civic engagement on psychosocial well-being. *Diversity and Democracy, 3*, 8–10.

Freire, P. (1970). *Pedagogy of the oppressed* (M. B. Ramos, Trans.). New York, NY: Continuum Publishing.

Freire Institute. (2015, June 27). *Concepts used by Paulo Freire*. Retrieved May 28, 2016, from http://www.freire.org/paulo-freire/concepts-used-by-paulo-freire.

Ginwright, S. (2015). *Hope and healing in urban education: How urban activists and teachers are reclaiming matters of the heart*. New York, NY: Routledge.

Hahn, T. N. (2003). *Creating true peace: Ending violence in yourself, your family, your community, and the world*. New York: Free Press.

Hicks, T. (2009). *Engaged scholarship and education: A case study on the pedagogy of social change*. Unpublished Dissertation, Claremont Claremont Graduate University, Claremont, CA.

hooks, b. (1994). *Teaching to transgress: Education as the practice of freedom*. New York, NY: Routledge.

hooks, b. (2000). *All about love: New visions*. New York, NY: William Morrow.

Iverson, S. V. D., & James, J. H. (2014). *Feminism and community engagement: An overview*. In *feminist community engagement: Achieving praxis* (pp. 9–27). Palgrave Macmillan US.

Keith, M. (1995). The irony of service: Charity, project, and social change in service-learning. *Michigan Journal of Community Serivce Learning, 2*, 19–32.

Keyes, C. L., & Haidt, J. (Eds.). (2003). *Flourishing: Positive psychology and the life well-lived*. Washington, DC: American Psychological Association.

Kezar, A., & Rhoads, R. (2001). The dynamic tensions of service-learning in higher education: A philosophical perspective. *The Journal of Higher Education, 72*, 148–171.

Kivel, P. (2007). Social service or social change. In Incite (Ed.), *The revolution will not be funded: Beyond the non-profit industrial complex* (pp. 129–149). Cambridge, MA: South End Press.

Kretzmann, J. P., & McKnight, J. (1993). *Building communities from the inside out*. Evanston, IL: Center for Urban Affairs and Policy Research, Neighborhood Innovations Network.

Levine, P. A. (1997). *Waking the tiger: Healing trauma*. Berkeley, CA: North Atlantic Books.

Levine, P. A. (2010). *Healing trauma: A pioneering program for restoring the wisdom of your body*. Boulder, CO: Sounds True Publishing.

Lewis, T. L. (2004). Service learning for social change? Lessons from a liberal arts college. *Teaching Sociology, 32*(1), 94–108.

Lorde, A. (1988). *Sister outsider: Essays and speeches by Audre Lorde*. Berkeley, CA: Crossing Press.

Macy, J., & Brown, M. Y. (1998). *Coming back to life: Practices to reconnect our lives, our world*. Gabriola Island, BC: New Society Publishers.

McIntosh, P. (1998). 'White privilege: Unpacking the invisible knapsack' *peace and freedom magazine* (pp. 10–12). Philadelphia, PN, July/August, 1989.

McIntosh, P. (2009). *White privilege: An account to spend*. Minnesota: The Saint Paul Foundation.

Mitchell, T. D. (2008). Traditional vs. critical service-learning: Engaging the literature to differentiate two models. *Michigan Journal of Community Service Learning, 14*(2).

Palmer, P. J. (2009). *A hidden wholeness: The journey toward an undivided life*. San Francisco, CA: Wiley.

Pitzer College. (2017). Mission and values. Retrieved August 25, 2017, from https://www.pitzer.edu/about/mission-and-values/.

Reich, J. (2013). *The well-being and flourishing of students: Considering well-being, and its connection to learning and civic engagement, as central to the mission of higher education*. Washington, DC: Bringing Theory to Practice.

Schreiner, A. L. (2010). *The "thriving quotient": A new vision for student success*. American College Personnel Association and Wiley Periodicals.

Shor, I. (1992). *Culture wars: School and society in the conservative restoration*. Chicago, IL: University of Chicago Press.

Simons. (2017, March 6). Happiness minister takes job seriously. *Los Angeles Times* (p. 1).

Simons, L., Fehr, L., Black, N., Hoogerwerff, F., Georganas, D., & Russell, B. (2011). The Application of Racial Identity Development in Academic-Based Service Learning. *International Journal of Teaching and Learning in Higher Education*. 23(1), 72–83.

Stevenson, B. (2016, March 29). American injustice: Mercy, humanity and making a difference. In *Criminal Justice Symposium*. Claremont, CA: Pomona College.

Vaccaro, A. (2009). Racial identity and the ethics of service learning as pedagogy. In S. Evans, C. Taylor, M. Dunlap & D. Miller (Eds.), *African Americans and community engagement in higher education* (pp. 119–134). Albany, NY: SUNY Press.

Valenzuela, A. (1999). *Subtractive schooling: U.S.-Mexican youth and the politics of caring*. New York, NY: State University of New York Press.

Walker, A. (2014). Activism is my price for living on the planet. In *Alice Walker: Beauty in truth*. Documentary film, written and directed by Pratibha Parmar, Kali Films. Aired 7 February, PBS.

Ward, K., & Wolf-Wendel, L. (2000). Community-centered service learning moving from doing for to doing with. *American Behavioral Scientist, 43*(5), 767–780.

Washington, J. M. (Ed.). (1986). *A testament of hope: The essential writings and speeches of Martin Luther King, Jr.* New York, NY: Harper Collins.

Watkins, M., & Shulman, H. (2008). *Towards psychologies of liberation*. New York, NY: Palgrave Macmillan.

West, C. (1999). *The Cornel West Reader*. New York: Basic Civitas.

CHAPTER 2

Disrupting Injustice and Mobilizing Social Change

This chapter will explore how to build strong communities that nurture individual and collective wellbeing while shifting paradigms of injustice. This chapter is guided by a four-step framework developed by criminal justice activist and lawyer, Bryan Stevenson (2016)[1]:

Step (1) *Becoming proximate*: In order to really understand and care about the complex social problems plaguing our society, it is necessary to get up close to them. Comprehending the nuances and urgency of any social issue requires becoming proximate to the lived experiences of injustice, and those living it.

Step (2) *Shifting the narrative*: Once we more intimately understand and care about a social issue and the communities it affects, we begin shifting the narrative we hold about that issue. The problem at hand often reflects a grander, dominant narrative that sustains the status quo, so recognizing and actively altering its narrative can disrupt broader systems of injustice.

Step (3) *Getting uncomfortable*: Shifting the narrative about a social problem unsettles one's beliefs, assumptions, and participation in oppressive structures in society. Coming into critical consciousness can elicit anger, fear, grief, or apathy, and can tap into the collective pain of oppression. This process necessarily involves an encounter with emotional discomfort and cognitive dissonance.

Step (4) *Cultivating hope*: We cannot rely merely on our proximity to others and raised consciousness alone to bring social change to fruition; we must also have a strong sense of purpose and hope propelling us. Cultivating

© The Author(s) 2018
T. Hicks Peterson, *Student Development and Social Justice*,
https://doi.org/10.1007/978-3-319-57457-8_2

hope involves connecting with others around shared lived experiences, radical visions of what our world could look like, and action strategies that will take us there. While Stevenson's step-by-step model frames this chapter, it is supplemented with concrete strategies for promoting social change that come from other scholar activists around the globe. Their methods draw on indigenous knowledge systems, theories of critical pedagogy, healing justice, and asset-based community development. Specific examples of what this looks like in action are sprinkled throughout the theoretical frameworks suggested.

Because theory should never be divorced from practice, this chapter also grounds these concepts in personal experience by promoting an iterant cycle of critical reflection. Each section concludes by offering a variety of proposed reflection prompts so the reader can explore the meaning, purpose, and growth that arises from actualizing social justice activism or community engagement experiences. Due to the intimate and sometimes challenging nature of critical learning and radical healing, it is recommended that readers create a conducive place in which to become centered and purposeful as they participate in these activities. I suggest that readers respond to the critical reflection prompts by journal-writing, letting the questions be a springboard for deeper considerations. Although the questions are seemingly simple, they can prompt deep personal and sometimes painful reflections so readers should be prepared for and mindful of any challenging reactions that surface. The mindfulness activities provided in Chap. 3 can also be put to use when responding to tough questions, as they enable readers to more effectively navigate any reactions triggered by provocative topics. The theories, critical reflection prompts and application strategies offered throughout this book can also be explored as a collective experience with others. Creating a "community of practice" (Lave and Wenger 1991)—whether amongst classmates within a course, colleagues in a community engagement support network, or in conversation with community partners—will allow the reader to engage in contemplative listening and meaningful dialogue around ideas or challenges that the questions of the book elicit. It is often in this space of experiential learning and collective critical reflection that our greatest insights emerge. When mobilized, the social change models presented and personal reflection ignited can have a profound impact on structural problems and the individuals who rally together to change them.

Becoming Proximate

Becoming proximate requires personally showing up in the context of injustice and social suffering. People who have never suffered from poverty, discrimination, mass incarceration, homelessness, or other social problems can only learn a limited amount about these issues from books or other media. Becoming proximate respectfully and ethically involves getting out of one's comfort zone and opening one's mind and heart to learn, care, and engage. At the same time, in this process there is great danger of exacerbating voyeurism, exploitation, or the distanced ethnographic gaze on "the Other."[2]

To avoid perpetuating "poverty tourism," individuals must investigate their motives for getting involved in social change activism.[3] Critically reflecting on one's motivations is explored in depth in Chap. 3, but we can note here the distinction between community engagement based on pity or curiosity and that founded on a sense of moral obligation and interdependence. The latter requires individuals to extend beyond wanting to "help" those that are suffering and instead becoming accountable to the interlocking systems of domination that marginalize some people while benefiting others. As Lila Watson and her Aboriginal activist group warned, "If you have come to help me, you are wasting your time. But if you have come because your liberation is bound up with mine, then let us work together" (1970).[4]

The shift from a shallow sense of moral obligation to a heartfelt commitment to work alongside others around issues of injustice cannot be forced. It emerges organically from authentic engagement, respect, understanding, and empathy built upon genuine experiences of proximity. Getting to know and truly care about each other leads to a deep understanding that every person's happiness or suffering is interdependent with others, including those that seem removed by differences in race, religion, culture, or location. Thich Nhat Hanh, the acclaimed monk and founder of Engaged Buddhism, describes the degrees of compassion and equanimity that can occur when we develop deep relationships with people different from ourselves: "In a deep relationship, there's no longer a boundary between you and the other person. You are her and she is you. Your suffering is her suffering. Your understanding of your own suffering helps your loved one to suffer less. Suffering and happiness are no longer individual matters" (2015, p. 21).

Cultivating such deep relationships first involves immersing oneself in environments where social problems are playing out and forming connections with those facing those problems. This must be done thoughtfully, using non-exploitative strategies such as working through an interlocutor who is known and respected by both parties and can facilitate relationship building based on mutual respect, clear communication, and reciprocity. The practices of deep listening, open-mindedness, humility, and patience are also inherent to becoming proximate. So too is an authentic commitment to exercise social responsibility and act as an ally around the issue at hand. As such, one must critically reflect on personal accountability or complicity in the problems that bring suffering to others. Through this process, one's heart seems to break open as they become intimate with the pain and suffering of real human beings facing real social problems and a sense of interconnectedness is deepened.

While everyone can learn something by becoming proximate to the experiences of another, becoming proximate to one's own personal experiences of suffering or injustice is another critical act of engagement, as history shows that the communities directly affected by injustice are typically the ones who lead movements to change it. In instances where one is advocating around social issues that directly impact one's own community, the process of proximation allows greater reflection and reflexivity about one's own lived experiences. This process of making the personal political involves reclaiming one's own expertise on the issue and discussing experiences of injustice with others who are similarly impacted.

Reflecting critically on one's own lived experience usually leads to formulating theories about the causes of injustice. This is what radical Brazilian pedagogist Paolo Freire called "naming the world," meaning naming the issues, responses, and associated power structures that frame one's experiences of injustice (1970). Renowned feminist scholar, bell hooks, has written extensively about the liberatory and healing effect that can emerge from crafting theories around one's own lived experience:

> I came to theory because I was hurting—the pain within me was so intense that I could not go on living. I came to theory desperate, wanting to comprehend—to grasp what was happening around and within me. Most importantly, I wanted to make the hurt go away. I saw in theory then a location for healing. (hooks 1994, p. 59)

Defining the larger political and social contexts of injustice raises both consciousness and empowerment amongst those who have suffered. Becoming critically conscious of the injustices that impact one's own community can be unsettling, but it is also a powerful, and, as hooks reminds us, healing process. Collectively raising consciousness from the inside out about issues of structural domination cultivates the power awareness and agency necessary to begin effectively dismantling the narratives and deconstructing the systems that cause suffering.

At the same time, becoming proximate to communities other than one's own can generate solidarity, another important ingredient of successful social change. According to Freire's conceptualization of *critical pedagogy*, a primary step toward challenging oppression is creating authentic relationships based on mutual learning, critical reflection, and reciprocity where a liberatory education of self and other can take place.[5] As such, critical pedagogy is both a methodology of teaching and learning and a site for socio-political activism. It is a community-based educational model that aims to deconstruct hierarchies of power and knowledge by re-centering common knowledge (knowledge/wisdom of the people, formed by lived experience) in a consciousness-raising process that mobilizes communities toward grassroots social change. Elevating respect for the knowledge of those most marginalized (and sometimes least educated) amongst us nullifies the idea that knowledge is a commodity (Freire 1970).

In my own experience of becoming proximate, I have been profoundly impacted by teaching college courses inside a local men's prison through a critical pedagogy approach. Following the Inside-Out Prison Exchange format, a dozen "outside" college students from my university merge with a dozen "inside" incarcerated college students to take a credit-bearing course, "Healing Arts and Social Change" within the prison.[6] The course explores the theories and practices of self-awareness, critical consciousness, and social change on which this book is based. Over the course of the semester, both inside and outside students are transformed deeply by becoming proximate and confronting their differences. The connection and learning stimulated by this act of engagement is simultaneously cognitive (intellectual) and affective (emotional). I, too, become deeply involved in the dialectic, reciprocal exchange of knowledge, consciousness-raising, and connection with this unique mix of students (Pompa and Crabbe 2004). The liberatory education that we co-create inside this punitive system temporarily disrupts the dehumanizing and oppressive norms that operate within the prison while simultaneously empowering both inside and out-side students to critically develop their own political and personal aware-ness. Simply being proximate to the workings of the prison and the experiences of those trapped inside has greatly deepened my and my outside students' comprehension of and commitment to dismantling the American system of incarceration.[7]

Through this proximation, both my mind and my heart opened to the realities of injustice and deep pain that exist in and as a result of our system of incarceration. With this, I realized the importance not only of becoming proximate to the issues of injustice or the communities facing such issues but also to the despair we feel about these issues. Systems theorist and Buddhist philosopher Joanna Macy calls this an act of allowing ourselves to feel "our pain for the world" (1998, p. 5).[8] Through her decades of facilitating activist groups around the world, she finds that this occurs best by forming genuine relationships with a community of people also invested in and willing to collectively reflect on the issues. Macy's version of be-coming proximate occurs through "the work that reconnects," a group process intended to "help people uncover and experience their innate connections with each other and with the systemic, self-healing powers in the web of life, so that they may be enlivened and motivated to play their part in creating a sustainable civilization" (Macy and Brown 1998, p. 58). Becoming proximate in these terms entails coming together in a group to participate in facilitated dialogues that create an atmosphere of trust, support, and safety. These dialogues cultivate the compassion and insight that in turn "arouse desire to act" (p. 60). The goals of the "work that reconnects" include the following:

- providing people with the opportunity to experience and share with others their innermost responses to the present condition of our world;
- reframing their pain for the world as evidence of their interconnect-edness in the web of life, and hence of their power to take part in its healing;
- providing methods by which people can experience their interde-pendence with, their responsibility to, and the inspiration they can draw from past and future generations, and other life-forms; and
- enabling people to support each other in clarifying their intention and affirming their commitment to the healing of the world (ibid).

The above approach is similar to the qualities of becoming proximate known as "*acompanimiento*" (accompaniment) that is a prominent practice in many Andean communities.[9] Through the connections of my mentor, over a dozen years ago I had the honor of accompanying a number of rural, native communities of *campesinos* and affiliated grassroots organizers throughout Peru with PRATEC (*Proyectos Andinos de Tecnologías Campesinas*, Andean Projects of Peasant Technologies).[10] This experience working with Quechua, Lamista, and Ayamara native communities and their *mestizo* allies helped me understand new ways of thinking about community building, wellbeing, and the connection of the personal to the collective. Through their teachings around the importance of mutual nurturing, interconnectedness, and reciprocity in communities, I came to see how these values must be embodied in all of our relationships, especially when attempting to accompany communities outside our own that are working for cultural affirmation in the face injustice.[11]

"Accompaniment" means sharing and participating with a community in their ways of being from a position of epistemological situatedness that honors the knowledge and lived experiences of the community (Tomlinson and Lipstiz 2013). The one who accompanies considers how best to participate in a relationship characterized by equivalency, respect, support, and thoughtful engagement. This involves critical reflection of one's positionality and any engrained beliefs that could inadvertently devalue the community one wishes to accompany. As my Peruvian mentor said, "Whoever wants to exercise the role of accompanist must realize s/he has been subjected to colonization. Colonization is dual" (Ishizawa 2006, p. 8). As important as relational accountability and reciprocity are to accompaniment, so too is the commitment to practicing decolonization and fostering intercultural understanding (which will be explored in greater length in Chap. 3).

Becoming proximate usually leads to caring deeply about a social justice issue and the desire to become an ally in working to change the social structures that sustain that form of injustice. Becoming an effective ally is delicate work, however. The desire to advocate for others can sometimes result in usurping their power to speak for themselves. Discovering what kind of support those you accompany want from you is of critical importance when getting involved in any social change movement.

"Accomplice" and "co-conspirator" are other terms that approximate the concept of being an accompanist. These terms have gained traction in recent years among criminal justice activists, advocates, and scholars who are intentionally politicizing the work of allies attempting to take down interlocking systems of domination through targeted analysis, planning, and action (Phillips 2015). Accomplices and co-conspirators shift focus away from simply breaking bread together to coordinating actions intended to disrupt the status quo. This centers the attention less on the ways individuals are affected (i.e., an outsider gains an understanding of another's suffering or the one suffering gains camaraderie and reassurance in knowing they have an ally, friend, or accompanist) to advocating for concrete legal, academic, or activist strategies for undoing injustice. This conceptualization encourages academics in particular to make their scholarship contribute concretely to the public good, or as Tomlinson and Lipstiz note, "rather than merely producing ever more eloquent descriptions of other people's suffering, scholars can join with others to address the suffering and to create ways of ending it" (2013, p. 13).

A successful example of this occurred during the Black Lives Matter protests at the Claremont Colleges in late 2015. That autumn, fervent protests led by young activists of color (many of whom also identified as low-income, queer, first generation, and/or undocumented) had erupted on college campuses across the nation. Students organized protests in the space of hours, days, and weeks to articulate demands concerning issues of access, equity, and wellbeing that were affecting their day-to-day experiences at college. They spoke to issues related to race, gender identity, sexual orientation, class, citizenship, ethnicity, ability, and more. They demanded to be treated fairly and to be included and cared for in all aspects of college life, from admissions to student affairs, financial aid to academic affairs. They spoke about the microaggressions from fellow students and professors that occurred in dormitories and classrooms. They argued for the necessity of having "safe spaces," wellness services, and student support resources on campus. They also demanded transparent, interactive dialogues with their administrations concerning the authentic meaning of such overused terms as "diversity" and "inclusion." They spoke about feeling underrepresented, underserved, and undervalued, institutionally and interpersonally.

Students expertly and expeditiously organized strategies to convey their feelings and demands, including occupying academic and administrative buildings, facilitating sit-ins, teach-ins, marches, and face-to-face meetings with the highest levels of student, faculty, and administrative governmental bodies at schools across the nation. In preparation for a massive, five college-wide Black Lives Matter march and protest at the Claremont

Colleges, Black students and other students of color came together around the injustices, insensitivities, and inequalities they confronted in their schools and created lists of demands to share with the administration.

They felt increasingly exhausted, fearful, and stressed as a result of organizing the protests in the midst of juggling classes, jobs, family obligations, and other responsibilities. As tensions mounted, white students who were their friends, roommates, and classmates expressed their desire to support the students of color who were organizing the demonstrations and become a part of the movement. These white students recognized that self-identified allies often hijack meetings, microphones, or agendas even when they intend to respectfully hold a space in partnership with marginalized communities. They asked what work they could do to support their peers, how to keep those being targeted by injustice at the forefront of the fight, yet not be alone in the struggle. The students of color discussed amongst themselves what would most support their cause, then, using an activist–ally model taught by Black Lives Matter movement leaders, came up with a list of things these potential allies could provide. The first item was providing logistical support in the form of organizing press, campus security, and march permits. The second involved providing physical support in the form of creating a buffer zone of protection by putting their (white) bodies in a circle around the Black Live Matters protesters, so that if the march was met with violence, the allies would act as the first line of defense. They also asked the allies to organize all this on their own, because the students of color did not have the time and energy to explain and lead them through yet another series of meetings. However, they ensured that one student of color organizer was present at each of the ally meetings to make sure that the allies were representing their needs accurately.

One of the students of color leaders on campus who was designated to sit in on the white ally organizing meetings shared with me her interpretation of this experience (R.C., *personal communication, 2016*). She was surprised and impressed by how thoughtful, conscientious, and reflective the white students were about their positionality and in figuring out how best to fulfill their roles as allies. She was also appreciative of how effective and respectful they were in carrying out these roles before and during the organized action.

A lesson that emerged from the Claremont Colleges protests was that diverse people can work together to foster social change provided they are willing to become proximate in transparent and respectful ways. In their willingness to collaborate, be held accountable, and respect students of color who were organizing the protests, these white students demonstrated their ability to effectively accompany, advocate for, and act as accomplices with those targeted for injustice. Activist students of color navigated this partnership by giving their allies important tasks to do while prompting them to actively and critically reflect on their own experiences and responsibilities in spaces where injustice and discrimination exist. They also encouraged them to seek the tools they needed to do the work, instead of relying on the students of color to tutor them. For example, the white students sought out non-violent, civil disobedience training to prepare for being buffers during the protests. Despite their disparate life experiences, these students felt compelled to create spaces where they could connect and share the work of change.[12]

Becoming proximate to others and to the (micro) lived experiences generated by (macro) social problems often results in developing a heartfelt commitment to changing society. Becoming proximate to others requires cultivating the same qualities needed to develop caring and awareness of ourselves: love, courage, humility, open-mindedness, and accountability.

To reflect on what becoming proximate might look like in practice in your own life, I encourage readers to pause here and explore the following prompts, either by free-writing responses individually or in a group conversation.

Critical Reflection: Becoming Proximate

1. Do you educate yourself about the culture and experiences of other racial, religious, ethnic and socioeconomic groups by reading and attending classes, workshops, cultural events, volunteering or creating community partnerships, etc?[13]
2. Where, with whom, how often, how deeply, and why have you attempted to become proximate to communities or social issues different from your own?
3. Where or in what contexts have you resisted becoming proximate? Why or what fuels that resistance?
4. In what ways do you become proximate to communities of which you are already a part?
5. How have you seen others outside your communities attempt to become proximate to your community? What have you

learned from observing their successes or failures in pursuing proximity?

6. What ethical issues are you cautious about in the work of becoming proximate?

7. What are the necessary ingredients for becoming a respectful and effective ally, accomplice, or accompanist?

SHIFTING THE NARRATIVE

Once we become intimately connected to a social issue, we begin to question the dominant beliefs and systems that underlie that issue. We open up to new ways of interpreting the historical trajectory of that social problem and the power structures and interlocking political and social contexts that effect it, thus shifting foundational narratives for how we understand the problem itself. This can then lead to figuring out the personal and systemic moves needed to change the problem, and a commitment to employing effective strategies for that change.

I began my own shift in narrative about indigenous knowledge when I was in the small village of Huito in the Peruvian Andes. At that time, as part of PRATEC, I was sitting in on a community-based education program on "mental decolonization." At the end of the program, I was asked to introduce myself. Then I was asked to talk about the native peoples living in Southern California. I quickly grew embarrassed both by my country's historic and current treatment of native communities and by my lack of knowledge about native tribes in Los Angeles. As a proud, second-generation local Los Angeleno, I thought knew the area well, but when asked, I realized I was not even sure who had originally lived there or what the status was of native communities there. The only story I could tell the students, parents, and teachers in Huito was that most of the native peoples in the USA had been decimated during periods of colonization and genocide and that the few that survived were still struggling to maintain traditional languages and practices. My shame deepened as I realized that, while I had become proximate to the peoples, cultures, and struggles of the indigenous communities I was accompanying in Peru, I had no proximation to the histories, communities, or stories of the peoples native to my home territory.

From this shame grew motivation to learn, to become proximate, and to see if my own narrative on native communities needed shifting—which, unsurprisingly, it did. When I returned home, a native colleague who had spent many years working with local native communities opened doors for me to accompany, learn from, and work with local native elders. These relationships developed into now nearly decade-long community engagement partnerships between members of local native tribes and students and colleagues from my college.[14] In fomenting long-lasting relationships with these elders, inviting them to be co-educators in my courses, collaborating on projects around indigenous knowledge, arts, and culture, and teaching about indigenous knowledge systems and decolonization in my classes, I not only learned a great deal, but also shifted the beliefs I had held about native rights, epistemologies, and histories. These shifts in narrative then informed how I saw myself as a product of settler colonialism. I investigated the epistemology I had been raised in and the cultural biases I held. I also reflected on my own practice of interconnectedness with others and the earth. These relationships and paradigm shifts in my thinking led me to invest in becoming an ally with local native communities working for social change. I also made a greater commitment to shifting the narratives in my academic community and work with my colleagues to address issues of equity, respect, and access to land and college education for our local tribal communities.

PRATEC's version of "shifting the narrative" focuses on undergoing mental, emotional, and spiritual acts of *decolonization* in order to reverse the effects of colonization. The decolonization process requires first recognizing the oppression of indigenous communities that began when they were first colonized over 500 years ago and then acknowledging that these communities continue to be socially, culturally, politically, and legislatively marginalized. Unlearning the ideologies of oppression and dominant assumptions that native customs, cosmologies, and forms of knowledge are backward, along with deconstructing narratives that underscore the primacy of western cultures or claim the absolute truth of western epistemologies, enables us to shift personal, institutional, and systemic narratives.

According to PRATEC, when we disentangle ourselves from oppressive, false teachings about indigenous cultures, we can generate new narratives that value indigenous forms of knowledge and culture.[15] We can honor demands that these be valued in educational and political contexts alongside western traditions. The methods and objectives of the educational system can shift to being informed by indigenous knowledge systems, respecting storytelling as a way of transmitting knowledge, providing different ways of understanding space, time, notions of individualism, and ownership, and recognizing how teaching and learning embody intellectual, spiritual, moral, and physical development (Mosha 1999; Smith 1999). While "Indigenous knowledge systems are themselves diverse (as are knowledge and traits ascribed to Western societies)," many indigenous epistemologies privilege the dynamic over the static, the subjective over the objective, the collective over the individual, the experiential and practical over the theoretical, and diversity over monoculture and standardization (Barnhardt and Kawagley 2005, p. 8).[16] Valuing and incorporating such notions and practices into conventional western schooling systems simultaneously affirms diverse cultures and ways of knowing while shifting colonial narratives about indigeneity.

PRATEC's decolonization process not only applies to "shifting the narrative" about indigenous communities, it can be used to understand any community and the institutions, norms, and laws that perpetuate oppression and injustice for members of that community. "Decolonization" is thus similar to the practice of "*conscientizacao*," or raising critical consciousness, as outlined by critical pedagogists. This process is designed to liberate both oppressors and oppressed by recognizing and shifting the narrative they hold about the interlocking systems of domination within which they operate. As stated by Freire, "Desocialized thinking called critical consciousness refers to the way we see ourselves in relation to knowledge and power in society, to the way we use and study language, and to the way we act in school and daily life to reproduce or to transform our conditions" (2006, p. 129).

There are four primary components to *conscientizacao* or raisingcritical consciousness:

Power Awareness: Knowing that society and history are made by contending forces and interests, that human action makes society and that society is unfinished and can be transformed;

Critical Literacy: Habits of thought, reading, writing, and speaking which go beneath surface meanings, first impressions, dominant myths, official pronouncements, traditional clichés, received wisdom, and mere opinions, to understand the deep meanings, root causes, social contexts, ideologies, and personal consequences of any action, event, object, process, organization, experience, text, subject matter, policy, mass media, or discourse;

Permanent Desocialization: Understanding and challenging artificial, political limits on human development; questioning power and inequality in the status quo; examining socialized values in consciousness and in society which hold back democratic change in individuals and in the larger culture; and seeing self and social transformation as a joint process;

Self-education/Organization: Self-organized transformative education to develop critical thought and cooperative action (Shor 1992, pp. 129–130).

Critical pedagogy's practice of *conscientizacao* advances shifts in narratives through providing popular education in critical thinking. It engages individuals in defining, naming, and restructuring the power structures that inform their social and political opportunities. The consciousness-raising process thus situates the individual within the power constructs of society.

Shifting narratives around knowledge production, power, and rights ideally results in a greater sense of personal agency, leading to strategies to confront and transform oppressive systems. However, learning about the systems that perpetuate social problems often leads to an initial period of devastation, hopelessness, anger, and grief, recalling again Macy's concept of feeling "our pain for the world" (1998, p. 5). This devastation often collides with anger at the conditions, policies, and people that perpetuate unjust environments. When anger toward oppressive or unjust systems is first expressed, it is often ignored or dismissed by the status quo. Black Lives Matter co-founded, Patrisse Cullores, has made the observation that proclamations about oppression and freedom made by Martin Luther King, Jr. and Mahatma Gandhi were initially considered outrageous; they were only memorialized after the social movements they instigated proved successful (On Being with Krista Tippett 2016a).[17]

Shifting the narrative also includes examining how we can use anger strategically instead of letting it generate more violence in the world and in ourselves. Expressing anger through art is one method of "shifting the narrative" about issues of oppression and agency. Examples include Augosto Boal's Theatre of the Oppressed, poetry slams, graffiti art, political murals, and political music.[18] Anger is transformed into social action "through the creation of radical culture, whether in the form of texts, movement, images, film, music, or performance, art is used as an effective medium and powerful tool for systemic change and transformation" (Ginwright 2015, p. 37).

As we will dive into in greater depth in Chap. 3, these "liberation arts" not only allow us to express ourselves, but enable us to cope with, heal from, and transform our suffering into a social good (Watkins and Shulman 2008).

Another way to shift the narratives is by transforming our social movements themselves. Transformative movement organizing and healing justice are emerging frameworks for reimagining social movements to include methods for both community healing and liberation.[19] "Healing Justice seeks to lift up resiliency and wellness practices as a transformative response to generational violence and trauma in our communities" (Page 2010).[20] Healing justice recognizes that individuals and communities are both chronically and acutely traumatized by oppressive social systems. These traumas can be healed through practices that address suffering and shift "how individuals, organizations, and communities relate to one another as they envision a new way of creating collective hope" (Ginwright 2015, p. 28) . Healing justice seeks "to regenerate traditions that have been lost; to mindfully hold contradictions in our practices; and to be conscious of the conditions we are living and working inside of as healers and organizers in our communities and movements." (Page 2010). The healing justice and transformative movement approaches shift the narrative about how we go about making change, which then alters the social change methods, goals, and movement environment.

Healing justice methods involve the creative arts, mindfulness and contemplative practices aimed at reimagining the world we want (not just what we are fighting against) and reorganizing our tactics and daily operations to bring about healing changes. Without such opportunities for healing, individuals and communities continue to carry unresolved traumas that may result in harming themselves and others. This shift in movement narratives ensures that changemakers do not end up internalizing their anger with unjust systems and projecting it internally within their move-ments and communities but instead work intentionally to create movement spaces that thoughtfully process anger and make room for healing.[21]

A key healing justice method is the healing circle. Similar to Macy's "work that reconnects," healing circles involve small groups of people creating the "group safety necessary for group members to share their experience and opinions" through dialogue, witnessing, and supporting each other (Ginwright 2015, p. 36). A similar shift occurs in the *restorative justice* model wherein community dialogues "restore group trust and fairness in cases where conflict occurs" (ibid). This approach re-envisions conflict in a way that disrupts conventional, polarizing conceptualizations of "victims" and "perpetrators." Instead of using punitive methods to separate individuals, these dialogues bring people together for the shared purpose of restoration and reconciliation as a form of justice and healing. Restorative and healing justice methods thus shift the narratives around oppression by focusing social change efforts on individual and collective healing as a means of creating the world we want to live in. "Rather than viewing wellbeing as an individual act of self care, healing justice advocates view healing as political action" (p. 8).

Based on his extensive research on hope and healing with young men of color in Oakland and San Francisco, scholar-activist Shawn Ginwright has articulated a number of factors necessary to shift the narrative of oppression toward hope. When facilitated in healing circles, these practices cultivate cultural affirmation, empowerment, community belonging, and hope, resulting in the motivation and sense of agency necessary to act personally and collectively against injustice. Principle components of such a shift include the following:

- *Culture*: Drawing on culture as "an anchor to connect young people to a racial and ethnic identity that is both historically grounded and contemporarily relevant" helps build connection and sense of purpose, belonging, and self-esteem. A sense of intercultural interconnectedness can be manifested by engaging communities in culturally appropriate (rather than appropriative) traditions such as rituals, music, sweat lodges, or healing circles.
- *Agency*: Defined as "the individual and collective ability to act in order to create desired outcomes and transform external conditions," agency is cultivated when groups "create space for youth voice [and] identify ways for young people to address community issues." Providing tangible projects for local change that are both achievable and empowering shifts the narrative from assuming that change is impossible to believing that anything is possible.
- *Relationships*: Defined as "the capacity to create, sustain and grow healthy connections with others," meaningful relationships are nurtured when groups "create healing circles where members share their interests, fears, and hopes." Developing meaningful relationships enables individuals and social activist groups to shift from being fragmented by oppression to being collectively empowered by community.

- *Meaning*: Cultivating meaning that supports "discovering our purpose, and building an awareness of our role in advancing justice" can
  be manifested when groups "have conversations about what gives life
  meaning [and] create discussions that foster self discovery," promoting a shift from apathy to purpose.
- *Achievement*: Achievement "illuminates life's possibilities and
  acknowledges movement toward explicit goals." It can be manifested
  when groups "build knowledge and skills about individual assets and
  aspirations" and work collaboratively to create the world they want
  (2015, p. 26).

Shifting the narrative toward acknowledging the need for healing and
connection amongst political activists and movements has been recognized
by some and resisted by others. Two well-known activist sisters recently
discussed this narrative shift:

Angela Davis: I think our notions of what counts as radical have changed
over time. Self-care and healing and attention to the body and the spiritual
dimension—all of this is now a part of social justice struggles. That wasn't
the case before.

And I think that now we're thinking deeply about the connection between
interior life and what happens in the social world. Even those who are
fighting against state violence often incorporate impulses that are based on
state violence in their relations with other people.

[…]

Fania Davis: The question now is how we craft a process that brings the
healing piece together with the social and racial justice piece—how we heal
the racial traumas that keep re-enacting.

Angela Davis: I think that restorative justice is a really important dimension
of the process of living the way we want to live in the future. Embodying it.

We have to imagine the kind of society we want to inhabit. We can't simply
assume that somehow, magically, we're going to create a new society in
which there will be new human beings. No, we have to begin that process of
creating the society we want to inhabit right now. (van Gelder 2016)

Healing ourselves so that we may connect and strengthen our combined
capacities to advocate for justice involves recognizing our strengths as
individuals and as collectives. One of the strengths of communities is their

ability to love, support, and assist their members so they can survive injustice and trauma. Honoring and mobilizing around such strengths is predicated upon another paradigm shift in how we think about communities and methods for social change. This kind of approach is promoted through the community-organizing model known as *Asset-Based Community Development* (ABCD), which is based on building relationships of trust, respect, and reciprocity among community members and then mapping out the capacities and assets of individuals, groups, and institutions. The notion of emphasizing human assets in this way disrupts a capitalist approach that measures the value of individuals based on their financial worth or ability to be financially productive and instead focuses on the inherent value of an individual based on their knowledge, skills, and capacities.

The ABCD model posits that traditional methods of assessing marginalized communities are inherently flawed because of the inclination to focus on problems, deficits, and needs rather than on assets, strengths, and capacities.[22] This former model leads to deficit-oriented service-providing models that promote temporary social services as solutions to community problems, instead of developing asset-building movements that are mobilized from the inside-out and generate long-term change. When service-providing agencies, foundations, universities, and even neighborhood residents define a neighborhood only in terms of its deficits, the community is quickly bound to rely on outside services for its wellbeing. Stereotypes are projected onto community residents as victims who lack agency. Community wisdom and knowledge, networks of support, and talents, abilities, and assets amongst residents are denied existence rather than drawn upon to solve problems and mobilize for change. Any solutions are usually temporary and fail to generate systemic change, since they are funded and provided by outside services rather than controlled by the community itself. This dynamic of reliance is unstable and unsustainable. An ABCD approach shifts this paradigm by recognizing the skills and abilities that exist within communities, connecting them to definitive needs, and ensuring that community members and groups design and execute agendas for change (Kretzman and McKnight 1993).[23]

Recognizing that marginalized communities possess internal assets does not hide the fact of real problems. Critiquing the power structures in society that contribute to oppression of such communities is imperative. Nevertheless, "all the historic evidence indicates that significant community development takes place only when local community people are committed to investing themselves and their resources in the effort" (Kretzman and McKnight 1993, p. 7). Acknowledging the value of community knowledge, bonds, strengths, and capacities promotes agency and supports communities in imagining and directing the changes they want, rather than being situated as recipients of the next fad in service provision.

Asset-based community development, healing and restorative justice, critical pedagogy, and practices of decolonization all provide ways of shifting the dominant narrative around oppression. These approaches change the lens through which we usually view social problems and alter our understanding of how to manifest social change. The largest shift we can make subsequently is to the issue of injustice itself. There are no one-size-fits-all methodologies for overturning injustice, however. These approaches all recognize that change is case specific and depends on the needs, assets, values, culture, norms, laws, institutions, politics, environment, and moral compass of each community and individual.

Some possibilities for shifting the narrative and mobilizing action around injustice occur in big, collective acts, such as shifting policies and community structures, while others occur in (equally important) small, personal acts, such as shifting beliefs and habits. Actions might include:

- giving money or time to organizations making change on the ground level;
- engaging with a local community or organization to conduct community-based participatory research or service aimed at creating larger structural shifts over time;
- calling or writing elected officials to voice support for or protest against specific legislation that impacts equity and justice;
- organizing or attending rallies, protests, marches, or teach-ins;
- educating yourself about and then voting in public elections for issues you believe in and candidates you think will best represent them;
- participating in neighborhood or city councils to push for local change;
- creating or attending gatherings in one's own neighborhood with others seeking to organize grassroots social change efforts;
- participating in organizational change within institutions (religious, professional, or civic) of which you are a part, including questioning

if/how your institution may be unwittingly colluding in upholding longstanding oppressive structures;
- participating in grassroots collaboratives that provide alternative community structures or systems;
- bearing witness to suffering and raising your voice against it;
- recognizing and changing personal biases;
- calling others up when unjust or discriminatory comments are made[24];
- engaging in difficult dialogues with people who have different life experiences or beliefs than you do to see if you can build common ground or bridges of understanding;
- re-learning history from the point of view of the oppressed;
- addressing the reproduction of inequalities in your own life (including in your intimate relationships and school or work communities);
- healing yourself and your community from the traumas of injustice.

The actions to shift injustice follow a shift in one's own understanding of the injustice itself and will vary from person to person. Before moving on to the next section, I encourage readers to explore what shifting the paradigmatic narrative might entail in your own life by responding to the following prompts:

Critical Reflection Activity: Shifting the Narrative

1. What dominant narrative have you inherited about a social issue you want to change?
2. Who authored, taught, or perpetuated this narrative? What is missing from it?
3. What counter-narratives undergird the issue? What narratives remain unspoken or silenced by the dominant narrative?
4. What would you need to learn more about to get a full picture of the factors, conditions, and histories influencing the issue and its dominant narrative?
5. Who might hold knowledge or a different way of seeing the world that you could learn from so as to promote a narrative shift concerning this issue?
6. What new ways might you imagine social change if you shifted the narrative around this issue?

7. What visions do you or people in your community hold for the kind of world you want to create? How are these visions distinct or similar to the world we have now?

8. What are concrete measures you can take in your life today that support shifting the narrative and creating real change?

GETTING UNCOMFORTABLE

Although coming face to face with community suffering and the narratives we hold that support them is crucial to social change, a great deal of discomfort can arise in the process. Joanna Macy dissects this discomfort in her discussion of "apatheia," a collective refusal to fully experience the pain of the world (1998). Most individuals often hesitate to acknowledge oppressive cultural, racial, and gender relations, economic inequalities, environmental degradation, and other realities of injustice for fear of experiencing despair, guilt, or powerlessness. Many tend to follow cultural norms that value stoicism over the risk of appearing weak, emotional, morbid, or unpatriotic and worry they may cause others distress by bringing social issues to the communal table (ibid). There are also great forces at work to repress this discomfort, including mass media, job and time pressures, social violence, and, for many, the need to direct all attention and energies to merely surviving.

Confronting this pain can seem unbearable, especially for those who have not been socialized to experience this level of emotional openness or do not have a place to process it. The findings of Shawn Ginwright demonstrated that young men of color who sought healing against a backdrop of state-sanctioned violence, poverty, discrimination, and poor schools were rarely given "permission to grieve and therefore find their own way to process their feelings [...] The streets had taught them that focusing on their emotions, such as fear, uncertainty, and sorrow made them vulnerable to the dangers of street life" (2015, pp. 49–51). Drawing attention to the pain of oppression can become a liability under such conditions.

In addition, critical thinking about social injustice is seldom part of the conventional educational experience. Assumptions about race, gender, sexuality, and other social identities are often opaque both to those who instruct people (i.e., teachers, clergy, program leaders) and to those being taught how to live. For many people, an encounter with the post-modern critiques that might disrupt such oppressive norms only occurs when they undergo a consciousness-raising experience, such as attending college, living abroad, or joining a social movement (J.C., *personal communication,* 2016).

Many activists and Cultural Studies theorists propose that hegemonic assumptions and norms are intentionally integrated into educational systems and political structures as operatives for oppression. Interlocking systems of domination cannot continue to function if those who are repressed by them become educated about the processes of exploitation. Repressing the truth about oppressive structures results in people living in "false consciousness," as explained through the traditional Marxist lens:

> Marx asserts that social mechanisms emerge in class society that systematically create distortions, errors, and blind spots in the consciousness of the underclass. If these consciousness-shaping mechanisms did not exist, then the underclass, always a majority, would quickly overthrow the system of their domination. So the institutions that shape the person's thoughts, ideas, and frameworks develop in such a way as to generate false consciousness and ideology. (Little 2007, p. 1)

Cultural Studies theorist Antonio Gramsci refuted the latent implication in Marxist theory that the oppressed do not have the agency or political capacity to break free from being "passive tool[s]" of the dominant ideology" (ibid). Gramsci argued that everyone has "the ability to influence the terms of [their] consciousness" and to contest the "terms of representation of the existing social reality" (ibid). Gramsci insisted that the oppressed can and do confront the ruling elite's hegemonic order by crafting their own "counter-hegemonic struggle." By facing their own pain and refusing to remain complacent about the dominant narrative, oppressed peoples all over the world ignite social change (Gramsci 1971).

Emotional discomfort can be a constant companion for those who personally, politically, or socially negotiate systems of oppression on a daily basis. bell hooks argues for intentionally developing a space for "radical openness" on the margins of dominant society. This is a place where oppressed peoples can craft liberatory consciousness and the tools of resistance. She says, "much more than a site of deprivation…it is also the site of radical possibility […] a profound edge. Locating oneself there is difficult yet necessary. It is not a 'safe' place. One is always at risk. One needs a community of resistance" (hooks 1989, p. 206). Raising consciousness about marginality and sitting with the discomfort generated by that position is a prerequisite to action and an opportunity to build solidarity with "a community of resistance."

Those who do not regularly experience oppression as a result of their racial, gender, class, or other social identities may initially encounter despair, anger, or guilt once they become aware of systems of oppression. Cognitive dissonance may arise when innocent beliefs such as "I am generally a good person, most people are generally good, and the world is generally a good place" are juxtaposed against the reality of injustice. Even greater personal and interpersonal turmoil emerges when those in privileged positions realize that they in fact benefit from systems of oppression (discussed further in Chap. 3). People who have had their consciousness raised about their deliberate or inadvertent complicity in such systems tend to gloss over their feelings of guilt or shame so they can move on to the "real work" of fighting oppression. It is true that any work intended to undo such systems should focus on those who are at the receiving end. However, those in power may undermine activist efforts if they are not willing to acknowledge their own guilt and shame.

In her study of "Integrating mindfulness into anti-oppression pedagogy," Beth Berila argues that discomfort "is the safety mechanism for systems of oppression to keep them intact" (2016, p. 140). When confronted with their roles in oppressive systems, those in positions of power typically react as if they are being attacked. As trauma therapist, Hala Khouri, explains: "One of the ways that people with privilege cope with their guilt and overwhelm is to dissociate from the injustice and oppression that they benefit from. Dissociation can take the form of denial ('it's not really that bad'), blame ('everyone can make it if they really try'), and/or conscious ignorance ('it's too much, I don't want to know')" (H.K., *personal communication*, 2016). They may automatically react with attempts to appear bigger by physically intimidating others or lashing out aggressively against allegations of privilege, they may attempt to appear smaller by shrinking away from social encounters and refusing to take responsibility for privilege, or they may distract or numb themselves in order to avoid the painful emotions triggered by awakening to their roles in oppression (Berila 2016). "All of these are part of the 'fight, flight, freeze' response of how one deals with an overwhelming event or circumstance. These coping strategies get passed on and even codified in cultural norms, beliefs and (re)actions in privileged communities" (H.K., *personal communication*, 2016). Activists should not permit people in positions of privilege to hurry past any discomfort they might feel about a social issue, but they also should not shame or blame them to the point where they become immobilized by guilt. Neither option moves us towards effective social change. Instead, we should all become consciously aware of where we experience privilege and participate in unjust systems and carefully attend to any emotional reactions that arise in this confrontational process. Beth Berila reminds us that:

> *What arises for us is the work.* The complex reactions are not things to get past in order to get to the 'real' social justice work. The grief, anger, pain, confusion, horror and denial that arise, those feelings, *is* the work. When we regularly reflect on what arises for us in discussions about oppression, along with our various attempts to examine them through various mindfulness practices, we will learn a great deal about our own role in oppressive systems and how to interrupt it. Only then can we imagine new possibilities into reality. (2016, p. 111)

Considering the systemic proliferation of oppression and violence against women, children, people of color, people with disabilities, people who identify as queer, people who are in prison, and so on, it seems unlikely that anyone is completely free of complicity in the structures that perpetuate harm. Recognizing ways in which we are implicitly or explicitly complicit in systems of injustice is a critical step in mobilizing the will and strategies necessary for making effective change. Whether we suffer or benefit from systems of injustice, facing our discomfort contributes to long-term individual and collective wellbeing more than ignoring such pain. Most people are taught to conquer their fears instead of sitting with them, but research demonstrates that suppressing emotional reactions to injustice can contribute to social fragmentation, alienation, blaming and scapegoating, political passivity, diminished critical thinking, avoidance of information about social issues, burnout, or feelings of powerlessness and despair (Macy and Brown 1998). In contrast, becoming mindful of how we embody the discomfort we feel about social injustice and our complicity in systems of oppression enables us to more effectively advance strategies for dismantling them.

Drawn from ancient secular and religious traditions, mindfulness practices such as meditation, introspection, and contemplation can help us tolerate uncertainty, confusion, and the contradictions that arise around social issues. They can also help us become better attuned to our embodied state and habitual forms of reaction. As Berila explains,

> Rather than merely seeing patterns of oppression in the society around us or even in our external behaviors, we can begin to recognize *how* they have insinuated themselves into our selves, bodies, and spirits. We can learn to recognize the effects in our rapid heartbeat, our anger, our deep shame or sadness. We can start to recognize how we want to lash out as a defense mechanism that both protects us from external threats and gives us something to focus on besides our pain. While there is a time and place when such lashing out is a necessary survival mechanism, with deeper reflection we might find that that behavior does not serve us in every moment. (2016, pp. 16–17)

Getting uncomfortable is one of the consequences of critical reflection, but sometimes people who have suddenly awakened to issues of injustice become so passionate about them that they begin policing or supervising other people's reactions. A provocative example of this occurred during one of my Inside-Out Prison Exchange courses. After reading Freire's *Pedagogy of the Oppressed*, the mix of inside (incarcerated) and outside (non-incarcerated) students were talking about where and how oppression manifested in their daily lives. After listening in silence to the discussion, one of the inside students, a 26-year-old Latino man, suddenly exclaimed, "Look, I don't know what you guys are talking about. I'm not oppressed! I've never had problems with the cops. I always did what I wanted to out on the streets. Now, I'm here in this place where I have free rent, free healthcare, free education, and time for meditation and reflection. I'm not oppressed!" Many of the outside students stared in him in disbelief, but said nothing. After leaving the facility, a number of the outside students, primarily white women, debated his claim. They argued that since he was incarcerated he was obviously oppressed but, due to false consciousness, he just did not know it yet. Another student, the only African-American woman in the class, then interjected that they had no right to decide if other people felt oppressed or not. She stated that the white students' positionality, which presumed the authority to determine a man of color's state of oppression, was extremely problematic.

Instead of consciously sitting with the complexity of this topic and the emotions and uncertainty that arose from it, students left that day feeling perplexed and angry. They needed time to digest and reflect on the nuances of the situation given that they were, in the moment, unable to bring differing perspectives into genuine conversation with each other. I believe that this interchange would have had a better ending if mindfulness activities had been integrated with critical reflection:

> Helping students to learn to pause, breathe, witness, and befriend their discomfort is a critical step in this process [...] With practices of mindfulness, we also can intentionally cultivate greater practices of compassion. The quality of compassion enables us to deeply connect with the suffering in ourselves and others, and once we feel connected to it, we are far more motivated to work to transform it [...] When the pain arises, we can breathe into our heart center, feel the pain, and use it to connect with others who have felt that pain. We can mourn the disastrous impacts of systemic oppression that robs all of us of our humanity, in different ways. Fierce compassion helps us connect with one another in a radical openness, offering us an alternative to hardening and cutting ourselves off. (Berila 2016, pp. 137, 140)

Becoming better equipped to handle discomfort within will increase the capacity of individuals to do so in relationship with others. This is key for becoming proximate with others that are different in background, values, or belief systems. "We live in an individualistic society full of anger, greed and violence. It is absurd to think that people working for social change have been spared these messages [...] we tend to take a highly polarized us-versus-them stance, isolating our movement from potential allies and partners" (Zimmerman et al. 2010, pp. 14 and 18). Real change involves changing how we view and treat those we see as opponents so that we are "engaging in real relationship building with [them] and developing ways to hold them accountable without demonizing them. We must help them (and our communities) to better act with love and compassion" (p. 31). Working across our divides is a site of both challenges and also the sweet spot of emerging compassion.

Taking a lesson again from transformative movement building, we must reflect critically on how our movements or organization for change negotiate the following:

- how much time and energy we put into attuning and aligning with others—and the work of relationship building that goes with it;
- how we "show up" to the work—and if we can be present, open, grounded, and sustainable *within* the daily grind;

- how we think about and utilize notions of power—enacting power *with* versus power *over* strategies so as not to replicate problematic hierarchies;
- how our actions mirror the world we wish to create—embodying the values of peace, love, and justice upon which their movements are based (Zimmerman et al. 2010).

"Moving from bystanding to compassionate engagement, facing one's own collusion with the perpetration of violence and/or injustice, and healing from the wounds of oppression require the development of dialogical skills" (Watkins and Shulman 2008, p. 176). We cannot hope for politicians and warring parties to create peace and justice if we are not willing to sit down and attempt to build bridges of understanding with those right beside us that are different from us or believe differently than we do. While invariably unsettling and challenging, engaging respectfully and effectively with folks with whom we may disagree is a key component of making change. Developing difficult dialogues across divides enables us to ensure that all voices are heard, that we learn from distinct points of view, develop patience and tolerance—and eventually, acceptance—of our differences, and build coalitions that can work together toward change.

Authentic dialogue with competing perspectives is a core value of a liberal arts education, though models of "affirming inquiry" emphasize connection over debate, where "mutual exploration of experiences/narratives by sharing" is valued more so than "seeking 'proof' or facts supporting discordant experiences/narratives to the inquirer" (University of Michigan 2016, p. 2). Affirming inquiry models of dialogue create "exchanges between participants seeking to surface and/or clarify particularly complex, potentially controversial or emotionally charged topics" (University of Michigan 2016, p. 1). Through the use of collaboratively created communication guidelines (see example in Chap. 5), participants can make space for multiple perspectives and "participate in sharing perspectives that they have critically, reflectively considered and can definitively identify what have informed their perspective" (ibid). Such dialogue requires mutual vulnerability, mutual contribution, and "expressions of appreciation, affirmation and/or gratitude" (ibid).

Similar to the "affirming inquiry" form of non-violent dialogue, the model known as "LARA" provides these tools for navigating the discomfort that arises in intergroup dialogue. These include the following:

- *Effective listening*: setting aside your own agenda while someone else is speaking, hearing what people mean, not just what they say and responding to a speaker's feelings.
- *Reflective listening*: listening for a feeling, relating to that feeling, and then reflecting, and restating that feeling back, affirming the connection you found when you listened.
- *Responding*: demonstrating that the other person's question deserves to be taken seriously and responding to it.
- *Adding information*: sharing resources, anecdotes, or other information that seems pertinent to developing greater understanding.
- *Empathy*: perceiving and responding to the feelings of another person while remaining in touch with your own feelings (University of Michigan 2014).

I don't believe we can reasonably expect broad social change to occur if we are unable to sit face to face with those with whom we disagree, negotiate the discomfort that will invariably surface, and seek bridges of understanding. This is of particular importance today as our country is torn apart by differing political beliefs, cultural backgrounds, and social value systems. From students to activists, politicians to organizational leaders, this coming together across difference is a key tool to heal our divided families, communities, states, and nations.

The mandate to "get uncomfortable" involves first recognizing the false consciousness we have been raised in and how we contribute to or are harmed by unjust systems. It also involves reflecting on how our implicit or explicit complicity in structures of domination relates to our complicity in perpetuating bias, microaggressions, or "othering" in our neighborhoods, work places, and schools. It also involves negotiating the discomfort or anger of that awakening. We must not be afraid to sit in the discomfort of our ignorance and biases, fears and apathy, oppression and pain. In the midst of confronting our own shortcomings, traumas, and the pain of the world, we must remember to find our breath, ground ourselves, push past our limitations, and extend compassion toward ourselves and others, including people we think are too different culturally, racially, and religiously from ourselves to understand (Corn 2015). Only then can we challenge the ideologies of oppression that limit us and begin to craft strategies for mental, physical, and political liberation.

Please take a moment now to respond to the prompts in the *Critical Reflection Activity: Getting Uncomfortable*

1. What makes you uncomfortable when participating in conversations about social justice?
2. What constitutes your comfort zone?
3. What scares you about going outside of your comfort zone?
4. What do you need to feel safe enough to get uncomfortable?
5. What forms of knowledge and understanding might you be missing as a result of your resistance to getting uncomfortable?
6. Do any of the communities, organizations or movements in which you participate perpetuate problematic social hierarchies? Are there any ways that their rhetoric, activist strategies, or interpersonal dynamics cause harm?
7. How do notions of power play out in your own life or work?
8. Which of your behaviors and activities require further critical reflection, healing, or shifting?
9. Are you able to remain emotionally grounded in the midst of challenging community work? If not, what practices might help you do so?
10. What can you do to contemplatively sit with *and* move through discomfort so it doesn't immobilize you?

CULTIVATING HOPE

One more ingredient is needed to transform the previous steps into action: *hope*. The sorrows and traumas of injustice are so great that "in order to survive, every human being must have a place that is furnished with hope" (Angelou 2016). Hope is shaped not only by individuals, but also by our social ecology. Cultivating hope is a collective action that draws on our convictions, faith, and interdependence to imagine a better world.

As Shawn Ginwright notes, "wellbeing is both a function of external opportunities such as access to jobs, good education, quality health care, *and* our capacity to hope for a more equitable, inclusive and safe society"

(2015, p. 17). The capacity for hope, wellbeing, and equal access to opportunities are thus entangled:

> Research suggests that both chronic and acute exposure to traumatic stressors erode young people's aspirations. The ability and capacity to envision a promising future is fundamental to having hope. Without hope, young people are more likely to experience depression, anxiety, and hostility and resort to substance abuse and are more prone to engage in violent behavior. (p. 20)

We must confront the fact that personal traumas as well as the persistent, collective traumas of injustice often erase hope and the capacity for self-care or community healing. Yet without hope and self-care, our chances of effectively building a movement for change become greatly diminished. Ginwright argues that "the presence of hope is one of the most significant factors to evoke social and community change. When people build a sense of collective hope, they are more likely to engage in activities that will improve their neighborhoods, schools, and cities" (ibid).

Collective hope is critical to surviving and thriving under conditions of social injustice. Ginwright conceptualizes collective hope as focusing "on those aspects of community life that provide meaning, purpose, happiness, and joy" (p. 21). Collective hope is predicated on "a salutogenic analysis of community which focuses on collective strengths and possibility, and views communities, groups, and collective action as key to wellbeing" (ibid). Hope is far more than a mood or feeling—it is the very basis of social will and political action, something born of our social belonging, something that propels us into a powerful collective force, an active *we* (Aaronson 2017).

Cultivating collective hope depends upon sharing "experiences from the conditions of everyday life," understanding the root causes of injustice, and imagining a radical future that embodies justice, peace, and freedom (Ginwright 2015, p. 22). Collective hope is generated when people connect with others in community—this may occur through healing circles, support groups, venues for popular education, religious or spiritual gatherings, activist gatherings, and other spaces dedicated to identifying shared experiences of suffering, learning about the larger structural issues that create or perpetuate injustice, and discussing collective methods for changemaking. In such groups, people discover their shared strengths, resilience, and the resources that can be called upon for surviving and thriving. People that develop a shared sense of connection in such groups can then work together to shift the narrative about the issues at hand, radically imagine the world they want to build, and cultivate the agency to pursue that vision.

In many instances, groups pay less attention to envisioning a better future than to "the struggle" itself. However, cultivating hope involves shifting the narrative around the work we do and how we do it. Another personal anecdote illustrates this point. Toward the end of my fieldwork in Peru, my Andean mentors asked me to share details about my work in Los Angeles. I explained that I was an *anti*-racist activist, working (at the time) for the *Anti*-Defamation League on *anti*-hate crimes legislation and facilitating *anti*-bias education programs. They began to laugh, then asked as respectfully as they could, "You are *anti*-everything; what are you *for*?!" Their question put me into an existential tailspin that lasted for a long time, but I now use it as a reminder not to get so caught up in what we are against that we forget to dream, imagine, and mobilize around what we are for. Activist scholar Robin Kelley reminds us that "without new visions we don't know what to build, only what to knock down. We not only end up confused, rudderless, and cynical, but we forget that making a revolution is not a series of clever maneuvers and tactics but a process that can and must transform us" (2002, p. 14). Cultivating hope thus requires not only changing the ways we understand social problems, but also dedicating time and energy to concretely envisioning a better world.

Another core component of cultivating hope is cultivating community connection and wellbeing. Mutual wellbeing is both the source of and feeds into collective hope. At the core of this is the belief that we are all interconnected. Mutual nurturing, interconnectedness, reciprocity, and attunement with each other and the natural world are the foundations of PRATEC's work toward decolonization and cultural affirmation. As explained by one of PRATEC's indigenous elders, Eduardo Grillo Fernandez:

> We are all relatives. We all belong to our community which we nurture and which nurtures us in turn. The contribution of each one of us is indispensable in the daily nurturance of our harmony and our harmony nurtures each one with the same love. Here there is no world in itself differentiated from ourselves. (Apffel-Marglin and PRATEC 1998, p. 128)

Engaging a sense of belonging, connection, and responsibility to others is necessary for the survival of our species and planet. We are intricately bound to those with whom we share lived experiences within our own communities as well as those who differ from us. As Martin Luther King, Jr. famously wrote during the civil rights movement: "Injustice anywhere is a threat to justice everywhere. We are caught in an inescapable network of mutuality, tied in a single garment of destiny. Whatever affects one directly, affects all indirectly" (Qtd in Washington 1986, p. 290).

Many social movement activists currently struggling to be effective deem King's notion of the "network of mutuality" as romantic or esoteric. Yet, messages of interconnectedness have long been foundational to indigenous communities and movements and have echoed throughout every successful social movement of our time, from the grassroots civil rights movement of the 1960s to the Truth and Reconciliation Commission efforts aimed to heal and unify post-Apartheid South Africa in the 1990's. (It was in this period that Bishop Desmond Tutu reminded the world that each of us "belongs in a greater whole and is diminished when others are humiliated or diminished, when others are tortured or oppressed, or treated as if they were less than who they are" [Tutu qtd in Watkins and Shulman 2008, p. 154]). This concept of interconnectedness extended even to the hope-embedded campaign of President Barack Obama, who offered a similar refrain in his keynote address at the 2004 Democratic National Convention:

> Alongside our famous individualism, there's another ingredient in the American saga: a belief that we're all connected as one people. If there's a child on the South Side of Chicago who can't read, that matters to me, even if it's not my child. If there's a senior citizen somewhere who can't pay for their prescription drugs and having to choose between medicine and the rent, that makes my life poorer, even if it's not my grandparent. If there's an Arab American family being rounded up without benefit of an attorney or due process, that threatens my civil liberties. It is that fundamental belief—I am my brother's keeper, I am my sister's keeper—that makes this country work. It's what allows us to pursue our individual dreams, and yet still come together as one American family. "E pluribus unum." Out of many, one. (Obama 2004, p. 5)

Joanna Macy affirms that interconnection not only inspires collective hope, it is key to our very survival: "To the extent that we allow ourselves to identify with the suffering of other beings, we can identify with their strengths, as well. This is very important for a sense of adequacy and resilience, because we face a time of great challenge that demands of us more commitment, endurance and courage than we can dredge up out of our individual supply" (Macy and Brown 1998, p. 192).

To this end, Macy encourages small groups of people wishing to recognize personal and collective wounds and work toward making great changes to allow themselves to actively express gratitude for their connection. She argues that "we can proceed, of course, out of grim and angry desperation. But the tasks proceed more easily and productively from an attitude of thankfulness" (1998, p. 82). She reminds us of some of the interconnections for which we can all be grateful, including for each other, our ancestors and "the inspiration offered by future generations," and "our bonds to other life-forms" (ibid, p. 89). Thankfulness is not simply a warm-and-fuzzy individual attitude. Research shows links between wholehearted gratitude, hope, and agency (Brown 2010; Ginwright 2015; Prilleltensky and Prilleltensky 2006), perhaps because gratitude "enables us to be aware of the vast resources we can draw upon, and...our strengths, too" (Macy and Brown 1998, p. 89).

Acknowledging our interconnections and taking collective action enable us to confront the despair or apathy that surface when we come face to face with injustice. As Flanagan and Budnick reveal in their study on the links between civic engagement and psychosocial wellbeing:

> The collective nature of public work is likely to benefit individuals due to an awareness that many problems that we feel are personal, in fact, have political roots and require collective solutions. Even when facing seemingly intractable social problems, the shared experience of tackling them together is likely to reduce anxiety; by acting collectively people are more likely to feel empowered and efficacious (Bandura 2000), and a sense of collective efficacy, in turn, may reduce psychological stress (Jex and Bliese 1999). Furthermore, collective action and the sense of common purpose engendered by it may build social trust; it may increase one's faith in humanity. (2011, p. 24)

Confronting social issues through community engagement not only decreases despair and anxiety, but it also increases feelings of connectedness, empowerment, faith, and hope. In fact, some believe that it is unusual that we would cultivate hope and then move to action; rather, it is in moments when it seems all hope is lost that our despair moves us to action (out of necessity, survival). It is the action itself, taken in concert with others, that moves us from hopelessness to a shared sense of energy, purpose, power, and hope (Aronson 2015).

I would like to share a tangible example that has resulted in the cultivation of both hope and social change through the creation of an urban farm called Huerta del Valle, which I am involved in through one of my community engagement courses. I teach a course, *Research Methods for Community Change*, in a semester-long, justice-oriented, interdisciplinary program focused on urban studies and community-based research called Pitzer in Ontario (see appendix I for this program description and course syllabus). While in the program, students study local community issues such as food justice, labor rights, incarceration, education, community health, and immigration. Students commit to 150 hours of community engagement with organizations in Ontario working for social justice and conduct a community-based research project relevant to these partnerships.

Ontario is in San Bernardino County, just 6 miles southeast of Pitzer College. Although San Bernardino borders Los Angeles County, its landscape is much less glamorous and its residents far less healthy. In 2015, the "Inland Empire" of San Bernardino and Riverside Counties had a poverty level of 20.9% (Cox 2015). California Enviroscreen data from 2014 showed that the 91761 zip code in Ontario was among the top most toxic areas in the state of California (OEHHA 2017). Ontario residents have an obesity rate of 67%, leading to chronic disease such as high blood pressure, diabetes, and heart disease (San Bernardino County 2015). The City of Ontario is not technically a food desert, but neighborhoods in the south of Ontario have high rates of poverty, low education, food insecurity, linguistic exclusion, stress, and other social determinants of health (Partners for Better Health 2017).

In 2010, the director of Pitzer in Ontario Program became interested in improving access to nutritious food in Ontario and she and our students began putting energy into collaborating with members of the local community to create an urban farm. This collaborative effort eventually involved Pitzer College, the City of Ontario, and low-income Latino residents—led by the hope of one community member in particular who wanted to bring positive change to her family and community. María Teresa Alonso originally came from Michoacán, Mexico, where she had worked as a registered nurse. After emigrating to the USA, she moved into a mobile home park in Ontario. She then became a community co-educator for Pitzer College's Spanish Practicum in the Community, an advanced course wherein students spend time every week with a local Spanish-speaking family to practice the language, get to know the culture, and build community. She learned about the concept of food justice and students' interests in this topic through her weekly dinners with Pitzer students.

As a community co-educator, María was able to share her concerns around access to healthy, fresh food with Pitzer students and faculty. Her interest in food justice was less political or theoretical than it was for most of the Pitzer students. Hers was born from the intimate needs of her own family. This mother of three recalls a medical visit in which her doctor recommended organic vegetables as the best treatment for her son's ADHD. The same year, her family's health problems with diabetes, obesity, and cancer came into sharp focus and she wanted to help her own and other families who struggled to gain access to affordable, fresh, organic produce.

María became the natural leader of the budding farm project. She got the word out by meeting with community members, students, city staff, and priests and making announcements at local aerobics classes and on a Latino radio program. Her tenacious hope and optimism were contagious. The students at Pitzer became just as dedicated to developing and sustaining the community garden. They conducted research on food needs in the community and wrote rigorous literature reviews on the socio-political, economic, cultural, and environmental barriers to food access and food quality. Working with Pitzer faculty and staff, the City of Ontario, and María and other community partners, the students used their research data to build relationships, write grants, and pursue a collective vision of what the community farm might look like. The collective imaginings of this group included building a large urban farm called Huerta del Valle that could be used by multiple families and that would operate as a hub for community education.

They started small, by putting a garden into unused land of a former elementary school. The collaborative faced myriad challenges in securing a larger city plot on which to farm. After an arduous process that lasted several years, their conversations with staff of the City of Ontario's Planning Department resulted in a 10-year land-use agreement to farm a four-acre parcel of land. After having been incubated through Pitzer College, members of the community farm collaborative secured pro bono legal support and became incorporated as a 501(c)3 non-profit. Another major triumph came in securing a small piece of a rather large pie when the farm became one of a nine-member consortium of community partners in a million-dollar Kaiser grant called "the HEAL zone" (the "Healthy Eating, Active Living" zone, which incorporated most of south Ontario).

Now in its seventh year of operation, Huerta del Valle has 62 plots available for gardening by local families. In addition to the family plots, a communal garden provides food for a Community-Supported Agriculture program and is sold to Pitzer's dining hall and local restaurants in the area. On Saturdays, Pitzer students and resident volunteers teach food justice literacy classes to children while their parents harvest their produce. A number of the community gardeners have now become community leaders and are being trained as "community health first responders" in order to be able to accompany, advocate for, and connect alternative health resources to community members suffering from mental or physical health problems. Huerta del Valle has now secured enough grant funding to pay moderate salaries to María, as director of the farm, and to Arthur Levine, a Pitzer alum who manages the farm and does outreach, as well as four other part-time farmers and development staff members. Indoor and outdoor classroom facilities are currently being planned for construction on the property. Huerta del Valle continues to be sustained by a team consisting of community members and leaders, Pitzer students, faculty, and alumni, and city officials. Huerta del Valle has received both local and national recognition for the innovative blend of urban farming with community gardening, and the unparalleled sense of community that sustains their work. In 2016, Huerta del Valle won its first major grant as an independent non-profit when was awarded a USDA grant.

The success of Huerta del Valle demonstrates that collective hope comes fully alive through critical action. When community members achieve a goal for change, it fosters empowerment, hope, and a sense of accomplishment that can come from civic engagement. This then creates further hope, creating an iterative process resulting in a greater shared sense of purpose and faith that encourages communities to collectively imagine and plan how they might achieve greater peace and justice in the future.

Pitzer College students who had only studied social justice issues in textbooks were provided a palpable example of food injustice when Maria communicated her despair over trying to meet her family's health needs without having access to organic produce. By becoming proximate to one another, two disparate communities—the mostly low-income, Latino population of southern Ontario and the mostly upper-middle class, white student population of Pitzer College—built authentic, trusting relationships and collaborated to create a community garden. The process of building the farm itself debunked dominant narratives claiming that immigrants are uninterested in community organizing and mobilizing for change. Students, faculty, staff, and community members all experienced discomfort as they navigated the uncertain terrain of building a community-campus partnership and sharing leadership and decision-making processes across differences of class, culture, geography, and concepts of social change. In the end, the despair that motivated the attempt to change the conditions of food injustice was matched by the collective hope that students and community partners could and would make such a change. The achievements of this community-campus partnership are many: securing land and creating the farm in more than one location, generating community buy-in and interest in the farm, conducting community-based research and organizing initiatives based on the results, and garnering financial support and public land-use agreements. None of these would be possible without collective hope, radical imaginings, and the mobilization of community assets, knowledge, and determination in an effort to disrupt injustice and create wellbeing in the local community.

As with the previous sections, please take a moment now to explore the prompts offered in the *Critical Reflection Activity: Cultivating Hope*

1. How do you define hope? What does hope *feel* like?
2. What does hope look like in action?
3. What stands between you and hope?
4. What stands between your community and hope?
5. What current locations furnish hope for you and your community?
6. What actions or beliefs might you embrace if you had more hope?
7. Can you think of any examples where hope fueled social change despite pre-existing barriers?
8. What vision do you have of a world built on hope and faith and characterized by peace and justice?

CONCLUSION

A variety of social change models and concepts, including decolonization, cultural affirmation, asset-based community development, the work that reconnects, critical pedagogy, transformative movement building, and

healing justice have been threaded together in this chapter in an exploration of methods for disrupting oppressive systems and creating community wellbeing. Their coming together has centered around the
four-step framework of "becoming proximate" to issues of social justice
and the people affected by them, including ourselves; "shifting the narrative" around the systemic scaffolding of the social issues that concern us;
"getting uncomfortable" with our own complicity, marginality, or pain
related to these issues; and "cultivating hope" by coming together and
imagining a new world into being. It is the responsibility of individuals,
groups, and institutions to grapple with these steps and imagine how they
can be embedded into daily operations, movements, and systems.

In reality, our social, educational, political, and professional institutions
rarely provide spaces and opportunities for diverse individuals and communities to heal, share, listen, and learn from one another in the ways suggested
here. If we wish to change policies and practices that sustain injustices and
inhibit our wellbeing, we must begin by transforming the institutions and
individuals that design and implement such policies and practices. Indeed,
since the focus of this book is on institutions of higher education, the bulk of
this book explores how the models and steps described in this chapter can be
integrated into community-campus social change partnerships. First, however, we move from this chapter's macro-analysis of community wellbeing
and social injustice to the micro-analysis of individual wellbeing and critical
awareness presented in Chap. 3.

NOTES

1. I came upon Bryan Stevenson's work through a talk entitled, "American
   Injustice: Mercy, Humanity and Making a Difference," which he gave on
   March 29, 2016 at the Criminal Justice Symposium at Pomona College.
   Stevenson founded and directs the Equal Justice Initiative in Montgomery,
   Alabama, where he works to challenge bias against poor people and people
   of color through his work in legal defense in hundreds of criminal justice
   cases that aim to upturn our country's unjust policies pertaining to incarcerated youth, condemned prisoners, and death row (http://eji.org).
   While his work focuses specifically on criminal justice, I found that his
   four-step approach can be stretched into a framework for addressing social
   change in a variety of contexts.
2. This phenomenon has been examined at length by post-modern,
   post-structural, feminist, and cultural studies researchers such as Anzaldua
   (1987), Clifford and Marcus (1986), Gannon and Davies (2012), Hall

(1997), Harding (1987), Hesse-Biber and Piatelli (2012), Minh-Ha (1989), Smith (1999), and Wolf (1992).

3. Poverty tourism has been defined as such: "Poverty tourism refers to cases in which financially privileged tourists visit impoverished communities for the purpose of witnessing poverty firsthand. Many visitors expect the trip will prove educational and help alleviate poverty" (Outterson et al. 2011, p. 39). Poverty tourism can be heavily unethical and problematic on a number of levels; "it plays with notions of the romantic sublime, almost celebrating a type of inverted aesthetics where the tourist wishes to see the drama of shanty towns, both literally and metaphorically, precariously and haphazardly holding on to the very margins of society" (Frenzel and Koens 2012, p. xv).

4. In an effort to accurately locate the citation for this now-famous quote, I discovered a blog from an activist artist who discussed it directly with the woman who is usually credited with the statement, Lila Watson. Ms. Watson indicated "that she was not comfortable being credited for something that had been born of a collective process [and] came to an agreement on how it could accurately be credited [...] 'Aboriginal activists group, Queensland, 1970s'" (Unnecessary Evils 2008).

5. Founded over 40 years ago by Brazilian educational theorist, Paolo Freire, the critical pedagogy model draws on the earlier works of John Dewey and Jean Piaget and has been expanded upon by more recent scholars such as Ira Shor, bell hooks, Henry Giroux, Peter McLaren, Michelle Fine, and Stanley Aronowitz. Discussions of critical pedagogy throughout this book draw primarily on Paolo Freire's principle text, "Pedagogy of the Oppressed" (1970) and Ira Shor's "Empowering Education: Critical teaching for social change" (1992), as well as my experience utilizing this methodology in my teaching and community work.

6. To date, I have taught five courses at the local men's prison, as well as helped facilitate a partnership with the prison that now allows faculty from the Claremont Colleges to teach up to eight credit-bearing inside-out courses in the prison each year. This has occurred through the framework of the national Inside-Out Prison Exchange Program: "The Inside-Out Prison Exchange Program increases opportunities for people, inside and outside of prison, to have transformative learning experiences that emphasize collaboration and dialogue, inviting participants to take leadership in addressing crime, justice, and other issues of social concern. Education through which we are able to encounter each other, especially across profound social barriers, is transformative and allows problems to be approached in new and different ways" (Inside-Out Prison Exchange 2017).

7. There are definitely contradictions and tensions that persist in negotiating a working partnership with a prison, and I am unsettled by the prospect that the partnership itself ends up supporting the current incarceration system to

some degree. Yet, I join others in the prison education community in the belief that one meaningful route for creating change is from the inside-out. This is work that is co-created and driven with those who are currently incarcerated, forging social change through the creation of liberatory education that attends to the academic interests and political empowerment of those inside. In so doing, we aim to create educational opportunities and raise critical consciousness which can fly in the face of the domination and dehumanization detention facilities embody.

8. Joanna Macy founded The Great Turning, a theory and small-group global practice, in the 1980s as an approach to planetary transformation that confronts apatheia (spiritual, emotional, and political apathy). It aims to disrupt individual and social destructive habits in order to shift our perceptions around the problems we face and explore alternative paradigms for manifesting a restored relationship with the earth and each other. To share this work I draw primarily on Joanna Macy and Molly Brown's book, "Coming back to life: Practices to reconnect our lives, our world" (1998).

9. This concept was originally developed by Archbishop Romero during the civil war in El Salvador. It has since been adopted by academics in American Studies and Anthropology as well as used as a key form of engagement within PRATEC, as described in Ishizawa (2006).

10. PRATEC (http://www.pratecnet.org) is a Peruvian organization co-founded in 1986 by Grimaldo Rengifo Vásquez, Eduardo Grillo, Francois Greslou, and Marcela Velásquez. It aims to regenerate traditional cultural knowledge and practices that support biodiversity, cultural diversity, interculturalism, and individual and systematic decolonization. I draw primarily on my Masters fieldwork research with PRATEC and its sister agencies, Urphichallay, CEPROSI, Waman Wasi, Suma Yapu, and Chuymaru, (Hicks 2005) and their book, "The spirit of regeneration: Andean culture confronting western notions of development" (Apffel-Marglin and PRATEC 1998).

11. For additional scholarship that speaks to the importance of engaging such values in the work of cross-cultural partnerships and decolonizing research, see Alfred (2005), Ishizawa (2006), ITK & NRI (2006), Smith (1999), Steinberg and Kincheloe (1998), Steinman (2011), and Wilson (2008).

12. Following this and other protests, as well as the well-orchestrated media storms that followed them, student, faculty, and administrative governmental bodies simply had no other option but to listen and respond to student demands. Some changes came with unexpected reactivity—across the country, presidents and deans were fired or resigned, policies were changed in real time, and new centers, programs, and staff positions were created with the intention to support diversity. Apologies were formally issued and promises were made to further the dialogue and response

strategies. Of course, the traumas experienced by students who live at the crossroads of multiple forms of oppression did not disappear because of a finite uproar on campus that made faculty, staff, and administrators feel temporarily outraged or nervous. In the nearly two years since these student protests occured, colleges across the country have been trying to figure out how to transform student demands into structural and behavioral changes in classrooms and residence halls to ensure that colleges promote learning and support for all students, not just some. This work necessarily involves integrating support services in academic and student affairs that will cater to all students, not just those that enter with the cultural capital that is modeled after the "typical" college student of the past: white, straight, cis-gendered, middle-class males. It means infusing diverse histories, epistemologies, value systems, learning styles, and communication styles representative of our multicultural society within disciplines, curriculum, and student affairs. It also means actively creating policies that confront and transform the reproduction of social inequality. The story of this movement and the changes it demands is still being written.

13. This question has been adapted from a handout entitled "Personal Self-Assessment of Anti-Bias Behavior" (Anti-Defamation League 2007).

14. In my role both as director of the Community Engagement Center and as a faculty collaborator, I have been a part of building these partnerships between our college and local native communities since 2008. I owe tremendous gratitude to my partners in these efforts, including Pitzer staff member Scott Scoggins (who originally opened the doors of the partnerships through his personal relationships), Pitzer faculty Erich Steinman, Gina Lamb, Brinda Sarathy, Paul Faulstich, and Joe Parker, and local native elders, Julia Bogany, Robert John Knapp, Tony Cerda, Barbara Drake, Kim Marcus, and Luhui and Mati Waiya, as well as the college students, other professors, and local tribal members who have helped shape the projects and relationships over the years.

15. These aims at "shifting the narrative" take place in PRATEC through programs of "Afirmacion Cultural" (Cultural Affirmation), "Ninez y Biodiversidad" (Children and Biodiversity), and "Conservacion In Situo" (In Situ Conservation)—all of which work to reinvigorate native traditions and agricultural methods that have cultivated the earth's highest levels of biodiversity for centuries. "Cultural Affirmation" workshops in Andean schools and communities support the revaluing of native traditions such as dance, music- and instrument-making, arts, language, sewing, ceramics, and tending the earth alongside more western epistemological practices in the school curriculum. In early childhood schools where the children are too young to participate in these activities, teachers instead paint the walls of their classrooms with murals depicting traditional indigenous practices so that the children are surrounded by visual representations revaluing their

customs. Community-supportive agricultural practices occur through "Ferias de Semillas," a seed exchange festival where farming families from various villages come together and trade and barter their different seeds in order to mutually support the biodiversity in each of their farms. Programs of "Interculturalismo" (Interculturalism) focus on action steps of reintegrating indigenous culture alongside western ways of knowing, being, schooling, governing, and engaging in community. For more details on this topic, see Apffel-Marglin and PRATEC (1998).

16. When characterizing indigenous knowledge, any "generalizations must be recognized as indicative and not definitive… these knowledge systems are constantly adapting and changing in response to new conditions" (Barnhardt and Kawagley 2005, p. 8). For more on scholarship about indigenous knowledge systems and their connection (and disconnection) from western epistemologies, see Apffel-Marglin and PRATEC (1998), Armstrong (2006), Delgado and Gomez (2003), Kirkness and Barnhardt (1991), Mankiller (2004), Mosha (1999), Semali and Kincheloe (1999), Smith (1999), Vasquez (1998), and Wilson (2008).

17. As King and West (2016) notes, even when our freedom fighters are honored, their declarations are often sanitized for posterity. Their more radical reactions and analyses of unjust social and economic systems are swept under the rug in favor of more palpable hero legends.

18. Theatre of the Oppressed was developed in the 1960s by Augosto Boal in Brazil (influenced by the principals and methods of Freire's Pedagogy of the Oppressed). Investigative, invisible, legislative, image, and forum theatre are specific theater forms used as a means of promoting social change, first "used by peasants and workers; later, by teachers and students; now, also by artists, social workers, psychotherapists, NGOs … At first, in small, almost clandestine places. Now in the streets, schools, churches, trade-unions, regular theatres, prisons." Greater detail on the use of this theatrical-activist method can be found at Theatre of the Oppressed (2017).

19. Transformative movement building aims to change the changemakers and the methods and approaches they take to making change. This leads to "more effective organizational communities that are better able to communicate, manage conflict, be self-aware and self-reflective, evolve and change. It also leads to changes in organizing models and social change practice as organizations reorient their goals and strategies to match the values they want to cultivate in the broader world, such as compassion, equity, love and non-violence" (Ginwright 2015, p. 35). A related practice of transformative movement building is healing justice.

20. The healing justice framework utilizes a variety of approaches, including restorative justice, transformative organizing, and contemplative practices, to both respond to and explore the conditions that create collective harm,

while actively restoring community wellbeing (Ginwright 2015). To share this work, I draw primarily on Shawn Ginwright's "Hope and Healing in Urban Education: How urban activists and teachers are reclaiming matters of the heart" (2015).

21. A more extensive discussion of this is eloquently addressed in a blog article by Kai Cheng Thom (2016).

22. A similar framework exists within community psychology, known as *appreciative inquiry*, which "rather than beginning by asking about difficulties and deficiencies, [practitioners] begin to inquire into what is generative and life-giving, knowing that it is these pieces that should be built on and nurtured [and] enables the community to name valuable resources and capacities that can be used as they work together toward mutually desired aims" (Watkins and Shulman 2008, p. 199).

23. Asset-Based Community Development is a theoretical and action-oriented model for building communities from the inside out, developed by John McKnight and John Kretzmann and based on community-organizing work with diverse communities across the country over the last 25 years. The ABCD methods include building relationships, mapping assets, sharing information, connecting assets and needs, and mobilizing neighborhood change initiatives from the inside. "Mapping assets" involves creating an inventory of the capacities of members in the community (from skills and abilities to enterprising interests and experience) and proceeds with an inventory of assets and capacities of local associations and institutions. An assessment of how to mobilize assets toward rebuilding the community's economy and leverage outside resources to support locally driven community development is a principal focus. For a complete overview of how to implement the praxis of the asset-based community development model, see Kretzmann and McKnight's (1993) *Building Communities from the Inside-Out: A Path Towards Finding and Mobilizing a Community's Assets.* Chicago: ACTA.

24. "Calling people up" is a phrase and practice used in many contemporary social movements and educational spaces as a means of pointing out unjust, insensitive, or oppressive comments in a way that invites conversation, curiosity, compassion, and solidarity. It intentionally moves from the practice of "calling people out" (which often aims to judge, criticize, and sometimes silence those who make inflammatory remarks). Similarly, "calling people in" suggests bringing them into a dialogue about the problematic aspects of what has been said; calling them up poses an invitation to speak in a more elevated, inclusive, and thoughtful way. Of the many articles that have been written about this in the online social activist blogosphere, for those interested in this topic I suggest "A note on call out culture" (Ahmad 2015).

REFERENCES

Ahmad, A. (2015, March 2). A note on call-out culture. *Briarpatch Magazine.* Retrieved February 2, 2017, from https://briarpatchmagazine.com/articles/view/a-note-on-call-out-culture.

Alfred, T. (2005). *Wasáse: Indigenous Pathways of Action and Freedom.* Peterborough, ON, Broadview Press.

Angelou, M. (2016, April 30). *Finding our families, finding ourselves.* Los Angeles, CA: Museum of Tolerance.

Anti-Defamation League. (2007). "Personal Self-Assessment of Anti-Bias Behavior," The Anti-Defamation League's Education Division, A WORLD OF DIFFERENCE Institute. Retrieved March 1, 2017. https://www.adl.org/sites/default/files/documents/assets/pdf/education-outreach/Personal-Self-Assessment-of-Anti-Bias-Behavior.pdf.

Apffel-Marglin, F., & PRATEC. (1998). *The spirit of regeneration: Andean culture confronting western notions of development.* New York: Zed Books.

Armstrong, J. (2006). Community: Sharing one skin. In J. Mander & V. Tauli-Corpuz (Eds.), *Paradigm wars: Indigenous peoples' resistance to globalization.* San Francisco: Sierra Club Books.

Aronson, R. (2015). *We: Reviving Social Hope.* Chicago, IL: University of Chicago.

Barnhardt, R., & Kawagley, A. O. (2005). Indigenous knowledge systems and Alaska Native ways of knowing. *Anthropology & Education Quarterly., 36*(1), 8–23.

Berila, B. (2016). *Integration Mindfulness into Anti-Oppression Pedagogy.* New York, NY: Routledge.

Brown, B. (2010). *The gifts of imperfection: Let go of who you think you're supposed to be and embrace who you are.* Center City: Hazelden.

Clifford, J., & Marcus, G. E. (1986). *Writing culture: The poetics and politics of ethnography.* New York: University of California Press.

Corn, S. (2015, February 5). *Tessa Hicks Peterson: Social justice, yoga and awareness of inequalities.* Interview with Tessa Hicks Peterson, Yoga Journal.

Cox, W. (2015, August 21). California: Land of poverty. *NewGeography.* Retrieved March 1, 2017, from http://www.newgeography.com/content/005026-california-land-poverty.

Delgado, F., & Gomez, F. (2003). Knowledge and belief systems in Latin America. In B. Haverkort, K. V. Hooft, & W. Hiemstra (Eds.), *Ancient roots, new shoots, endogenous development in practice.* London: Zed Books.

Freire, P. (1970). *Pedagogy of the oppressed,* (M.B. Ramos, Trans.). New York, NY: Continuum Publishing.

Freire, P. (2006). *Pedagogy of the oppressed.* 30th anniversary edition. New York, NY: Continuum Publishing.

Frenzel, F., & Koens, K. (2012). Slum tourism: Developments in a young field of interdisciplinary tourism research. *Tourism geographies, 14*(2), 195–212.

Gannon, B., & Davies, S. (2012). Collective biography and the entangled enlivening of being. *International Review of Qualitative Research, 5*, 357–376.

Ginwright, S. (2015). *Hope and healing in urban education: How urban activists and teachers are reclaiming matters of the heart.* New York, NY: Routledge.

Gramsci, A. (1971). *Selections from the Prison Notebooks.* New York, NY: International Publishers.

Hahn, T. N. (2015). *How to Love.* Berkeley. CA: Parallax Press.

Hall, N. (1997). Creativity and incarceration: The purpose of art in a prison culture. In D. Gussak & E. Virshup (Eds.), *Drawing time: Art therapy in prisons and other correctional settings* (pp. 25–41). Chicago, IL: Magnolia Street Publishers.

Harding, S. G. (1987). *Feminism and methodology: Social science issues.* Bloomington: Indiana University Press.

Hesse-Biber, S. N., & Piatelli, D. (2012). The feminist practice of holistic reflexivity. In S. N. Hesse-Biber (Ed.), *Handbook of feminist research: Theory and praxis* (2nd ed., p. 2). Thousand Oaks, CA: Sage.

Hicks, T. (2005). *The interconnected community: Lessons from the Andes on ecological regeneration and interculturalism.* Unpublished thesis. Claremont, CA: Claremont Graduate University.

hooks, b. (1989). Choosing the margin as space of radical openness. *Framework: Journal of Cinema and Media, 36*, 15.

hooks, b. (1994). *Teaching to transgress: Education as the practice of freedom.* New York, NY: Routledge.

Inside-Out Prison Exchange Program. (2017). *Inside-out prison exchange program: Social change through transformative education.* Retrieved March 10, 2017, from http://www.insideoutcenter.org/.

Ishizawa, J. (2006). *From Andean cultural affirmation to Andean affirmation of cultural diversity—Learning with the communities in the central Andes.* Sweden: Dag Hammarskjold Foundation.

ITK., & NRI. (2006). Negotiating Research Relationships with Inuit Communities: A Guide for Researchers. In S. Nickels, J. Shirley & G. Laidler (Eds.). *Inuit Tapiriit Kanatami and Nunavut Research Institute: Ottawa and Iqaluit.*

Khouri, H. (2016, April 27). Guest lecture: "Trauma and Justice". In *Healing arts and social change course.* Norco: California Rehabilitation Center.

King Jr, M. L., & West, C. (2016). *The Radical King.* Boston, MA: Beacon Press.

Kirkness, V. J., & Barnhardt, R. (1991). First Nations and higher education: The four R's-respect, relevance, reciprocity, responsibility. *Journal of American Indian Education*, 1–15.

Kretzmann, J. P., & McKnight, J. (1993). *Building communities from the inside out.* Evanston, IL: Center for Urban Affairs and Policy Research, Neighborhood Innovations Network.

Lave, J., & Wenger, E. (1991). *Situated learning: Legitimate peripheral participation.* Boston, MA: Cambridge University Press.

Little, D. (2007). False Consciousness. Understanding Society: Innovative thinking about a global world. Retrieved 12 February 2017. http://www-personal.umd. umich.edu.

Mankiller, W. (2004). *Every day is a good day: Reflections by contemporary indigenous women*. Golden, CO: Fulcrum Publishing.

Macy, J., & Brown, M. Y. (1998). *Coming back to life: Practices to reconnect our lives, our world*. Gabriola Island, BC: New Society Publishers.

Minh-ha, T. T. (1989). *Woman, native, other: Writing postcoloniality and feminism*. Bloomington: Indiana University Press.

Mosha, R. S. (1999). The inseparable link between intellectual and spiritual formation in indigenous knowledge and education: A case study in Tanzania. In M. S. Ladislaus & J. L. Kincheloe (Eds.), *What is Indigenous knowledge? Voices from the academy* (209–223). New York, NY: Routledge.

Obama, B. (2004). *Keynote address*, 2004 Democratic National Convention. Fleet Center, Boston, MA. Retrieved March 1, 2017.

OEHHA. (2017). *CalEnviroScreen*, OEHHA science for a better California. Retrieved November 3, 2016, from https://oehha.ca.gov/calenviroscreen.

On Being with Krista Tippett. (2016a, February 18). Radio podcast. *The resilient world we're rebuilding now*. Interview with Patrisse Cullors and Robert Ross. Minneapolis. Retrieved February 23, 2016.

On Being with Krista Tippett. (2016b, November 10). Radio podcast. *Is America possible?* Interview with Vincent Harding, Minneapolis. Retrieved November 17, 2016.

Outterson, K., Selinger, E., & Whyte, K. (2011). Poverty tourism, justice, and policy: Can ethical ideals form the basis of new regulation. *Public Integrity, Winter, 12*(14) 1, 39–50.

Page, C. (2010, August 5). Transforming wellness & wholeness. *INCITE blog reflections from Detroit: Transforming wellness and wholeness*, web log post. Retrieved March 1, 2017, from https://inciteblog.wordpress.com/2010/08/05/reflections-from-detroit-transforming-wellness-wholeness/.

Partners for Better Health. (2017). *Build health challenge*. Retrieved November 3, 2017, from http://p4bhealth.org/build-health-challenge/.

Phillips, S. (2015). Prison ethnography and activism. *Anthropology and mass incarceration*. Denver, CO: Annual Meetings of the American Anthropological Association.

Pompa, L., & Crabbe, M. (2004). *The inside-out prison exchange program: exploring issues of crime and justice behind the walls*. Instructor's Manual. Rev. ed. Philadelphia: Temple University. http://www.insideoutcenter.org.

Prilleltensky, I., & Prilleltensky, O. (2006). *Promoting well-being: Linking personal, organizational, and community change*. New York, NJ: Wiley.

San Bernardino County. (2015). *Community indicators report.* Retrieved February 1, 2017, from http://cms.sbcounty.gov/Portals/21/Resources%20Documents/CIR_2015_Report.pdf.

Semali, L., & Kincheloe, J. L. (1999). *What is indigenous knowledge? Voices from the academy.* New York, NY: Routledge.

Shor, I. (1992). *Culture wars: School and society in the conservative restoration.* Chicago, IL: University of Chicago Press.

Smith, L. T. (1999). *Decolonizing methodologies: Research and indigenous peoples.* London: Zed books.

Steinberg, S. R., & Kincheloe, J. L. (1998). *Students as researchers: Creating classrooms that matter.* London: Falmer Press.

Steinman, E. (2011). Making space: Lessons from collaborations with tribal nations. *Michigan Journal of Community Service Learning, 18*(1), 5–19.

Stevenson, B. (2016, March 29). American injustice: Mercy, humanity and making a difference. *Criminal justice symposium.* Claremont, CA: Pomona College.

Theatre of the Oppressed. (2017). *International theatre of the oppressed website.* Jana Sanskriti International Research and Resource Institute. Retrieved June 6, 2016. http://jsirri.org/.

Thom, K. C. (2016). *8 steps towards building indispensability (Instead of disposability) culture.* Retrieved February 10, 2017, from http://everydayfeminism.com.

Tomlinson, B., & Lipsitz, G. (2013). American studies as accompaniment. *American Quarterly, 65,* 1–30.

University of Michigan. (2014). LARA/LARI and empathy. *The program on intergroup relations.* Ann Arbor, Michigan.

University of Michigan. (2016). Deepening dialogue through "affirming inquiry". *The program on intergroup relations.* Ann Arbor, Michigan.

Unnecessary Evils. (2008). "Attributing words," November 3. Retrieved March 7, 2017. http://unnecessaryevils.blogspot.com/2008/11/attributing-words.html#links.

Van Gelder, S. (2016). *The radical work of healing: Fania and Angela Davis on a new kind of civil rights activism.* Yes! Magazine. Spring. Retrieved March 1, 2017, from http://www.yesmagazine.org/issues/life-after-oil/the-radical-work-of-healing-fania-and-angela-davis-on-a-new-kind-of-civil-rights-activism-20160218.

Vasquez, G. R. (1998). Education in the modern west and the Andean culture. In F. Apffel-Marglin & PRATEC (Eds.), *The spirit of regeneration: Andean culture confronting western notions of development* (pp. 172–192). New York: Zed Books.

Watkins, M., & Shulman, H. (2008). *Towards psychologies of liberation.* New York, NY: Palgrave Macmillan.

Wilson, S. (2008). *Research is ceremony: Indigenous research methods.* Black Point: Fernwood Publishing.

Wolf, M. (1992). *A thrice-told tale: Feminism, postmodernism, and ethnographic responsibility.* San Jose, CA: Stanford University Press.

Zimmerman, K., Pathikonda, N., Salgado, B., & James, T. (2010). *Out of the spiritual closet: Organizers transforming the practice of social justice.* Oakland, CA: Movement Strategy Center.

CHAPTER 3

Self-Awareness and Radical Healing

Traumas of injustice occur when humanity is denigrated, rights are seized, and wellbeing and security are physically, emotionally, or spiritually threatened. Creating peace and justice today means not only navigating methods for effective social change, but also cultivating self-awareness and self-care in the face of such injustice. This work comes alive when we investigate personal identity, positionality, woundedness, sense of purpose, and strategies for caretaking ourselves and others. This chapter threads together consciousness-raising in conjunction with practices that nourish wellbeing, fortify radical healing, and disrupt injustice.

Radical healing begins by becoming aware of how the traumas of injustice influence our own behaviors and the behaviors of others. For many people, the desire to work on a specific social conflict issue stems from personal experience with that issue. While taking action around that issue can be personally transformative and even help heal some wounds, unacknowledged trauma or unfinished healing process can end up being unfairly projected onto others. As Thich Nhat Hanh explains, "We should not try to help others in an effort to escape our own sorrow, despair, or inner conflict. If you are not peaceful and solid enough inside yourself, your contributions will not be as useful. We must first practice mindfulness and grow compassion in ourselves, so that peace and harmony are in us, before we can work effectively for social change" (2003, p. 59). In other words, if we seek to aid in the liberation of others, we must be committed to the ongoing work of internal liberation.

© The Author(s) 2018
T. Hicks Peterson, *Student Development and Social Justice*,
https://doi.org/10.1007/978-3-319-57457-8_3

When an individual struggles with dis-ease (literally being without ease or out of balance in mental, physical, emotional, or spiritual dimensions), the ripple effect goes beyond those in intimate proximity and leaks into the larger community.[1] Those of us interested in forwarding social change are thus obliged to become conscious of our personal wounds, trigger points, and underlying motivations for social activism. We must be willing to be vulnerable and open to examining where and how our own traumas have a grip on our thoughts, behaviors, and reactions and may influence our work in the community. Even when community engagement is indeed a vehicle for healing, we can avoid putting others at risk by differentiating working on ourselves outside the community from our social justice work inside the community. By committing to consciously and consistently reflecting on our own healing, "we become empowered to act from a place of awareness and compassion rather than an impulsive agenda motivated by our fear and our wounds. When we are *reactive* without consciousness around our trauma or triggers, we may become part of the problem we wish to address. When we are *responsive*, we are 'able to respond' from a more grounded and self-regulated place" (Khouri 2010). Getting intimately familiar with and consciously addressing our own wounds or traumas makes it less likely they will control our actions. In order to advocate for justice and wellbeing in our communities, we must simultaneously attend to the wellbeing of ourselves.

Wellbeing is defined here as the distinct and intentional presence of social, psychological, and emotional health, including: "self-acceptance, positive relations with others, personal growth, purpose in life, environmental mastery and autonomy" (Keyes 2002, p. 208). Beyond these primarily psychological components of individual wellbeing, "social wellbeing" can also be cultivated. Social wellbeing occurs when individuals "see society as meaningful and understandable, when they see society as possessing potential for growth, when they feel they belong to and are accepted by their communities, when they accept most parts of society, and when they see themselves contributing to society" (ibid). The reverse is also true. When people do not feel valued and understood or have little sense of belonging and social connectedness, both social wellbeing and collective wellbeing suffer. Thus, devoting time to critical reflection, self-care, and personal growth not only gives us the stamina to sustain our social change efforts, but it also enables us to remain open, grounded, responsible, and effective within the community.

These practices are particularly important for young people in college who are coming into their own sense of self as well as critical consciousness of the world around them. While navigating both intra- and interpersonal development, they uncover who they want to become in the world and often become interested in having a positive impact on the world. Given the opportunity to connect with others about the challenges they face in nourishing their personal wellbeing (especially in the face of injustice), as well as on the strengths and resiliencies they possess or could develop, students often recognize that others experience similar injustices or challenges to wellbeing. Cultivating critical awareness of self and other through introspection and community engagement can thus result in profound shifts in understanding of both social biases and interconnectedness.

Although processes of introspection and self-care have not been given much attention in most service-learning, community engagement, and activist literatures, they are inescapably tied to community building and social change. To become more effective in the world, we must pursue provocative lines of inquiry around our identities, sense of purpose, relationship to injustice, and strategies for radical healing. In this chapter, these lines of inquiry are framed around the following concepts:

- *Self-awareness*—becoming aware of the life experiences and the formation of values that have informed and influenced who we are and why we feel drawn to the work of social change;
- *Self-identity*—identifying positionalities based on race, class, religion, culture, gender, ability, citizenship, and sexual identity and orientation that determine how we see and are seen in the world;
- *Intersectionality*—disrupting identity binaries, cultivating interconnectedness, and honoring an integrated sense of self in relation to others;
- *Radical healing*—nurturing practices that sustain personal and community wellbeing and social change activism.

This chapter weaves together critical theories intended to raise awareness of our positionalities and motivations for community engagement with practices that attend to our personal and collective wellbeing. Through free writing or in conversation with others, readers are invited to mindfully engage with the critical reflection prompts that correlate with each section of this chapter. Interactive exercises for cultivating mindfulness are also provided to help readers sit with and move through the discomfort and dissonance that the consciousness-raising process may elicit. I encourage readers to utilize the reflection prompts and activities provided throughout the Chapter as a handbook, or perhaps, a journal, to record and reflect on how the concepts presented here take shape in your own life.

DEVELOPING SELF-AWARENESS

Self-awareness (of one's values, biases, and positionalities) has a reciprocal relationship with community awareness (of local and global examples of domination and liberation). When we become more cognizant of and committed to addressing the challenges and assets within ourselves, we also become more available and invested in addressing the challenges and assets of our community. Furthermore, becoming mindfully aware of our inner conflicts and fostering harmony within ourselves cultivates our abilities to negotiate social conflict and become compassionate toward those who are similar or dissimilar to us in the communities within which we work.

The inverse is also true: our connections with others are intertwined with a sense of being connected to ourselves. Research in the field demonstrates strong correlations between community engagement and emotional, social, and psychological wellbeing.[2] Sometimes the positive individual outcomes of connecting with others come at the expense of the communities within which we work, however. The community should not be used in order for individuals to feel better about themselves. Self-awareness practices can assist us in uncovering our underlying motives for doing community service work. For example, some of us want to be seen as "good" people, even heroes, but this motivation can result in participating in tasks that will be publicly applauded, while leaving more challenging and necessary work untouched. Others do community work out of a never-ending sense of obligation, but that can lead to caring for others at the expense of their own wellbeing, resulting in eventual burnout and even resentment (Beath 2005).

The intimate work of introspection and self-development must not be divorced from awareness of the larger collective. As Alexander explains, "It requires the work of each and everyone, to unearth this desire to belong to the self *in* community as part of a radical project, which is not to be confused with a preoccupation with the self. The one has to do with a radical self-possession, the other with self-preoccupation on which individualism thrives. Self-determination is both an individual and collective project" (2003, p. 632). While self-serving naval-gazing can drive obsessive individualism to the detriment of collective wellbeing, becoming "solid enough inside yourself" to participate effectively in social change requires exploring multiple dimensions of the self (Hanh 2003, p. 59). Reflecting on who we are and how we come to see the world, our values, motivations, and sense of purpose are all crucial to developing critically conscious and effective approaches to social change work. Critical reflection carried out within the cradle of community adds a deeper layer to personal introspection. By engaging in critical reflection with others, we can bear witness to suffering, listen to and learn from different perspectives, and develop mutual accountability. Critical reflection, conducted individually or collectively, is a vital component of social change work.

To engage directly in your own practice of critical reflection around who you are, what your values are, what you are passionate about and fearful of, and what community engagement means to you, explore the *Critical Reflection Activity: Self-awareness.*

1. Who are you? List five adjectives that describe your persona or the way you portray yourself to others. Then list five adjectives that describe the self inside that is less known or silenced.
2. Who do you want to become?
3. Where are you from? Geographically? Politically? Culturally? Spiritually?
4. To whom are you responsible? Accountable? Connected?
5. What is your inheritance, figuratively speaking?
6. List the five most basic beliefs or values that guide your life.
7. Where do you find your greatest sense of belonging and purpose?
8. What are you most passionate about? What scares you the most?
9. Is the life you are living the life you want? Is it in line with your visions for a just society?
10. What do you imagine are or will be your greatest challenges and greatest joys in doing social change/community work?[3]

DEVELOPING AWARENESS OF IDENTITIES

In addition to exploring the potential impact of our values or motivations for engaging in social change, we must reflect on the various societal positions and identities we hold. Awareness of self and social identities is necessary to developing an understanding of systems of oppression and what roles we play in them. Actively listening to those who occupy different societal positions is also important if we are to build bridges across difference and increase our consciousness of accountability. Both these processes can lead to a conscientious effort to consider how our identities influence how we respond to the trauma of injustice and how we engage in coalitions for social change.

In addition to becoming curious about the impacts of our positionality, we also must recognize the prejudices we hold and how that influences our work in the world. Almost everybody has had the experience of being prejudiced in some ways and being targeted by prejudice in other ways. Some people fear that acknowledging the wide range of experiences of prejudice in our society insinuates that all people have equal access to the power necessary to exclude or oppress others. Of course, that is not the case. An individual being prejudiced against another individual is not the same thing as having a power structure that supports and integrates individuals' prejudices within a backdrop of systemic oppression. Recognizing the complexity of prejudice also generates cognitive dissonance, since it clashes with static "oppressed" versus "oppressor" labels and with the desire to be seen as wholly "good," unprejudiced people. Nonetheless, candid reflections on the personal biases we hold are a key step in confronting our individual parts in perpetrating the divides in our society.

A great deal has been written about the development of self-identity, especially as it relates to race, gender, and sexual orientation, and how this impacts our interactions with others and the formation or dissolution of bias.[4] Most pertinent to this book's discussion of campus-community partnerships is Simons and colleagues' application of Cross' (1991) and Helms (1990) well-known racial identity development models to students in service-learning programs (2011). They examined the ways in which the racial identity of students developed in conjunction with community engagement experiences. Simons and colleagues (2011) noted several stages in racial identity development that come alive through the process of community engagement:

- preencounter/contact stage: prior to entrance into a community placement program, most students hold colorblind views of race along with pre-conceived notions about racial groups; they then experience some culture shock upon exposure to communities constituted of people who have different racial backgrounds than their own.
- encounter/disintegration stage: students recognize the social implications of their race for "out-group" members; "most students acquired awareness (89%) and understanding (74%) of racial differences between themselves and service recipients, and 86% of them provided examples illustrating White or class privilege" (Simons et al. 2011, p. 201).
- immersion–emersion stage: greater understanding emerges about racism and the social problems that can be attributed to racial privilege, which can lead to greater understanding of the systems affecting the people students are engaged with their community placement; however many "white individuals are resistant to acknowledge that race is an underlying cause of social and educational inequities," while students of color often experience heightened interest in their own ethnic heritage and racial identity (ibid).
- internalization–commitment stage: students are fully enmeshed and accountable to the members of the community in their placements; this is often correlated to a greater sense of social responsibility towards issues of racism and community responsibility (and reward) related to the relationships built in the community; advanced self-awareness, capacity for critical self-reflection, and increased self-esteem are related to the ability to effectively work in diverse communities (Simons et al. 2011).

While this study is helpful in articulating the ways in which racial identity develops through involvement with service learning, there are limitations to its application of the identity models and perhaps to the original models themselves. The first limitation is the focus on the experience of white students entering communities racially different than their own. Unfortunately, most of the scholarship around community engagement follows this trend. We need additional research on how the developmental experience varies for students of color and how other factors such as class, sexual orientation, and geography influence the development of students who enter communities that do and do not reflect their own identities. Second, we must recognize that identity development is fluid, iterant, and does not follow the same step-by-step process for all members of any given racial group. While this is changing, for many years the identity development literature neglected multiple or intersectional identities (e.g., mixed race), non-conforming identities (e.g., non-binary gender), and the influence of non-racialized identities (e.g., class, ability, sexual orientation) on identity development. Third, researchers should determine the stage of development students are in before they arrive at college or enter a community engagement program, the climate of personal or group awareness and reflection on identity issues on campus, and whether or not the communities the students engage with reflect their own identities before attempting to correlate identity development with community engagement. Finally, researchers should examine whether the racial identity development of college students is occurring at the expense of the communities in which they are engaged. Does having students learn about their biases and ignorance through exposure to marginalized communities put the wellbeing of those communities at stake?

AnneMarie Vaccaro's research speaks to this last point (2009). She demonstrates that white students who have an underdeveloped racial identity and related racialized biases and assumptions have harmed community partnerships. Many students remained unaware of, discounted, or did not actively reflect upon their privileges, biases, or positionality while becoming engaged with communities. Community engagement in such cases resulted in aversive racism, entrenched racist attitudes and microaggressions, and the perpetuation of unequal benefits to the service-learning partnership for communities of color. Even when white students learned a great deal about themselves through community engagement, their beliefs and behaviors often ended up causing more harm than good to the communities and the benefits of service learning were often lopsided. While white college students engaging in communities of color often attain "skill enhancement, resume-building experiences, and course credit," they also end up engaging in microaggressions and "adding to the sense of invisibility, frustration, and exhaustion of youth of color," effectively mitigating any other positive results of the service partnership (p. 129). Other research indicates that such cross-cultural service relationships can result in further cementing prejudicial attitudes and stereotypes (Moely et al. 2008; Dunlap et al. 2007). With this book, I join a small but growing group of scholars interested in further assessments that examine the potential for inequities, stereotype threats, and other harmful impacts that can dispro-portionality impact students of color involved in community engagement (Simons et al. 2011; Finley and McNair 2013; Harper 2009). Essentially, community engagement programs that are not planned with these con-cerns at the forefront or that do not facilitate student reflection on identity development and biases can potentially cause harm both to students and community members involved in community engagement programs.

Over the course of their lives, individuals encounter varying levels of privilege or marginalization aligned with different aspects of their identity. Everyone is therefore responsible for recognizing their biased beliefs and behaviors and accountable for shifting them. We can begin to make this shift by exploring the many identities we inhabit and the levels of power assigned by society to each of those identities. We then reflect on how the structural and interpersonal advantages or disadvantages associated with such identities have affected our families and identity groups over time. Through critical reflection, we can come to recognize the manifestations of colonization, white supremacy, patriarchy, capitalism, and heteronorma-tivity in thinking, speaking, behaviors, belief systems, and social norms. This ideally results in taking greater responsibility for educating ourselves on the broader implications of our identities and understanding how we are impacted and impact others by the personal biases that uphold structural biases, social exclusions, violence, and oppression.

A specific exercise to help facilitate this critical reflection follows. While intentionally crude in its evaluation of identity, this reflection exercise helps illustrate where society does and does not assign privilege to individuals and the impact of such assignments. It also helps us choose how to react to socially imposed identities. As with all reflection activities, attempt this exploration mindfully and honestly, initially through personal writing, followed by small-group debriefing conversations.

Critical Reflection: Self-identity

1. Which identities and levels of privilege do you inhabit? On the left column, fill in the blank for how you identify in each category and then circle the associated levels of privilege on the right, *as determined by the assigned value society gives towards these labels:*

   a. Race: _____ a. +/−
   b. Gender Identity: _____ b. +/−
   c. Religion: _____ c. +/−
   d. Class: _____ d. +/−
   e. Sexual Orientation: _____ e. +/−
   f. Citizenship status: _____ f. +/−
   g. Language: _____ g. +/−
   h. Ability: _____ h. +/−
   i. Ethnicity: _____ i. +/−
   j. Age: _____ j. +/−

2. Do the levels of privilege society assigns you as a result of these identity traits correlate with how you view yourself or your experiences in the world?
3. What challenges and strengths or insecurities and securities are attached to these identities?
4. How have these identities shaped the lens with which you view the world and are treated in the world?
5. Where does privilege show up in your life, explicitly and implicitly?
6. Where does exclusion or discrimination show up in your life, explicitly and implicitly?
7. If you are plagued with guilt, how can you recognize it without being immobilized by it?
8. If you are racked with anger, how can you use it strategically to make change?

9. Are there ways you dissociate from injustice and oppression (i.e., by going into denial, blame, ignorance, apathy, distraction, numbness, rage, lashing out, or shrinking back)?

10. What price do you pay or have others paid for you to stand where you are?

11. Provide real examples of what it would look like if you were to use or lose your areas of privilege in the name of peace and justice.

Reckoning with Privilege

At some point, most individuals confront both oppression and privilege, in different circumstances and based on their different identities. Whether those benefiting from privilege explicitly or implicitly, intentionally or unintentionally participate in hierarchical and unjust systems, they are nonetheless participants in systems from which they benefit. Investigating systems of domination (however absurd and baseless) and the feelings, beliefs, and reactions they incur is a critical step in the work of everyone who benefits from oppressive systems and wishes to change them. This work is particularly important for those whose identities have been highly valued politically, socially, and historically. People who have multiple levels of privilege (i.e., because of being white, male, wealthy, able-bodied, or heterosexual) are not often cognizant of the extent of the advantages, opportunities, access, and security accorded to them. The ways in which privilege colors the lens through which one sees the world and influences how one is treated in the world impacts most facets of life, yet often remains invisible to the ones with privilege (McIntosh 1989, 2009). They may not even recognize that *not* having to think about one's positionality on a daily basis is itself a privilege.

When one's values, notions of common sense, and cultural norms mirror those promoted by the ruling classes, judging others who live with a different set of identities and cultural orientations results not only in personal biases but also in institutional and systemically perpetrated exclusion and oppression of others. Some researchers note that oppressive systems also have deleterious effects on those who are positioned as oppressors.[5]

Those who are assigned dominant roles in terms of power, access, privilege, and reputation obviously benefit directly from their positionality, but they are also negatively affected by having their investments, benefits, and sense of self-worth tied to a hierarchical system in which they succeed at the expense of others. While the negative impact of living within an unjust society on people with privilege cannot be compared to the trauma experienced by marginalized people, the systems and practices of oppression implicate all involved in a set of toxic beliefs and hierarchies. Thus, it is of critical importance for individuals coming from multiple positions of privilege to reflect on how their positionality influences their movement through the world and how unjust social policies perpetuate their positions of power.

If we want to have integrity in our work to end oppression and create justice, peace, and wellbeing, we must start by looking in the mirror at our own positions of privilege. It is particularly important for teachers or community leaders who wish to thoughtfully walk their talk in their facilitation of community engagement programs to model critical reflection around issues of positionality and privilege.

In my own journey of self-reflection, I have asked myself many questions concerning privilege and accountability, which may be applicable to some readers, especially seasoned activists or faculty with multiple levels of privilege.

Critical Reflection: Privilege and Accountability

1. What personal biases and acts of discrimination are a part of your personal repertoire or cultural lens that you cannot or choose not to see?
2. What ways does privilege buffer you from injustice and trauma that you may not even notice?
3. What ways do you contribute to unjust systems as a result of the positions you hold in society, advancements you've reaped in your education or career, policies you adhere to, or even conversations you are a part of?
4. Since advantages and access enjoyed today by certain groups with privilege are the result of advantages and access afforded to similarly privileged ancestors (who may have benefited from such oppressive systems as settler colonialism or slavery), what

reparations can you make for these discrepancies in opportunity, access, and financial gain that were (and may still be)
unavailable to others?

5. What social buffers keep you healthy, safe, protected, and
   respected on a daily basis that may not exist for others simply
   because of the differences in identities?

6. How are you keeping yourself accountable to disrupting unjust
   systems through your community engagement work in the
   world today?

In the course of such critical reflections, resistance to acknowledging
either the privileges or the disadvantages correlated to our different identities may emerge. When first discovering the injustices of the world and
one's part in them, those in positions of privilege usually experience an
onslaught of feelings of disbelief, sadness, anger, defensiveness, and grief.
Individuals who have multiple identities of privilege are often plagued with
feelings of guilt and shame, followed by feeling helpless to do anything to
change the unjust system from which they benefit. This is particularly
challenging when their privileges are unearned, when individuals have not
sought out or asked for them, but have simply received them as a benefit of
their identities, as is usually the case. Beth Berila explains the sources of
such dissonance:

> The dissonance that arises from learning about oppression is more than a
> cognitive one. It is also an emotional and psychological one, because the
> ideas we are challenging are often embedded in the students' very sense of
> selves. These are not merely facts we are challenging but also worldviews that
> have long structured their worlds. Students and faculty alike have been so-
> cialized, often learning ideologies that uphold social inequalities, regardless of
> the cultural framework of that socialization. Dominant group identity, for
> instance, has been constructed with an invisible sense of entitlement already
> embedded into its very definition, so to challenge it inevitably creates fun-
> damental dissonance. (2016, p. 122)

Initially, realizing the reality of oppression and our complicity in it feels like
an affront to our very understanding of the world and the information we
have been fed about what it means to hold the identities we have. Intense

emotional reactions are expected to arise in this process. Anticipating such reactions and cultivating awareness so that we can bear witness to them as they unfold within ourselves or in others allows us to learn from this dissonance. With critical self-reflection, deep listening and learning from people who hold other perspectives on these topics, people who hold unearned privileges can recognize the ways in which participation in social change work is an act of resistance to the continuation of institutional oppression. However, only undoing privileges will enable such efforts to be fully realized:

> We can begin to see that each time we peel away another layer of oppression, we can learn to have more choice in what messages we learn and what we choose to integrate into our sense of self. For many of us, the ideologies of privilege were internalized without our even knowing it. So unlearning them means we have more choices about the role we play in the world, how we relate to others, and how we understand ourselves. While the process of unlearning privilege can be deeply unsettling, the potential results are liberating, for marginalized groups and for ourselves. (Berila 2016, p. 112)

The tension between possessing unearned privileges and working to dismantle them must be wrestled with head on in order for social justice work to be conducted consciously, with accountability, and true commitment to reversing these privileges.

Reckoning with Oppression

As vital as analyzing privilege is to working effectively in movements for peace and justice, it is also important not to rush past reflecting on how we have been personally affected by oppression and injustice. For many, recognition is rendered daily around the personal impact that results from holding an identity that is not part of the hegemonic order. Sometimes this recognition is welcomed and celebrated in acts of cultural affirmation, but more often than not it is something imposed externally with implicit or explicit aims to dehumanize, delegitimize, or limit the full freedom and capacity of the individual to take action. Reflecting on positionality and how it affects all facets of our day-to-day lives births a reckoning with our beliefs and actions as well as the systems that support or deny them in society.

PRATEC promotes a three-part process for addressing and transforming experiences of oppression into a regeneration of personal and collective affirmation (Apffel-Marglin and PRATEC 1998). While this process concentrates explicitly on the impacts of colonization on Native communities, it can be applied to any marginalized groups who have borne the brunt of institutionalized and systematic oppression, as "the recollection of a repressed or denied history is a key element in reclaiming vitality" for all oppressed groups (Watkins and Shulman 2008, p. 5). The following three-part process comes to life through introspection, group dialogue, ceremony, lessons in reclaiming history, and culturally affirming practices imbued with resistance and resilience.

a. *Decolonizacion Mental* (Decolonization of the Mind): The first step begins by recognizing the ways colonization of lands and nations as well as of spirits and minds occurred in the past and continue to occur. People examine historical and contemporary practices of settler-colonial imperialism, white supremacy, and other forms of domination that have divorced communities from their lands, spiritual practices, cultural traditions, epistemologies (ways of knowing), and ontologies (ways of being in the world) and then taught people that these ways were backward and barbaric. Decolonizing the mind involves intentionally unlearning the colonizing norms and values that have oppressed the minds of the colonized during and long after colonization occurred.

b. *Afirmacion Cultural* (Cultural Affirmation): Once decolonization of the mind has been ignited, community members focus their energies on regenerating and reaffirming their cultural practices, identities, values, knowledge systems, and traditions. Cultural affirmation of ways of thinking, believing, dreaming, communicating, teaching, learning, practicing rituals, making art, building community and relationships, governing, relationship-building, and so on occurs at the levels of the individual and the collective.

c. *Interculturalismo* (Interculturalism): The final step encourages people to interact with people from other cultures (even those that have been in the colonizing position) in ways that neither negate their own cultural practices nor shut out different cultures and practices. The intention of this step is to find ways to foster intercultural understanding and exchange; it thus reflects the indigenous values of mutual nurturing and coexistence in an interconnected world.

Following this three-step process enhances our understanding of how our identities, minds, and actions are affected by—but can yet be freed from—the underpinnings of domination. It provides an opportunity for increasing our critical consciousness about our positionalities and how they correlate to greater systems of oppression, a vital step for any personal or political move towards liberation   (Freire 1970; Gramsci 1971; hooks 1994; Shor 1992) .

Personal introspection around the impacts of oppression that develop insight on how to make meaningful movement towards cultural affirmation and intercultural understanding is worthwhile for everyone. Even those with multiple levels of privilege can benefit from engaging in such reflection, as it shows how much was lost and needs to be regained in the collective process of decolonization. For reflection prompts on these topics, please explore *Critical Reflection: Decolonization, Cultural Affirmation, and Intercultural Understanding*.

1. What beliefs were you taught about your identity as a result of colonization or oppression?
2. What did these beliefs tell you about those in power in terms of morals, values, intelligence, knowledge, access, rights, and so on?
3. Where did you pick up these beliefs (e.g., from school, media, religion, family)?
4. How do these beliefs translate into oppressive norms and systems in society?
5. How have such beliefs affected you physically, emotionally, mentally, or spiritually?
6. What impact has this had on your sense of identity, value, self-esteem, or pride?
7. What culturally affirming practices, rituals, knowledges, histories, and traditions in your community have been colonized, stolen, or repressed?
8. Describe instances where you have seen oppressive beliefs or actions confronted and refuted.
9. Who can you learn from and work with to reaffirm cultural practices in your daily life and the communities or institutions you belong to?

10. How can you create intercultural understanding or build coalitions with other groups or people with other identities? What would that look like in action?
11. What are the connections between cultural affirmation, resistance, and resilience?

INTERSECTIONAL IDENTITIES

Equally as important as raising consciousness around identity, privilege and oppression is challenging the social categories that limit us from experiencing our identities as whole, integrated and pliant. Society molds us to fit into rigid identity boxes according to race, ethnicity, gender, class, sexual orientation, religion, ability and citizenship through the use of census forms, quotas, and representational politics. In this section, I challenge the perpetuation of identity binaries and seek to appreciate the fullness and unevenness of our many different identities. The concept of "intersectionality" helps in recognizing the importance of contextualizing and connecting the impacts of disparate but related oppressed identities. The Black feminist scholars who originally conceived of the notion of "intersectionality" encouraged a critical analysis of how multiple identities (such as race and class) intersect and thereby add to or diminish access to power and opportunity and the degrees to which different forms of oppression inform and influence one another (Combahee River Collective 1977; Colins 1990; Collins and Bilge 2016; Crenshaw 1987).

Discussing our positionalities in stark binary terms, such as when we identify ourselves strictly as members of distinct groups with static labels, inhibits the rich expression of our multifaceted selves and diminishes the complex nuances of our intersectional identities. In *Borderlands/La Frontera*, Gloria Anzaldua warned us of the perils of such compartmentalized identities when she wrote, "What we are suffering from is an absolute despot duality that says we are able to be only one or the other" (1987, p. 41). Beyond an understanding of how distinct oppressions are interdependent and compounded by others, Anzaldua called us to honor the interstitiality and blurring between our expressions of race, gender, ethnicity, culture, language, and sexuality, to "embrace ambiguity, complexity, and multiplicity, and encourage resistance to repressive and alienating cultural norms" (Watkins and Shulman 2008, p. 171).

Perpetuating limitations within and separateness between our different identities not only impacts our own coherent and integrated sense of self, but also adds tension to our attempts to work in coalition across difference. As M. Jacqui Alexander warns:

> Oftentimes when we have "failed" at solidarity work we retreat, struggling to convince ourselves that it is indeed the work we have been called upon to do. The fact of the matter is there *is* no other work but the work of creating and recreating ourselves within the context of community. Simply put, there is no other work. It took five hundred years, at least in this hemisphere, to solidify the division of things that belong together. But it need not take us five hundred more to move ourselves out of this existential impasse. (2003, p. 632)

When we "solidify the division of things that belong together," we perpetuate politically motivated cultural polemics that were thrust upon us centuries ago (i.e., with the creation of racial categories, powell 2015). We perpetuate a cycle of divisiveness by drawing lines around ourselves and enclosing ourselves within distinct identity groups that are not nearly as flexible as our experiences of them. Our whole selves become fragmented into many parts and our whole communities into many subgroups. When we "internalize a worldview based on fragmentation and dichotomization" and adhere to dualistic self-identifications, our full humanity becomes diminished (Reynolds and Pope 1991, p. 177). We lose the nuanced, fluid sense of self that permits us to not strictly be one thing or another and to change over time, rather than ignoring the reality that many people consider themselves to be a mix of races, cultures, or ethnicities, that many people view their gender expressions, sexual identities, and sexual orientations not as static or fixed but as occurring along a continuum, and that many people experience shifts in some aspects of their identity over their lifetimes (i.e., in identities of class, religion, citizenship, and ability). Since "to be oppressed is to be socialized into a worldview that is suboptimal and leads to a fragmented sense of self" (Myers et al. 1991, p. 56, quoted in Reynolds and Pope, 1991, p. 177), classifying our diverse, intersectional identities into fixed, dualistic categories is itself a form of oppression. "When the fluidity, malleability, and multiplicity of identity go unrecognized, dehumanizing the Other is more possible" (Watkins and Shulman

2008, p. 172). If we do not interrogate the means of dicing up our identities, we may end up perpetuating paradigms of hierarchical dualism in our own language and actions, which then continue to inform oppressive systems and patterns.

Unfortunately, the traditional terminology of identity politics often sustains the very hierarchical dualisms that cemented us into rigid identity categories in the first place. Even when we splice our identities into distinct categories for the sake of raising consciousness around privilege and oppression, as was done in the *Critical Reflection on Self-identity* activity, we exacerbate the use of binaries that break down the whole person into many fragmented pieces and separate whole groups of people from "the Other." Using binary categories continues to divide "us" from "them," "victim" from "perpetrator," and "oppressed" from "oppressors." As Audre Lorde reminds us, "the master's tools will never dismantle the master's house" (1984, p. 2). Discussions of identity and oppression are linked in that we want to dismantle the house altogether, yet we keep using the master's tools (such as finite identity boxes and binary notions of oppression) that maintain its foundation in society.

A tension thus arises around how we choose to define our identities and understand ourselves. Many people refute the validity of any socially imposed categorizations. This is seen in the common desire to defy the concept of "race" altogether, since racial categories are predicated on the arbitrary measurement of skin color and thereby erase multifaceted cultures, personalities, values, and ancestry. Taking this approach is problematic, however, because it disavows the real and meaningful cultural and political identities that have been borne out of racial categorizations. For many, such identities are a source of community and survival. Furthermore, choosing not to acknowledge the existence of racialized identities in such stark terms risks failing to recognize the many instances of systemic and historic discrimination that have occurred along the rigid, dualistic lines of race, class, gender, and so on. The question remains: Can we simultaneously accept that identity is neither fixed nor fragmented while recognizing that the static way our identities are perceived in society impacts our access to rights, power, resources, and dignity?

Identity Holism

Our identity experiences that correlate with privilege in some instances and disadvantage in others are in a dialectic relationship with one another. They juxtapose, define, and sometimes balance each other through their differences (Baxter and Montgomery 1996; Chung and Ting-Toomey 2011). Understanding these opposing forces within our own diverse, intersectional identities requires that we negotiate the security that comes with privilege and insecurity that comes with disadvantage. Since some of our identities change as we develop and as our environments and relationships change, we must constantly adapt to these different parts of ourselves, the experiences they bring, and how they impact our self-definition (Chung 2017). Negotiating the challenges and strengths that come from these different components of our identities is also part of the self-identity development process (Ting-Toomey 2015). Negotiating the fullness and multiplicity of our identities not only makes our internal identity development experience more coherent, it fosters greater compassion towards other people's experiences. We have all been in the "out group" at some point. Reflecting on this experience can help us better understand the pain others feel who are caught in an "out-group" position in opposition to a particular "in-group" identity we hold. A clear understanding of inclusion and differentiation enables us to engage in social interactions that respect and support those who are different from us and moves us toward external inclusion as well as internal cohesion of our dialectical differences. If we do not successfully negotiate our dialectical identities, we may be less practiced at successfully negotiating diversity with others (Chung and Ting-Toomey 2011; Ting-Toomey 2015).

We cannot experience the fullness of our being unless we transcend the rigid categories we or others have pinned to us; otherwise, we end up limiting ourselves to the surface narratives of identity. One way to disrupt these binaries is to adopt what Reynolds and Pope (1991) call "diunital reasoning." Diunital reasoning "challenges the dualistic and either-or beliefs found in the dominant Western worldview and is centered on the notion that all things or beliefs can occur simultaneously and in harmony with each other" (Reynolds and Pope, 1991, p. 177). While "check the box" identity groups are critical components of self-identity, they are not the entirety of it. Limiting our biographies to these identity labels not only has the unwanted consequence of fragmentation, it also inadvertently limits the soulfulness of our inner landscape and shortchanges the possibility of having a more mystical or poetic relationship with our interiority (On Being 2015; Palmer 2000). Fragmenting our identities also separates us from our connection to our ancestors, the earth, and dreams and visions of how we and the world might better operate together if we escaped these historic narratives of division (Anzaldúa 1987). Disrupting binaries allows us to reconnect and integrate the multi-faceted and fluid aspects of ourselves in a more holistic identity. The concept of holism is nothing new. Most indigenous ontologies have long been situated in a belief and experience of holism. Indigenous scholar Jeannette Armstrong has much to teach us about holism as she recounts the ways in which Okanagan people self-identify:

> When we say the Okanagan word for ourselves, we are actually saying 'the ones who are dream and land together.' That is our original identity. Before anything else, we are the living, dreaming Earth pieces […] We are tied into and part of everything else. It refers to the dream parts of ourselves forming our community, and it implies what our relationships are. We say, 'This is my clan,' or, 'This is my people. These are the families that I came from. These are my great-grandparents,' and so on. In this way I know my position my responsibility for that specific location and geographic area. That is how I introduce myself. That is how I like to remember who I am and what my role is. […] One of the reasons I explain this is to try to bring our whole society closer to that kind of understanding, because without that deep connection to the environment, to the earth, to what we actually are, to what humanity is, we lose our place and confusion and chaos enter. We then spend a lot of time dealing with that confusion. (2006, pp. 35–36)

Holistic forms of self-identification do not divide identities into separate, fixed categories. They do not juxtapose our similarities and differences to others. Holistic self-identification instead reminds us and others of the sacred notion of interconnection. It suggests that at some energetic, cellular, or spiritual level, we are all one and thus have obligations to others—community, ancestors, land, and culture. As bell hooks says, we embrace "a global vision wherein we see our lives and our fate as intimately connected to those of everyone else on the planet" (2000, 88).

Holistic oneness does *not* mean sameness or equality nor does it negate the realities of injustice. Holism instead disrupts the personal and systemic patterns that have fragmented our internal identities and our diverse communities. It acknowledges that a fragmented identity leads to a fragmented spirit, fragmented community, and fragmented relationships across difference. It reminds us that disrupting the binaries of identity requires using alternative languages and frameworks to empower individuals and build unified communities. We thus relinquish the very limiting tools that have sustained the master's house for so long.[6]

Cultivating Interconnectedness Through a Love Ethic

Radical love, also called *agape* or the "love ethic," is one of these alternative concepts that can disrupt the binaries that separate us from one another. A love ethic honors our deep connections in creating a just world and is both an affective and a political tool:

> All the great social movements for freedom and justice in our society have promoted a love ethic. Concern for the collective good of our nation, city, or neighbor rooted in the values of love makes us all seek to nurture and protect that good. If all public policy was created in the spirit of love, we would not have to worry about unemployment, homelessness, schools failing to teach children, or addiction [...] Embracing a love ethic means that we utilize all the dimensions of love—'care, commitment, trust, responsibility, respect, and knowledge'—in our everyday lives. We can successfully do this only by cultivating awareness. Being aware enables us to critically examine our actions to see what is needed so that we can give care, be responsible, show respect, and indicate a willingness to learn. [...] Loving practice is not aimed at simply giving an individual greater life satisfaction; it is extolled as the primary way we end domination and oppression. (hooks 2000, pp. 76, 94, and 98)

Some are thrown off by the notion of inserting love where oppression prevails. When a rhetoric of hate is exchanged between conflicting parties that are deeply polarized by their differences, the concept of love seems almost counter-intuitive. Yet, it is precisely in such conditions that embracing interconnectedness and the actualization of love become pillars of social change. To interrogate the meaning and use of the word love I point to the definitions provided by Dr. Martin Luther King, Jr., who espoused it as a key strategy of the civil rights movement:

> In speaking of love at this point, we are not referring to some sentimental or affectionate emotion. It would be nonsense to urge men to love their oppressors in an affectionate sense. Love in this connection means understanding, redemptive goodwill. [...] *Agape* is disinterested love. It is a love which the individual seeks not for his own good, but the good of his neighbor (I Cor. 10:24). *Agape* does not begin by discriminating between worthy and unworthy people, or any qualities people possess. It begins by

loving others *for their own sakes*. It is an entirely neighbor-regarding concern for others, which discovers the neighbor in every man it meets. […] In the final analysis, *Agape* means a recognition of the fact that all life is interrelated. All humanity is involved in a single process, and all men are brothers. To the degree that I harm my brother, no matter what he is doing to me, to that extent I am harming myself. (qtd in Washington 1986, pp. 19–20)

The call to embrace a love ethic requires us to take responsibility for being aware of ourselves and our own suffering at the same time that we become more expansive and compassionate toward the suffering of others. The love ethic demands much of us personally. I write this thinking specifically about the importance of cultivating awareness of our biases while at the same time demonstrating openness, patience, and kindness to others who are likewise discovering their own biases, even when their discoveries occur at our expense. This deep practice of compassion is neither easy nor enjoyable. Furthermore, it is not necessarily right that we should suffer because of another person's ignorance, much less their hate. Yet, remembering that we are all lifelong learners on the topic of injustice and that at some point our own learning process may require other people to show patience and generosity toward us helps us develop our own compassion. It also enables us to counteract kneejerk reactions that otherize those that are different from ourselves or lead us to cast aside those that enact oppressive behavior.

Intentionally upholding our sense of interconnectedness alongside our demands for justice creates a space for both compassion and accountability: "When I am mindful of the moments when I inadvertently uphold oppression, I have more compassion for those people who inadvertently marginalize me. That does not mean I do not get angry, challenge them, or hold them accountable. But it does prevent me from demonizing them because I recognize that we are all in this together" (Berila 2016, p. 24). This forwards the premise that no matter how distant or distinct from one another we seem, we are all connected. Because of our interconnection, harboring hate or intolerance for others not only perpetuates a cycle of hate but poisons our own hearts and spirits in the process. Martin Luther King, Jr. reiterates:

> In the struggle for human dignity, the oppressed people of the world must not succumb to the temptation of becoming bitter or indulging in hate campaigns. To retaliate in kind would do nothing but intensify the existence of hate in the universe. Along the way of life, someone must have sense

enough and morality enough to cut off the chain of hate. This can only be done by projecting the ethic of love to the center of our lives. (qtd in Washington 1986, p. 19)

Yet, engaging a love ethic does not mean denying the anger we feel in response to oppression. In response to enduring discrimination and violence, Maya Angelou has advised:

If you're not angry, you're either a stone, or you're too sick to be angry. You should be angry. Now mind you, there's a difference. You must not be bitter. Now let me show you why. Bitterness is like cancer. It eats upon the host. It doesn't do anything to the object of its displeasure. So, use that anger, yes, you write it, you paint it, you dance it, you march it, you vote it, you do everything about it. You talk it. Never stop talking it (2006).

The love ethic does not mean accepting someone else's anger or their expression of an oppressive ideology directed at you. It does not let you or anyone else off the hook for harmful actions or complicity in systems of domination. The love ethic instead recognizes that anger is a fundamental and instinctual human reaction to threats to survival. It is very hard and sometimes impossible to navigate the immensity of our emotions when we are isolated, however. We need communal support to process, manage, and utilize our emotions effectively. Community itself can become a container for our anger and pain as well as our joy.

If uncontained or misdirected anger can take over community activism, resulting in burned-out activists and defensive opponents. "Righteous anger," on the other hand, is anger that is at once justified and strategic. Self-discipline is required so that we can recognize and honor our righteous anger, learn when to let us guide us and when to step back, and try to approach the situation from a different point of view. Non-violent civil disobedience is another vehicle for processing anger. The disciplined practice of non-violent disobedience demands that we cultivate not only self-awareness and knowledge but also community awareness and connection (Conn 2016).

With "the principle of love" standing "at the center of nonviolence," righteous anger can be turned into a springboard for direct action, mobilizing individuals and communities to no longer tolerate abuse and demand change (King qtd in Washington 1986, p. 19). Righteous anger can be used as motivation to engage in strategies that will at once disrupt violence and oppression while nurturing community. Combining righteous anger with an ethic of love enables us to become mindful of our responses to oppression and recognize our interconnectedness in the fight for justice. In short, dismantling the master's house of toxic hatred and oppression requires that we strategically navigate our anger, cultivate a love ethic in our social movements, and develop the fullness of our intersectional identities in the embrace of an interconnected community.

To investigate how identity binaries, intersectionality, and an inter-connected love ethic might exist in your own life, please engage with the prompts in the *Critical Reflection Activity: Interconnected Community*

1. Do you feel boxed into any identity binaries? How so?
2. What terminology or means of self-identification can you imagine employing that would celebrate your multiple identities in all their fullness and integration instead of limiting or boxing them in?
3. How might embracing your own dialectical identities help advance intercultural understanding?
4. How can you acknowledge divisive and oppressive systems without perpetuating an "us versus them" mentality?
5. Can you recall any instance when your learning about other cultures and communities and issues of injustice may have occurred at someone else's expense?
6. What would you need to support you in being expansive enough to educate others about your culture, community, or experience of injustice, even when such generosity might come at a cost to you?
7. How can we recognize the depths of our interconnectedness and cultivate a beloved community that is big enough for both our ignorance as well as our compassion?
8. How can we strategically utilize righteous anger to actively but peacefully disrupt injustice?
9. What might employing a love ethic look like concretely in your life?

HEALING THE TRAUMAS OF INJUSTICE

With a clear understanding and appreciation of the fact that we are all interconnected, we discover that any effort to tackle issues of injustice cannot separate personal change (towards individual wellbeing) from social change (towards collective wellbeing). Ginwright notes that activists are increasingly "seeking strategies that both address oppression (racism, sexism, homophobia, poverty) *and* suffering (anxiety, fear, stress, despair) [my italics]. These strategies are directed at fostering social change by shifting how individuals, organizations, and communities relate to one another as they envision a new way of creating collective hope" (2015, p. 28). Since the structural realities of oppression can result in persistently traumatic experiences, both personal and shared wellbeing requires concentrated efforts for healing from trauma. Trauma is "something that overwhelms us, that makes us feel helpless, that makes us feel paralyzed. And it's something that happens to our bodies and our brains, something that happens to our nervous system, to our whole organism, that doesn't un-happen" (Levine 2010). As such, public involvement in social change efforts also includes private examinations of how our own experiences with trauma might influence our responses to injustice and distress in the community.

Traumatic events are nearly unavoidable given the pain and suffering that exists in the world. Many people have suffered from traumatic experiences at some point in their lives, often at critical junctures in their development as children or adolescents. Sometimes trauma is "big" and imposed impersonally (e.g., war, social violence, state-sponsored violence, natural disasters). Other times trauma occurs on a more intimate scale (e.g., physical, emotional, verbal, or sexual abuse). Often the individual, intimate experience is linked to systemic oppression, as in the case of sexual violence. Some forms of trauma are one-time events with a high negative impact; this is known as "shock trauma." By contrast, "developmental" or "complex trauma" refers to an ongoing series of traumatic events.

Personal instances of shock or developmental traumas are further exacerbated by social and historic traumas of injustice, i.e., that of state-sanctioned violence, poverty, or discrimination. The potential of undergoing harm related to getting basic needs met is exacerbated for those living in conditions of oppression, including those without access to quality food, water, land, jobs, homes, education, childcare, and health-care, as well as basic dignity, respect, political representation, power, and capital. As such, traumas of injustice have direct personal and collective impact.

Research shows that "nearly seven in 10 adults in the USA (69%) report having experienced discrimination" and that "experiencing discrimination is associated with higher reported stress and poorer reported health" (APA 2016, pp. 6 and 8). Discrimination-related stress is not only related to the poor treatment marginalized communities experience but also to the ways these experiences then impact their future behavior and mental health. "For many adults, dealing with discrimination results in a state of heightened vigilance and changes in behavior, which in itself can trigger stress responses—that is, even the anticipation of discrimination is sufficient to cause people to become stressed" (APA 2016, p. 8). Many people aiming to work for social change are often personally reeling from the traumas of injustice that are not singular events but ongoing experiences embedded in the fabric of everyday life. Responding to the impacts of both personal and systemic trauma is another layer of stress and pain that cannot be overlooked for activists personally assaulted by oppression. This also impacts communities that are working together for change, but also reeling together from trauma.

To thoughtfully consider how stress or traumas show up in your own life and impact your interest in community work, please explore the *Critical Reflection Activity: Personal Motivation and Woundedness*

1. What motivates you to do work around social change?
2. What memories and feelings emerge when you visualize what originally motivated you?
3. Are there ways in which these motivations are personally connected to your own traumas or wounds and not related to the activist issue itself?
4. In what ways do any traumas you've personally experienced still have a grip on your thoughts, behaviors, somatic experiences, or emotional reactions today?
5. What can you do to remain conscious of your own healing process? How might your healing process influence your work for social change?

6. What factors must be in play so that your work in the community can be a source of personal healing without causing any harm to the community in the process?
7. What do stress and disconnectedness look like to you?
8. What does a sense of thriving and interconnectedness look like to you?
9. What do both stress and thriving *feel* like in your physical and emotional bodies?
10. What support systems and people can you reach out to in order to support your own healing so you can be a more effective peace worker?

While most traumatic events can be negotiated successfully in the moment or in the immediate aftermath to negate long-term impact, other traumas stay in the emotional and physical body and memory long after the traumatic incident occurred. These kinds of trauma continue to inform our responses to unassociated "triggers" well into the future (Levine 1997; Van der Kolk 2014). Studies show that when trauma occurs, we naturally react with one of three responses: fight, flight, or freeze. The adrenaline that courses through our veins at the moment of trauma enables us to respond immediately with an appropriate strategy for self-preservation and survival. However, we often maintain a heightened level of stress and continue to apply these life-or-death survival strategies when we encounter non-traumatic but triggering events that consciously or unconsciously resonate with the original trauma (Khouri 2010). When our neurological pathways practice these physiologically and emotionally exhausting reactions again and again, they become engrained patterns of behavior (Daugherty 2014).[7] In the end, these responses do not serve us or the situations to which we are responding.

Trauma symptoms often emerge because an unexpressed impulse to respond to a traumatic event is still lying dormant in the body. It is important to find safe ways to discharge the adrenaline that was stored up in fight–flight–freeze reactions and express the unexpressed impulses that were first mobilized during the traumatic event (Levine 2010). If we do not find healthy and appropriate ways to express these impulses and discharge suppressed energy, we may end up acting out personal pain in a "just" battle in the community within which we are active (Khouri 2010).

As noted in Chap. 2, we must find ways to sit with our discomfort instead of fleeing from it or using activist scenarios as locations to play out our triggers.

In addition to traumatic stress, most people today are assaulted by heightened levels of anxiety and daily sources of stress that have a strong negative impact on their physical, emotional, and mental capacities.[8] As Thich Nhat Hanh notes,

> Stress accumulates in us every day. If you do not know how to protect yourself, stress will overcome your mind and body. All parts of our body—our liver, heart, lungs, kidneys—send us SOS signals constantly; they are suffering, and we are often too busy to listen. We have become alienated from our own body and rarely allow it to rest or restore itself. We continue to eat, drink, and work in ways that deplete our body of its well-being. We need to learn how to listen to our bodies again. (2003, 47)

Learning to regulate our responses to stress or when a triggering interaction occurs in the course of community work—that is, when something in the present brings up feelings and memories from the past—is critical.[9] Self-regulation refers to the ability to manage stress and emotional reactivity and center yourself in an embodied way back into a safe space at the very moment you are feeling triggered. Self-regulation usually helps us better respond to triggering situations rather than letting another's ignorant or harmful actions (and our reactions to them) hijack our capacity for a thoughtful and empowered response. When we are self-regulated, it impacts those around us since our energies and nervous systems resonate with one another. Internal coherence often results in external and collective coherence. Self-regulation is thus a critical component for becoming an effective changemaker.

The *Self-Regulation Exercises* provided here offer specific steps towards orienting, grounding and breathing which readers can take to self-regulate when a triggering interaction occurs. These derive from Alane Daugherty's *Heartfully Engaged Awareness Reprogramming Tools* (*HEART*), (2014, 160–161) and from Hala Khouri's Self Regulation technique (2016), respectively:

Heartfully Engaged Awareness Reprogramming Tools (HEART)[1]

1. *Notice*—This step invites you to pause, turn inward, and begin to notice what is present for you. Notice any reactivity coming up [in reaction to a challenging situation] and take a few intentional breaths. Try to disengage from the reactivity's charge; observe and witness your response rather than being hijacked by it. Notice your thoughts, feelings, and any emotional responses without engaging them. Attempt to foster non-reactivity, ground yourself in your breath and Inner Being if possible.

2. *Refocus*—This step calms your system and creates receptivity to a heartful shift. Establish an intentional, calm, natural breathing pattern. Focus on your eyes and let go of all the tension or stress in the tiny little muscles around them and throughout your eye sockets. Let go of all the tension in your shoulders and release into your breath. Bring your awareness to your torso where it feels right for you as a place to focus your breath. With all your awareness on your breath, breathe slowly and deeply, but most of all comfortably and naturally. You can silently repeat the word 'release' to yourself on the out breath if it helps. Notice if you begin to create a 'felt sense' of openness.

3. *Nurture*—This step nurtures a heartful way of being and responding to difficult situations that can transform your overall experience. Intentionally engage in an emotional shift to heartful awareness. It could be something about the situation that you generally appreciate or an emotional shift to focus on something else in your life for which you are truly grateful. It could be an intentional state of being that you would like to create or it could be a state of self-understanding or self-compassion for any difficulty you are experiencing. The key is that it needs to be a genuine shift to a heartful state of being. And it needs to be felt.

Trauma-Informed Self-Regulation Exercise

- *Orient yourself:* When you feel a heightened reaction to a triggering moment, bring awareness back to your present moment. Look around to register the room you are in, notice the sounds and smells, the presence and stability of your body and your breath. This helps you tangibly recognize that this is not your past, not the moment when an original trauma occurred, but the here and now. Orient yourself to the present moment with all your senses.
- *Ground yourself:* Feel your legs and feet on the floor, bring awareness to your breath, and reflect on your current somatic experience and the trigger that has been ignited. Stay present without judgment to your emotional reaction and mindfully invite yourself back into regulation.
- *Find your breath:* Take some deep breaths. Imagine the breath filling you from the ground up. Find strength within your body —even if it's just your pinky toe that feels strong! Pull that sense of stability and groundedness into the rest of your body through your breath. Use your breath to ground and stabilize you. You may also use soothing images or memories to restore a sense of calm, safety, and even joy.

In order to disrupt and unlearn both oppression and trauma, we must learn to recognize it in our lives and in our bodies, to sit with the discomfort and become compassionate to the reactions that may arise. Connecting mindfully, curiously, and compassionately to our experiences of trauma, stress, or despair is an important step in self-awareness.[10] The next step involves seeking self-care and radical healing practices so that we can operate more thoughtfully and with greater awareness in all of our relationships—intimate, social, and political.

RADICAL HEALING AND SELF-CARE

If we are going to candidly confront issues of individual and collective trauma and injustice, we must cultivate practices for self-care and community care. Many scholar-activists of color have emphasized the importance of connecting social justice activism to radical healing practices, not only as strategies for change, but for survival itself (Alexander 2003; Anzaldúa and Moraga 1981; Bernal et al.; Lorde 1984; Okazawa-Rey and Sudbury 2015; Kelley 2002). Dealing with issues of bias and discrimination, responding to microaggressions, and educating people about the suffering that your community faces can be thankless, tiring, and frustrating work. Self-care provides refueling, grounding, and self-love for folks who might otherwise be debilitated by experiencing structural or personal violence. Furthermore, self-care is a radical act because it puts the power of re-establishing wellbeing into the hands of the people whose wellbeing is being threatened. When daily wellbeing suffers as a result of the realities of oppression, individual and collective practices of care become critical forms of resistance, resilience, and rebuttal. As Audre Lorde claims, "Caring for myself is not self-indulgence, it is self-preservation, and that is an act of political warfare" (1988, p. 131).

Taking care of oneself and taking time to recognize the need for personal healing and self-integration is a critical component of being able to take care of others and being effective in long-term efforts of collective social change. This is sometimes hard for activists to value, as the demands of the struggle always seem to take precedence. Many see the work of self-care as an extravagant distraction from the real work of social change. Others resist self-care because they believe that it is an unnecessary, expensive, or even an irresponsible indulgence, given one's obligation to care for others. There also exists suspicion around calls for self-care as issues of privilege generate an imbalance around who has access to support in terms of care. Feminist theorist Sara Ahmed points out:

> Privilege is a buffer zone, how much you have to fall back on when you lose something. Privilege does not mean we are invulnerable: things happen, shit happens. Privilege can however reduce the costs of vulnerability, so if things break down, if you break down, you are more likely to be looked after. [...] Lorde says self-care is *not* self-indulgence but self-preservation. Some have to look after themselves because they are not looked after: their being is not cared for, supported, protected. [...] When a whole world is organised to promote your survival, from health to education, from the walls designed to keep your residence safe, from the paths that ease your travel, you do not have become so inventive to survive. You do not have to be seen as the recipient of welfare because the world has promoted your welfare. The benefits you receive are given as entitlements, perhaps even as birth rights. (2014)

In addition to the fact that self-care is a privilege not afforded equally by all, many activists find it more critical to focus their energy toward dismantling oppressive structures rather than focusing on self-care because the undoing of these systems will itself halt subsequent experiences of pain. (And indeed it sometimes seems we are encouraged to work more on improving our resiliency strategies than actually questioning why we have to be so dang resilient in the first place!) Yet I argue that working to end oppression does not mean we must endure suffering as we wait for utopia to come. Self-care is not a temporary band-aide applied to keep us going while we do the real work of social change. Care of self and community are means of creating a world that prioritizes the wellbeing of our bodies, minds, and spirits just as much as it values justice.

Self-care practices are particularly crucial for anyone living in a hyper-industrial, materialistic, and individualistic society that fragments identities, families, communities, and interconnected relationships. Yet, the concept of self-care has been used in so many different ways that its meaning has become diluted and hard to pin down. The self-care I am advocating for here does not necessarily mean going to the spa or paying exorbitant fees for a therapy session. Self-care may simply mean allowing yourself to pull back and ask someone else to carry the load so you can replenish the energy it takes to continue the struggle. It may mean remaining present to your activist work but not giving it your all—re-serving some of your heart space, head space, time, and energy for yourself (Chung 2017). In yet other instances, the activist work itself can be a form of self-care, as being in community with others who face similar struggles as you do provides support, nourishment, and empowerment. Directly confronting bias and injustice can renew your personal arsenals of energy, so that you are indeed able to do your part in continuing the legacies of activism that came before you. Self-care practices are ones that balance, strengthen, and nourish activists so they can be more grounded, giving, and sustainable in their activism. Activists must build their capacity for compassion, love, resilience, and coherence internally so they can effectively project that into the external world.

Most of us need to restore some basic self-care practices to ensure that our fundamental physical needs are being met in our pursuit of social change. This requires intentionally creating time to foster wellbeing in the following domains:

- *Safety*—relationships and surroundings that make you feel safe and secure, physically, emotionally, mentally, and spiritually;
- *Food*—eating regularly, mindfully, and without haste; using food as a source of connection by eating joyfully and with people you love; and eating healthily (food that is as close to the source as possible) but without judgment or scorn;
- *Sleep*—sleeping as much as the body requires for sound operation, ideally averaging 8 hours a night; using meditation or visualization to calm the body and mind and encourage deep sleep (i.e., no working, social media, or arguing before going to bed);
- *Exercise*—whatever movement feels good and challenges the body; ideally 30 minutes daily or an hour three times a week (in many communities, of course, exercise occurs naturally as part of the daily physical work of childrearing or manual labor).

Beyond meeting basic survival needs, Thich Nhat Hanh (2003) gives us "food for thought" about how to maintain a mindful and grounded experience by considering what we imbibe that either plants seeds of peace or seeds of violence within. He suggests we become more mindful about consuming the following four "foods":

1. *Edible food*, a commitment to consuming food that is "produced and distributed in a sensitive, nonviolent way that does not harm us or other species (79)";
2. *Sense impressions*, meaning considering what we consume with all our senses and committing "to avoid things that can bring toxins into our consciousness such as violent media, music, sights, sounds and ideas" (80);
3. *Mindful intentions*, investigating if "we are acting for the cause of peace, love, and understanding when in fact we may be working for our own fame, profit, and power" (83);
4. *Consciousness*, "if we allow ourselves to be nourished by delusion, ignorance, fear and violence, our consciousness will bring about the kind of life that makes us and those around us suffer. By ingesting the right kinds of mental, physical and spiritual food, we grow in wisdom, compassion, and nonviolence" (84).

Sometimes we may be in circumstances that preclude us from deciding what we want to imbibe or how much we can eat and sleep, but whenever we do have options, we should practice being present and thoughtful about what we do with our choices. The key is to continually check in with yourself about what will help sustain your involvement for the long term, then be wise and kind enough to follow up on the form of self-care that is most needed in that moment. These practices around the "four foods" suggest several ways of embodying mindfulness and becoming more aware of our surroundings and ourselves, including our thoughts, beliefs, actions, and illusions. Mindfulness practices can also enhance healing and compassion for ourselves and others, as discussed next.

Mindfulness Practices and Self-love

Most of us carry the deep pain of trauma and/or injustice around with us every day. Such pain can separate us from our inner radiance and self-love. It can separate us from others in self-defeating acts of self-protection. And it can push us into unhealthy activities in an attempt to ease, numb, or suppress our pain. These habits become ingrained in neurological and biochemical pathways that maintain us in a rut that is incongruent to the self-love we crave. Since our emotional, neurological, and physiological bodies are interdependent, however, we can address and diminish the pain of oppression within ourselves by practicing mindfulness and cultivating self-love (Daugherty 2014).

Mindfulness practices do not mask or try to put a positive spin on the heavy burden of suffering. Instead, they give power back to those who feel disempowered by ensuring that the reins of control for emotion and wellbeing are in their hands. While the amount of pain rendered from forces that thwart wellbeing is often beyond our control, the amount of suffering in response to it is actually something we can influence directly. When individuals become "mindful of their choices, rather than controlled by their environment," it results in "subtle shifts in their sense of agency, power and perception of the world" (Ginwright 2015, p. 57). Instead of avoiding or suppressing emotion (which keeps us from feeling both pain and joy), becoming more familiar with one's inner landscape through mindfulness practices creates a more expansive ability to feel, process, and respond effectively to all kinds of emotion. Thich Nhat Hanh notes that "when we hold back our feelings and ignore our pain, we are committing violence against ourselves. The practice of nonviolence is to be here, to be present, and to recognize our own pain and despair. We do not make war on our feelings or reject them, but just recognize, embrace and transform them" (2003, 16).[11] Similarly, Beth Berila has found that "we have to first become aware of our responses and learn to understand them before we can hope to change them. This early part of the process cannot happen if we automatically judge our responses. To accept our responses with compassion is NOT the same thing as accepting oppression. On the contrary, it is a critical first step in dismantling oppression as it operates within our very beings" (2016, 52).

The practice of mindfulness reunites "our body and mind" (Hahn 2003, p. 47). Research has shown that a variety of mindfulness or contemplative practices have "the potential to quiet our fear response system, and allow our calm and connection system to flourish" (Daugherty 2014, p. 160–1). Mindfulness simply consists of calling ourselves to attention in the present moment, to recognizing and accepting how our emotional, physical, and spiritual bodies feel and how we can intentionally respond to the stimuli around us without becoming reactive. One way is by concentrating on breathing as a way to ground the body. Mindful breathing sends signals to the nervous system that we can relax and calm our internal systems (Siegel 2007). This is effective because "the physiologically detrimental effects of anxiety, worry, fear, and other ungrounded emotions are in direct biochemical and neural opposition to positive loving emotions and a sense of inner calm—and it is physiologically impossible to feel both states at once" (Daugherty 2014, p. 39). As we release tension, we ease and support the flow of intra- and interpersonal bioelectric energy. We connect our embodied experience to the energy we emit and receive from others (Siegel 2007).

Loving kindness meditation is a self-care practice that can be especially powerful for those suffering from the trauma of injustice or a lack of self-love. By "looking through a lens of self-love," we become able to "appreciate how past reactions, patterns, and behaviors have helped protect us in the past, and 'update' the parts that are no longer serving us" (Daugherty 2014, p. 42). We cultivate loving kindness by attuning to the present moment, ourselves, and others with an intentional, non-judgmental acceptance. Although the threats of external and internal violence may be quite real, personal and collective peace can be strengthened when "we approach our here-and-now experience with curiosity, openness, acceptance and love...With mindfulness seen as a form of intrapersonal attunement, it may be possible to reveal the mechanisms by which we become our own best friend with mindful practice. We would treat our best friend with kindness, after all. Attunement is at the heart of caring relationships of all sorts" (Siegel 2007, pp. 15–16).

Practicing loving kindness sends the message that we care enough about ourselves and our worth to "claim authentic selfhood and act it out" (Palmer 2000, p. 32). Self-love thus emerges as a form of resistance to oppression, "a revolutionary intervention that undermines practices of domination" (hooks 2014, p. 20). It is an affront to systems that attempt to marginalize, devalue, or neglect care for ourselves and entire communities.

Contemplative practices that support becoming mindfully aware of oneself, the present moment, and the cultivation of loving kindness as a tool for sustained and engaged activism are critically important. Mindfulness activities are also helpful when integrated at the beginning of a community gathering or in the midst of a challenging discussion to help individuals self-regulate, begin to gain fuller consciousness of their embodied experience, consider the ways in which they react on autopilot rather than respond mindfully, and exercise concrete tools for being present with discomfort in order to become more attuned with self and other. Such activities can be conducted individually or collectively, during moments of strife or adopted as a long-term, consistent practice.

The following activity is a recommended practice for cultivating mindfulness and comes from Thich Nhat Hanh's *Mindful Breathing Exercise* (2003, p. 31):

Mindful Breathing Exercise

Breathing in, I am aware that I am breathing in.
Breathing out, I am aware that I am breathing out.
Breathing in, I am in touch with the energy of mindfulness in every cell of my body. Breathing out, I feel nourished by the energy of mindfulness in me.
Breathing in, I am in touch with the energy of solidity in every cell of my body. Breathing out, I feel nourished by the energy of solidity in me.
Breathing in, I am in touch with the energy of wisdom in every cell of my body. Breathing out, I feel nourished by the energy of wisdom in me.
Breathing in, I am in touch with the energy of compassion in every cell of my body. Breathing out, I feel nourished by the energy of compassion in me.

Breathing in, I am in touch with the energy of peace in every cell of my body.
Breathing out, I feel nourished by the energy of peace in me.
Breathing in, I am in touch with the energy of freedom in every cell of my body. Breathing out, I feel nourished by the energy of freedom in me.
Breathing in, I am in touch with the energy of awakening in every cell of my body. Breathing out, I feel nourished by the energy of awakening in me.

Engaging in such somatically centered mindfulness exercises may be challenging or irritating at first, but resistance to such practices often has more to teach us than the practices themselves. Becoming curious about the resistance opens us up to learning more about the woundedness that may dwell within and that has not yet been dealt with. Resistance might indicate that mindfulness practice does not work for you, however. What is most important is finding and putting into practice any activity that nourishes, connects, and holistically integrates your mind–body–spirit in your life.

Since we experience stress, oppression, trauma, and suffering in our bodies, unlearning or regulating them also occurs at the level of the body. Just as generating social change through action (walking the walk instead of simply talking the talk), releasing trauma in the body through movement is critical to healing and the place where key transformation often occurs. Practicing embodied ways of releasing trauma, stress, and other kinds of physical or emotional pain leads to long-lasting changes in our biochemistry, our neurological and nervous systems, and our habits of mind and heart (Daugherty 2014). Examples can include mindful breathing, meditation, systems of energy movement such as Chi Gong and Tai Chi, walking, yoga, dance, sports, sweat lodge ceremonies, singing, or chanting. These can be practiced alone or in communities together as a means of cultivating greater connections between social change and personal transformation. The main aim is to find a practice that helps renew the spirit, engage the heart, regulate the nervous systems and create new pathways for thriving in the brain and body and in interactions with others.

Note that each practice is based on a different cultural, emotional, or spiritual understanding of self, trauma, and wellbeing. In taking on any such exercise, it is important to recognize the potential for and intentionally refrain from any acts of cultural appropriation. If you are interested in engaging in a cultural practice that is not from your own cultural tradition, you can avoid appropriating it by taking a respectful approach to intercultural understanding. Learn about it by connecting to someone who has the cultural knowledge and standing to invite you into their practice. Explore where the practice emerged and how it survived oppression to remain alive today. Investigate the role it plays in diverse communities today and what role you can respectfully play within them, as well.

RADICAL HEALING IN COMMUNITY

Connection is a basic human need, one that gives us a sense of safety, belonging, purpose, and meaning. In fact, connection already exists; it is our job simply to recognize it (powell 2015). Supporting and feeding connection, as well as incorporating regular practices that nurture oneself, family, and community, is vital to resisting injustice and creating peace. Being surrounded by a caring community also improves the odds of surviving and thriving in the face of injustice; "having emotional support appears to improve the way that individuals view their coping abilities with discrimination" (APA 2016, p. 9). It is in the cradle of care of our community that we learn how to love and heal ourselves and others. Some people feel that they do not have access to a safe space where they can bring their true emotions to the surface and acknowledge the trauma, vulnerability, grief, and hopelessness that are liabilities to their survival. Cultivating such spaces and sense of community are fundamental ways of acknowledging the physical, mental, and emotional attacks that people targeted for their identities endure. Cultivating supportive and safe community spaces in which to process such things creates opportunities for self-care and the development of resilience, hope, and belonging—unsurprisingly, the same things needed for social change (Ginwright 2015) .

Radical healing is thus a means for not only dismantling systems of oppression and our parts in them, but also for rebuilding systems of support and wellness that nurture personal and community wellbeing. When facing destruction of community, rights, or tradition, a key act of resistance is coming up with new creations or regenerating old traditions that celebrate community, rights, and tradition. Standing up for your beliefs and cultivating empowerment with others as you create change heightens a sense of purpose, belonging, and wellbeing for individuals and the community. Community engagement itself *is* radical healing!

Through the interdisciplinary lens of psychologies of liberation (Watkins and Shulman 2008), communities that cultivate healing, community building, and movements have been called "communities of resistance" (ibid) though I prefer to call them "communities of affirmation" so that the emphasis draws primarily on personal and cultural empowerment. Yet, of course, these spaces conjure both affirmation and resistance for communities reeling from the trauma of injustice: "amid and in opposition to violence and injustice, it is necessary for people to join together to create communities where justice and peace on a small scale are possible. Such communities resist the dehumanizing forces present in the dominant culture" (p. 209). When one's wellbeing is being threatened by the status quo, connecting with others suffering from similar repression creates solidarity, belonging, and resilience. It is here that communities create new ways of being together that disrupt oppressive ideologies and practices and that nourish more life-sustaining and healing ways of being.

With western trends of obsessive individualism, many have lost previously common spaces of coming together for food preparation, shared child rearing, or ritual—spaces that also lent themselves to public dialogue and connection. The social disruption that has resulted creates feelings of separation and isolation (Watkins and Shulman 2008). Rebuilding such spaces allows those grieving these losses to come together to confront dehumanization, reclaim dignity, and create visions for change and the solidarity necessary to move towards them. Creating or regenerating communities of affirmation is also a crucial component of reclaiming individual and group healing, given that many daily private rituals as well as communal ceremonies of healing have been lost in the disconnected bustle of modern times or suppressed by acts of cultural oppression. It is here that we affirm that spending time in deep listening and dialogue, making or listening to music, slowing down to laugh and play, connecting to nature, bearing witness to suffering together, engaging in writing or art-making, and participating in rituals or any traditional practices that connect to source, spirit, or spirituality (however you choose to define it) are just as important to wellbeing as healthy eating and sleeping.

Binding healing and activism, communities of affirmation are spaces where systems of domination are named, confronted, and analyzed, where new visions for empowered and liberated communities are formed and methods for their (re)creation are imagined and where healing from the traumas of injustice occurs within the embrace of a loving community. It is here where we often see the emergence of shared creativity, an unleashing of the imagination that allows us to question what is and imagine what could be:

> Imagination is a psychological phenomenon that occurs at the level of the local in individuals and communities. It gives those in isolating, asphyxiating, and exhausted social structures new possibilities. To create cultural alternatives, people have to break with taken for granted ways of thinking that prevent them psychologically from interrupting the status quo. (Watkins and Shulman 2008, p. 3)

It is with imagination and poetic knowledge that together we create "freedom dreams," revolutionary visions of transforming society, emancipating our thoughts, structures, and ideologies, and dreaming up a world of our own creating, one that allows for the fullness of our humanity, our politics, and our poetry (Kelley 2002). Key to crafting these visions is the creativity found in "liberation arts." "Liberation arts" are collective creative practices that

- resurrect and develop symbolic resources that have the potentiality of helping individuals rethink possibilities and solidarities,
- awaken imagination,
- uncover hidden feelings that have not yet been owned,
- [build] shared understanding of history and social contexts in a community environment that will witness past events in order to prevent future violence and exclusion,
- build up possibilities for constructive social change, and
- [enable participants to] enter long-term sustainable process of local critical dialogue about the past, present, and future (Watkins and Shulman 2008, p. 263).

Given the healing nature of art-making and the criticality of the arts to help us imagine and create new realities of liberation, they have been a key component of most movements of change.

> Art-making loosens the mind, opens the heart, and leads to dialogue. People begin to imagine that things could be otherwise. They dream of the world as it should be. They realize they share a common vision. Together people

begin reaching for goals that everyone agrees are of utmost importance....
(hooks qtd in Watkins and Shulman 2008, p. 211)

Civil rights movement veteran Vincent Harding speaks to the importance of creativity, especially music making, in his story about participating in the epic march from Selma to Montgomery, Alabama in 1965, during the campaign to secure equal voting rights. As he joined Martin Luther King, Jr. and others at the front lines of the Selma bridge crossing, they were confronted with tear-gas, biting dogs, charging police in riot gear, and racist chants. The response of this group of hundreds of protesters was not to respond in kind, but instead to sing in unison "This little light of mine, I'm going to let it shine," and continue marching on with heads held high. The power of their love and faith in the face of hate and the impact of intentionally singing songs that promoted self-worth, empowerment, and determination in the face of violence were key components to the success of the movement (On Being 2016). The use of spiritual songs as tools for political change was a key practice firmly grounded in the civil rights movement (On Being 2016; Watkins and Shulman 2008).

The Zapatista movement of Chiapas, Mexico likewise exemplifies the power that can develop when radical political changemaking is integrated with radical community healing, art-making, and connection. The Zapatistas combine unique socialist analysis with an indigenous cosmology, traditional practices, education, environmentalism, and the arts. This movement fights against the economic, educational, and land-based violence and discrimination born of neoliberalism that has destroyed the autonomy, rights, and communal land ownership of countless indigenous communities. For over 25 years, Zapatistas have successfully advanced autonomous self-government, education, healthcare, and collective development under the mandate "*mandar obedeciendo*" (lead by obeying) to represent radical democracy, an experiment in devolution of power to the community level, and indigenous teachings that aim to build a world in which all worlds have a place. The Zapatista movement places primacy on unearthing ceremonial spaces for imagination and connection, translating dreams of freedom into poetry and art. The movement demonstrates that vibrant demonstrations valuing love, community, earth, and spirit are not divorced from political and social change but in fact vital pillars of them (Mexican Solidarity Network 2017).

Unfortunately, practices that connect the spiritual to the political have become increasingly atypical in the modern, hyper-industrial world and are often looked at as warm-and-fuzzy distractions from the real work of political change, rather than as fortifying elements that make social movements heartfelt and sustainable.

> While progressives can and do point to a rich legacy of leaders and move-ments grounded in spiritual practice — Mahatma Gandhi and the Indian Independence Movement, Rev. Martin Luther King Jr. and the Civil Rights Movement, and César Chávez and the Farm Workers Movement, to name a few — the Left is also deeply shaped by staunchly secular social justice work influenced by Marxist thought that is suspicious or even hostile to religion and spirituality. These secular traditions have made important contributions to our understanding of material conditions and revolutionary change, but they have also reinforced a deep split between our mind, our bodies and our spirits. This Western cultural bias draws a sharp line between inner and outer transformation, defining them in opposition to each other. Nonetheless, many within the Left have challenged this split, seeking to synthesize wisdom and practice from spiritual traditions (often focused on deep inner transfor-mation) with social change traditions of the Left (generally focused on social analysis and systems change). This kind of leadership is not new. Even at the moments in history when these approaches to transformation have been most polarized, leaders have always emerged who sought to integrate them and bring them into balance with each other. (Zimmerman et al. 2010, 5)

Drawing on traditions of radical healing is critical to social change move-ments, as are efforts to sustain daily wellbeing in communities of affirma-tion. The following lists some examples of communal healing acts, with the understanding that these should be conducted by invitation and in a spirit of cultural understanding and connection (as opposed to cultural appropriation):

- council (the indigenous tradition of group dialogue, following the simple rules of speaking to a specific issue, from the heart, without excess, one person at a time)[12];
- healing circles (safe spaces to support, witness, and genuinely embrace the sharing of one's lived experience, both the joy and the suffering)[13];
- circles of trust (loosely facilitated groups devoted to meaningful dia-logue and self-discovery)[14];
- meditative, spiritual, or devotional communities and gatherings;

- experiences in nature (being present and active in the wilderness, growing food, etc.);
- collective art-making (such as murals, theatre, dances, and music-making);
- community vigils (bearing witness to suffering or death); and
- community collaborations or activist actions for social change.

Individuals can conduct many other simple radical healing practices fostering wellness and grounding either alone or within community:

- gratitude practices,
- lighting candles,
- music-making,
- healing movement,
- silent meditation,
- centering prayers,
- contemplative journaling, and
- consciousness-raising scholarship, poetry, music, and art.

To consider what role and impact radical practices of healing for self and community can have in your life explore the prompts in the *Critical Reflection Activity: Radical healing of self and community.*

1. What self-care practices or community-care practices do you engage in regularly?
2. Do you engage in any activities that prompt self-reflection, self-regulation, or self-love?
3. Do you engage in any activities of radical, communal healing with others?
4. What activities can you imagine participating in that physically embody peace, healing, and interconnectedness (in culturally appropriate ways)?
5. Why might you resist such practices? Can you become curious about this resistance?
6. What do you need to be able to be present, vulnerable, and listen well in doing community change work?
7. What can you do to encourage self-care practices or community-care practices with others?

8. How can you imagine "liberation arts" fitting into community practices of healing and social change?
9. How can you support movements or communities that you are a part of integrate self-care and radical healing as a collective value and practice?

Engaging radical healing practices that embody peace and interconnectedness are key not only to our own holistic self-development, but also to the development of collective change. When our healing activities become, in fact, sacred practices aimed at positively impacting the web of life of which we are a part, we engage in what many now call "subtle activism," an "activity of consciousness or spirit, such as prayer, meditation, or ecstatic dance, intended to support collective healing and social change" (Gaiafield 2017, para. 1). Linking the spiritual and political for the purpose of transformative change on both levels has also been called "sacred activism:"

> Sacred Activism is a transforming force of compassion-in-action that is born of a fusion of deep spiritual knowledge, courage, love, and passion, with wise radical action in the world. ...[It is] focused on inviting concerned people to take up the challenge of our contemporary crises in order to become inspired, effective, and practical agents of institutional and system change, in order to create peace and sustainability. (Andrew Harvey 2017, para. 1)

Many people who have been silenced by oppression find voice, courage, support, compassion, consciousness, and love by engaging in these forms of activism. Such practices also create intentional space for community efforts in "resymbolizing and resignifying the world, [and] enlarging possibilities for restructuring economic, social, and personal realities" (Watkins and Shulman 2008, p. 234).

CONCLUSION

Individuals undergirded by a holistic integration of their myriad roles, identities, and values that enjoy a rich inner landscape honoring both their wounds and resilience and that are committed to radical healing are ultimately better able to contribute to building community and social change.

Radical healing reignites practices that reclaim interconnectedness and the relationships we have lost (to ourselves, to our neighbors, to our communities, and to our environment) as a result of the fragmenting impacts of oppression and our country's devotion to individuation. Cultivating a greater sense of accountability and care (for ourselves, for our neighbors, for our communities, and for our environment) is inherent to the reclamation of community healing. By bringing awareness to the impact of the traumas of injustice and integrating the mind, body, and spirit in sacred practices of healing, we raise our capacities for hope, consciousness, and social change. It is time for society to more boldly honor these multiple forms of radical healing and activism that encourage internal and external transformation and peace.

NOTES

1. A version of this concept is explored by Phylameana Lila Desy on her blog (Desy 2016).
2. Astin et al. (2000), Harward (2016), Finley (2012a, b), Flanagan and Bundick (2011), Markus et al. (1993), Thoits and Hewitt (2001), Youniss and Yates (1997), Swaner (2005).
3. Some prompts here were inspired by the work of Sharon Bridgeforth, http://www.sharonbridgforth.com.
4. See Atkinson et al. (1989), Banks (1984), Chickering; Cross 1991, Delworth (1989), Helms (1990), Hoffman and Myers (1988), Reynolds and Pope (1991), Tatum (1992).
5. Berila (2016), Freire (2006), Macy & Brown (1998), Manuel (2015), McIntosh (1989, 2009), powell (2015), Vasquez (1998).
6. Portions of this section were previously printed as: Hicks, T. 2006. "Humanizing the Other in 'Us and Them.'" *Peace Review: A Journal of Social Justice*, Vol. 18, No. 4. Fall.
7. "[T]hreat, anxiety, and reactivity perpetuate themselves. As we consistently and routinely expose ourselves to the physiology, biochemistry, and energetics of these states, significant physical adaptations occur in our bodies and brains that continue to worsen the whole cycle" (Daugherty 2014, 36).
8. "The projected cost of American healthcare by 2017 has been estimated at over $4 trillion. At least 50% of these costs will be due to preventable disease, including diabetes, cardiovascular conditions, and strokes" (Gallup 2017). Instead of individually and collectively valuing health and wellbeing, by our actions it seems that Americans typically end up ignoring, suppressing, or only temporarily regulating stress and preventable diseases.

9. The related trauma-informed self-regulation exercise provided in this section was adapted from work on trauma-informed self-regulation (Levine 1997) and facilitated by trauma therapist, Hala Khouri, in her guest lecture in my course, *Healing ourselves, healing our communities.*

10. For excellent inquiries on the topics of trauma and mindfulness, see Daughtery (2014), Hahn (2003), Hanson (2009), Levine (2010), Siegel (2007) and Van Der Kolk (2014).

11. Thich Nhat Hanh offers a useful breathing practice related to this recognition of difficult emotions: "When anger or fear is present in us, we bring awareness to it. We smile to it and call it by its true name. Hello, my fear, I know you are there. We can follow our mindful breathing to help calm our feeling. Breathing in, I am aware fear is present in me. Breathing out, I calm my feeling of fear" (2003, 16).

12. "Council and circle practices (Zimmerman and Coyle 1996; Baldwin 1998) draw on traditional ways of calling people to enter a circle with one another to mindfully listen to themselves and to one another. They provide basic, foundational ways of listening for feelings, thoughts, and visions that are living within us and others. Through a structured format that allows space for each participant to come forward as well as listen quietly, children and adults can begin to disengage from monological practices, entering instead a dialogical rhythm" (Watkins and Shulman 2008, p. 191).

13. In his facilitation of healing circles with young men of color in the Bay area, Shawn Ginwright found that "Healing circles provide spaces for young people to both reflect on the wounds resulting from their personal struggles, and be supported and guided to a political understanding and action" (2015, p. 53).

14. "The Circle of Trust® approach is distinguished by *principles* and *practices* intended to create a process of shared exploration—in retreats, programs and other settings—where people can find safe space to nurture personal and professional integrity and the courage to act on it" (Center for Courage and Renewal 2017). For more on circles of trust, see also Palmer (2009).

REFERENCES

Ahmed, S. (2014). Self care as warfare. *Feminist killjoys.* 25 August. Retrieved July 8, 2017, from https://feministkilljoys.com/2014/08/25/selfcare-as-warfare/.

Alexander, M. J. (Ed.). (2003). *Sing, whisper, shout, pray!: Feminist visions for a just world.* Edgework Books.

American Psychological Association. (2016). *Stress in America: The impact of discrimination.* Stress in America Survey.

Angelou, M. (2006). *Interview with Dave Chappelle*. Iconoclasts, season 2, episode 6. 30 November. http://www.imdb.com/title/tt0874578/.

Anzaldúa, G. (1987). *Borderlands: La frontera* (Vol. 3). San Francisco: Aunt Lute.

Anzaldúa, G. & Moraga, C. (Eds.). (1981). *This Bridge Called My Back: Writings by Radical Women of Color*. London: Persephone Press.

Apffel-Marglin, F., & PRATEC. (1998). *The spirit of regeneration: Andean culture confronting western notions of development*. New York: Zed Books.

Armstrong, J. (2006). Community: Sharing one skin. In J. Mander & V. Tauli-Corpuz (Eds.), *Paradigm wars: Indigenous peoples' resistance to globalization*. San Francisco: Sierra Club Books.

Astin, A. W., Vogelgesang, L. J., Ikeda, E. K., & Yee, J. A. (2000). *How service learning affects students*. Los Angeles, CA: Higher Education Research Institute, University of California.

Atkinson, D. R.., Morten, G., & Sue, D. W. (Eds.). (1989). *Counseling American minorities: A cross-cultural perspective* (3rd ed.). Dubuque, IA: William C. Brown.

Banks, J. A. (1984). Black Youths in Predominantly White Suburbs: An Exploratory Study of Their Attitudes and Self-Concepts. *The Journal of Negro Education, 53*(1), 3–17.

Baxter, L. A., & Montgomery, B. M. (1996). *Relating: Dialogues and dialectics*. New York: Guilford Press.

Beath, A. (2005). *Consciousness in action: The power of beauty, love and courage in a violent time*. New York, NY: Lantern Books.

Berila, B. (2016). *Integrating Mindfulness into Anti-Oppression Pedagogy*. New York, NY: Routledge.

Center for Courage and Renewal. (2017). *The circle of trust approach*. Retrieved March 10, 2017, from http://www.couragerenewal.org.

Chung, L., & Ting-Toomey, S. (2011). *Understanding intercultural communication* (2nd ed.). Oxford: Oxford University Press.

Chung, L. (2017). The whole student: Intersectionality and well-being. In *Building Public Trust in the Promise of Liberal Education and Inclusive Excellence, Annual Conference of the American Association of Colleges and Universities*, San Francisco, CA.

Collins, P. H. (1990). *Black feminist thought: Knowledge, Consciousness, and the Politics of Empowerment*. Routledge, New York, NY.

Collins, P. H., & Bilge, S. (Eds.). (2016). *Intersectionality*. Malden, MA: Polity Press.

Combahee River Collective. (1977). *The Combahee river collective statement*. Retrieved March 1, 2017, from http://www.circuitous.org/scraps/combahee.html.

Conn, J. (2016). Personal communication. Sierra Madre, CA.

Crenshaw, K. (1987). Demarginalizing the intersection of race and sex: A black feminist critique of antidiscrimination doctrine, feminist theory, and antiracist politics. *University of Chicago Legal Forum, 1989*, (pp. 139–167).

Cross, W. (1991). *Shades of black: Diversity in African American identity*. Philadelphia, PN: Temple University Press.

Daugherty, A. (2014). *From mindfulness to heartfulness: A journey of transformation through the science of embodiment*. Bloomington: Balboa Press.

Delworth, U. (1989). Identity in the College Years: Issues of Gender and Ethnicity. *NASPA Journal, 26*(3), 162–166.

Desy, P. L. (2016). Disease: Healing term. *ThoughtCo*, 17 February 2016. Retrieved December 2, 2016.

Dunlap, M., Scoggin, J., Green, P., & Davi, A. (2007). White students' experiences of privilege and socioeconomic disparities: Toward a theoretical model. *Michigan Journal of Community Service Learning, 13*(2).

Finley, A. (2012a). *Making progress? What we know about the achievement of liberal education outcomes*. Washington, DC: AA&U.

Finley, A. (2012b). The joy of learning: The impact of civic engagement on psychosocial well-being. *Diversity and Democracy, 3*, 8–10.

Finley, A., & McNair, T. (2013). *Assessing underserved students' engagement in high impact practices*. Washington: AAC&U.

Flanagan, C., & Bundick, M. (2011). Civic Engagement and Psychosocial Well-Being in College Students. *Liberal Education, Spring, 97*(2), 20–27.

Freire, P. (1970). *Pedagogy of the oppressed* (Myra Bergman Ramos, Trans.). New York: Continuum Publishing.

Freire, P. (2006). *Pedagogy of the oppressed. 30th* (anniversary ed.). New York, NY: Continuum Publishing.

Gaiafield Project. (2017). What is subtle activism? *Gaiafield project: Subtle activism for global transformation, para. 1*. Retrieved March 7, 2017, from http://gaiafield.net/what-is-subtle-activism/.

Gallup Healthways *WellBeing Index*. (2017). Retrieved February 12, 2017, from http://www.gallup.com/poll/106756/galluphealthways-wellbeing-index.aspx.

Ginwright, S. (2015). *Hope and healing in urban education: How urban activists and teachers are reclaiming matters of the heart*. New York, NY: Routledge.

Gramsci, A. (1971). *Selections from the prison notebooks*. New York: International Publishers.

Hanh, T. N. (2003). *Creating true peace: Ending violence in yourself, your family, your community, and the world*. New York: Free Press.

Hanson, R. (2009). *Buddha's brain: The practical neuroscience of happiness, love, and wisdom*. Oakland, CA: New Harbinger Publications.

Harper, S. R. (2009). Race-conscious student engagement practices and the equitable distribution of enriching educational experiences. *Liberal Education, 95*(4), 38–45.

Harvey, A. (2017). What is sacred activism. *Andrew Harvey Institute for Sacred Activism.* Retrieved March 7, 2017, from, http://www.andrewharvey.net/sacred-activism/.

Harward, D. W. (Ed.). (2016). *Well-being and higher education: A strategy for change and the realization of education's greater purposes.* Washington, DC: Bringing Theory to Practice.

Helms, J. (1990). *Black and white identity development: theory.* Greenwood, Westport, CT: Research and Practice.

Hicks, T. (2006). Humanizing the Other in "Us and Them". *Peace Review: A Journal of Social Justice, 18*(4).

hooks, b. (1994). *Teaching to transgress: Education as the practice of freedom.* New York: Routledge.

hooks, b. (2000). *All about love: New visions.* New York: William Morrow.

hooks, b. (2014). *Black Looks: Race and Representation.* New York: NY: Routledge.

Kelley, R. D. G. (2002). *Freedom Dreams: The Black Radical Imagination.* Boston, MA: Beacon Press.

Keyes, C. L. (2002). The mental health continuum: From languishing to flourishing in life. *Journal of Health and Social Behavior,* 207–222.

Khouri, H. (2010). Guest Lecture: "Conscious Activism". In *Healing Ourselves in Healing our communities course.* Claremont, CA: Pitzer College. 6 April.

Khouri, H. (2016). Guest lecture: Trauma and justice. In *Healing arts and social change course.* Norco: California Rehabilitation Center. 27 April.

Levine, P. A. (1997). *Waking the tiger: Healing trauma.* Berkeley, CA: North Atlantic Books.

Levine, P. A. (2010). *Healing trauma: A pioneering program for restoring the wisdom of your body.* Boulder, CO: Sounds True Publishing.

Lorde, A. (1984). *Sister outsider: Essays and speeches by Audre Lorde.* Berkeley, CA: Crossing Press.

Lorde, A. (1988). *Burst of Light: Essays by Audre Lorde.* Ithaca, NY: Firebrand Books.

Macy, J. & Brown, M. Y. (1998). *Coming back to life: Practices to reconnect our lives, our world.* Gabriola Island, BC: New Society Publishers.

Manuel, Z. J. (2015). *The way of tenderness: Awakening through race, sexuality, and gender.* Somerville, MA: Wisdom Publications.

Markus, G. B., Howard, J. P., & King, D. C. (1993). Integrating community service and classroom instruction enhances learning: Results from an experiment. *Educational evaluation and policy analysis, 15*(4), 410–419.

McIntosh, P. (1989). White privilege: Unpacking the invisible knapsack. *Peace and Freedom Magazine,* 10–12. Philadelphia, PN. July/August.

McIntosh, P. (2009). *White privilege: An account to spend.* Minnesota: The Saint Paul Foundation.

Mexico Solidarity Network. (2017). "Zapatismo" Autonomous University of Social Movements. Retrieved 27 January 2017. http://www.mexicosolidarity.org.

Moely, B. E., Furco, A., & Reed, J. (2008). Charity and Social Change: The Impact of Individual Preferences on Service-Learning Outcomes. *Michigan Journal of Community Service Learning, 15*(1), 37–48.

On Being with Krista Tippett. (2015). radio podcast. *The Inner Landscape of Beauty.* Interview with John O'Donahue, Minneapolis. Retrieved 1 September, 2016.

On Being with Krista Tippett. (2016). radio podcast. *Is America Possible?* Interview with Vincent Harding, Minneapolis. November 10, 2016. Retrieved November 17, 2016.

Palmer, P. J. (2000). *Let Your Life Speak: Listening for the Voice of Vocation.* San Francisco, CA: Jossey-Bass.

Palmer, P. J. (2009). *A hidden wholeness: The journey toward an undivided life.* San Francisco, CA: John Wiley & Sons.

powell, j. a. (2015). *Racing to justice: Transforming our conceptions of self and other to build an inclusive society.* Bloomington: Indiana University Press.

Reynolds, A. L., & Pope, R. L. (1991). The complexities of diversity: Exploring multiple oppressions. *Journal of Counseling and Development, 70*(1), 174–180.

Shor, I. (1992). *Culture wars: School and society in the conservative restoration.* Chicago, IL: University of Chicago Press.

Siegel, D. J. (2007). *The mindful brain: The neurobiology of well-being.* New York, NY: WW Norton & Co.

Simons, L., Fehr, L., Black, N., Hoogerwerff, F., Georganas, D., & Russell, B. (2011). The application of racial identity development in academic-based service learning. *International Journal of Teaching and Learning in Higher Education., 23*(1), 72–83.

Sudbury, J., & Okazawa-Rey, M. (2015). *Activist scholarship: Antiracism, feminism, and social change.* New York, NY: Routledge.

Swaner, L. E. (2005). Educating for personal and social responsibility: A review of the literature. *Liberal Education, 91*(3), 14–21.

Tatum, B. D. (1992). Talking about race, learning about racism: The application of racial identity development theory in the classroom. *Harvard Educational Review, 62*(1).

Thoits, P. A., & Hewitt, L. N. (2001). Volunteer work and well-being. *Journal of Health and Social Behavior,* 115–131.

Ting-Toomey, S. (2015). Identity negotiation theory. *The international encyclopedia of interpersonal communication* (pp. 1–10).

Van Der Kolk, B. (2014). *The body keeps the score.* New York, NY: Viking.

Vaccaro, A. (2009). Racial identity and the ethics of service learning as pedagogy. In S. Evans, C. Taylor, M. Dunlap & D. Miller (Eds.), *African Americans and community engagement in higher education* (pp. 119–134). Albany, NY: SUNY Press.

Vasquez, G. R. (1998). Education in the modern west and the Andean culture. In Apffel-Marglin, F. & PRATEC (Eds.), *The spirit of regeneration: Andean culture confronting western notions of development* (pp. 172–192). New York: Zed Books.

Washington, J. M. (Ed). (1986). *A testament of hope: The essential writings and speeches of Martin Luther King, Jr.* New York, NY: Harper Collins.

Watkins, M., & Shulman, H. (2008). *Towards psychologies of liberation.* New York: Palgrave Macmillan.

Youniss, J., & Yates, M. (1997). *Community service and social responsibility in youth.* Chicago, IL: University of Chicago Press.

Zimmerman, K., Pathikonda, N., Salgado, B., & James, T. (2010). *Out of the spiritual closet: Organizers transforming the practice of social justice.* Oakland: Movement Strategy Center.

Critical, Contemplative Community Engagement

This chapter integrates the social change theories and wellbeing strategies explored in the previous chapters into the arena of higher education. This chapter's introduction of the Critical, Contemplative Community Engagement (CCCE) model provides a theoretical framework for investigating how individuals, institutions, and communities can create effective and meaningful social justice-oriented community partnerships. This chapter examines this model through three main foci: critical and contemplative learning and teaching theories, the need for a social justice orientation of engagement, and considerations for ethical and reciprocal community-campus partnership development. Drawing on my research and that of others in the social justice and community engagement fields, this chapter explores concrete factors that should be included when developing community-campus partnerships and community engagement courses.

LEARNING AND TEACHING THEORIES OF CRITICAL, CONTEMPLATIVE COMMUNITY ENGAGEMENT

The empowerment gained from education has long been perceived as connected to an obligation to give back to the public good in order to sustain a democratic society. Despite this admirable aim, the educational system itself was founded as a means to ensure the continuity and protection of the status quo. We must not forget that the American schools first created by colonists were explicitly and exclusively reserved for white,

© The Author(s) 2018   119
T. Hicks Peterson, *Student Development and Social Justice*,
https://doi.org/10.1007/978-3-319-57457-8_4

Christian men as a means for proper civic and religious socialization and apprenticeship (Cremin 1970). The schooling system has since endeavored to maintain a class of educated citizens who will produce knowledge that will advance our society, uphold the laws of the land, and increase the economy. Students are trained to become not just socially responsible citizens, but obedient ones. Thus, while schools have been revered as sites of knowledge production that contribute to the public good, there has been little contestation regarding *whose* good they are aiming to serve (Butin 2010; Westheimer and Kahne 2004).

Because of this, "systematic or formal education, in spite of its importance, cannot really be the lever for the transformation of society" (Freire and Shor 1987, p. 129). Because "the problems of school are deeply rooted in the global conditions of society," even when teachers use the critical pedagogy approach to inspire "democratic participation," their classes *alone* cannot create widespread change (ibid). Classroom learning must be connected and accountable to community-based movements for change. As Freire explains: "To change the concrete conditions of reality means a tremendous political practice, which demands mobilization, organization of the people, programs, all these things which cannot be organized just inside a classroom or a school" (Freire and Shor 1987, p. 134).

Fortunately, connecting education to social change by partnering with organizing efforts outside the classroom has a long and rich history. For generations, young people have been central to forwarding most social movements around the globe, movements which have been intricately connected to their own learning about peace and justice. In the United States, students have been engaged in community-based education and community engagement programs since the establishment of land grant colleges in 1862. The Civilian Conservation Corps and the Experiment in International Living programs of the 1930s provided other opportunities, theoretically supported by the pedagogical shift to experiential education around the same time (Dewey 1938). Students also engaged by fighting Jim Crow and speaking out about other socio-political issues during the civil rights era, between 1954 and 1974 (Oden and Casey in Calderon 2007; Stanton et al. 1999). The federal volunteer program (VISTA) created in 1964 and the National and Community Service Act in 1990 authorized grants to schools to support service learning and demonstration grants for national service programs to youth corps, non-profits, and colleges and universities, all of which led to the burgeoning of "service-learning" trends in colleges in the early 1990s (Boyer 1994; Jacoby 2003; Giles et al. 1991; Stanton et al. 1999). The charge to more clearly prioritize and forward practices of community-based learning, engaged teaching, civic engagement, and public scholarship in institutions of higher education has grown ever stronger over the years. National agencies, foundations, and universities and colleges have supported the development of promising practices, policies, curricula, research, and assessment protocols on the topic.[1]

"Community Engagement" is one of the most popular terms used currently for the work of students and engaged scholars who see the academy as inextricably tied to the challenges and movements of social systems and communities outside the walls of the university. Community engagement can include "service learning," which is usually defined as "a form of experiential education in which students engage in activities that address human and community needs together with structured opportunities intentionally designed to promote student learning and development" (Jacoby 2003, p. 3). I and many other scholars, teachers, and activists consider the "service-learning" concept to be limiting, however. It often assumes a hierarchical relationship about who is being served and who is doing the learning and it excludes the scholarship of engagement (i.e., community-based, participatory research). I prefer to use community engagement to broadly represent practices that create respectful, ethical, and reciprocal partnerships among engaged faculty, students, and staff of colleges and universities with community members, organizations, and institutions utilizing methods of civic engagement, community building, service providing, political organizing, participatory action research, advocacy, or accompaniment. These collective efforts aim to shift paradigms of injustice and increase engaged and civic education.

As I have written elsewhere, various learning theories ground the practice of community engagement.[2] Some of the most foundational derive from well-known educational theorists John Dewey, Paulo Freire, Ira Shor, and David Kolb. Dewey believed that you can't sever knowing and doing; one's greatest learning occurs in cycles of action and reflection. Dewey was interested in the learning that results from the mutual exchange between people and their environment. Kolb's work expanded notions of experiential learning to concentrate on the skills that observation, reflection, and analysis play in enabling students to take charge of their learning and engage in cycles of continuous learning (Stanton et al. 1999). Freire furthered these concepts by exploring the power dynamic that exists in traditional roles of teacher as the knower and student as the empty receptacle into which the teacher deposits knowledge. He not only dismantled the inherent power dynamics in that relationship but also the idea that learning is something that is done to you, given to you, rather than something you co-create and exchange in a consciousness-raising process that involves literacy, reading, writing, action, reflection, self-awareness, relationship building, and reciprocity. According to critical pedagogy, by engaging in this dialectic, a critical reflection of one's own positionality within community, culture, and knowledge production becomes essential (Freire 1970; Shor 1992; hooks 2003).

A feminist twist on critical pedagogy is called "engaged pedagogy." It was introduced to the field by bell hooks to emphasize a pedagogy concerned with "radical openness" and a form of wellbeing or "care of the soul" that "involves a knowledge of oneself and an accountability for one's actions, as well as a deep self-care, for both students and professors" (hooks as qtd in Berila 2016, p. 7). Similarly, Owen Barfield has introduced the notion of "participatory epistemology" in which "the learner is actively connected to what is being learned, and diverse forms of contemplative practice become conduits to elicit deep awareness, focus, compassion, social change, transformation, creativity, and inspiration, as well as intellectual understandings" (Rendón 2014, p. 134). Finally, an inclusive concept that weaves these pedagogies together is called "integrative learning." Contemplative pedagogist Laura Rendon describes the multifaceted nature of integrative learning:

> In one view, integrative learning connects skills and knowledge from diverse sources and experiences, as well as crosses disciplinary boundaries (American Association of Colleges and Universities & Carnegie Foundation for the Advancement of Teaching, 2004). The second view recognizes connections among diverse ways of knowing but also emphasizes the relationship between mind, body, and spirit, and the connection between the outer life of vocation and professional responsibility and the inner life of personal development, meaning and purpose. (ibid)

Critical, Contemplative Community Engagement promotes this critical and integrated approach to education grounded in the belief that knowledge is socially and culturally structured and influenced by those structures. As such, knowledge is neither value neutral nor objective (Lather 1986). To study knowledge construction is to recognize the factors impacting the situatedness of knowing (Butin 2010; hooks 2003; Steinberg and Kincheloe 1998). To this end, critical classroom settings, instruction, and content must be inclusive, multicultural, integrative, reflective, collaborative, democratic, dialogic, empowering, transdisciplinary, and experiential (Calderon 2007; Freire 1970; hooks 1994; Rendón 2014; Shor 1992). The second main principle of the CCCE model is contemplation. To better link student and community wellbeing to community engagement programs, we need to pay more attention to the value of introspection and contemplation, qualities of participation that have been less attended to in the field of community engagement. Contemplative or meditative practices not only improve personal and collective wellbeing, they can "involve stirring the soul, shaking the learner's belief system, fostering a social justice consciousness, developing wisdom, and in the end transforming the self" (Rendón 2014, p. 141). Contemplation thus connects the cultivation of peace and wellbeing amongst students and communities to the social change aim of disrupting the roots of injustice. When community engagement is both *critical* and *contemplative*, it can "highlight an 'embodied reflexivity' in which participants learn to reflect on their own ideologies and experiences, question their ways of thinking, and imagine alternatives" (hooks qtd in Berila 2016, p. 15). Threading together the critical with the contemplative will promote critical learning, radical healing, and social change on campuses and in partnerships with local communities.

As a key component of the CCCE model, integrative learning is grounded in the belief that knowledge is constructed and partial, yet extends beyond rational and empirical ways of knowing to value the knowing that comes from within. It encourages introspective practices that enable "students to cultivate a nuanced discernment of their own experience" (Berila 2016, p. 15). Through contemplation and introspection, a deeper understanding of course material, of each other, and of personal meaning, insight, and interpretation of knowledge can take place, along with "a deepening sense of the moral and spiritual aspect of education" (p. 14). This ensures that emotional, physical, mental, and spiritual forms of wellbeing are being attended to. Students do not have to leave their personal experiences at the door in order to increase their cognitive development or become actively engaged in the community, nor do they have to deny the links between learning, engaging, and developing. Incorporating student development into the aims of community engagement encompasses a number of aspects of student mental health, identity development, and sense of purpose, all of which are increasingly being linked in the literature to the social connectedness found through community engagement activities.[3]

At the core of the CCCE framework is grounding the engagement in a weekly classroom forum where students can connect their field experiences to theories on social change and the larger structural and historical issues informing or creating community problems. Dynamic intellectual growth, political awareness, and social responsibility can be thoughtfully addressed, taught, and reflected upon in a classroom context that frames the community engagement activity. Research indicates that "adequate time, contact, in-class reflection, and talking about service experiences make a difference in students' civic and academic outcomes' (Mabry 1998, p. 39). In most community engagement programs, students have weekly commitments to a community organization or association and receive credit (academic or work study) for their community internship.[4]

The aim here is to support students in deepening their learning, critical consciousness, and personal growth while also connecting the community engagement experience to relevant theoretical and political frameworks. Explicitly articulating student learning outcomes that include these aims along with the disciplinary focus of the course provides a roadmap to such learning. In addition, it is necessary to create classroom discussions, lectures, reading, and writing assignments that engage reflections and analysis around the structural, political, social, economic, and/or environmental conditions (and any other root causes) that have resulted in the need for the social change partnership while also exploring the benefits and potential pitfalls of community-campus collaborations. The CCCE approach incorporates course readings and discussions intended to enable students to challenge the hegemonic structures and practices that further social injustice and oppression and develop strategies for disrupting or removing systemic barriers to equality and inclusiveness (Pitzer College 2016). It is also helpful to orient the students about the communities they will be working in (and correlating economic, racial, social, political, and historic contexts that have resulted in the existing problems, needs, and assets in that community). Such an orientation can drive home expectations that students will be respectful, accountable, professional, and self-reflective in their partnerships. Finally, building a classroom space that encourages a safe (enough) space for students to learn, grow, be challenged, get uncomfortable, gain new perspectives, and reflect critically is key.

Contemplative community engagement classrooms can be set up in a way that creates a conducive environment for processing the emotional labor of doing social justice-oriented community work. A critical reflection classroom fosters a place to reflect on experiences, the impact of involvement, and responsibility and accountability to community partners. This kind of setting enables students and faculty members alike to negotiate the emotions or tensions that may surface both in and out of the classroom as they engage in social change efforts. Including contemplative practices that invite emotions, intuition, and other ways of learning, knowing, and being in the classroom may help ensure "the design of a relationship-centered classroom based on caring, trust, support and validation [and] a curriculum that is inclusive of multicultural perspectives and worldviews and that is focused on social justice" (Rendón 2014, pp. 136–137). McAdam's longitudinal research of student allies that were engaged in the civil rights movement, in particular in the 'Freedom Summer' effort, provides one example of the need for a space to process the discomfort that can arise through community engagement:

In 1964, students from elite Northern universities volunteered to register voters in Mississippi. Compared to those who were interested in the project but did not participate in Freedom Summer, those who engaged in this intense encounter with injustice in America ultimately became more cynical about the government. Afterward, some had social adjustment problems including loneliness, isolation, and loss of emotional control; one in ten became estranged from loved ones in subsequent years. Such intense political activism is not the typical form of civic engagement for most undergraduate students. Nonetheless, it is a reminder of the importance of continuing social support as young people grapple with unjust social conditions and seek to make change. (Flanagan and Bundick 2011, p. 22)

As this example demonstrates, becoming proximate to injustice does not allow practitioners to walk away and resume a more comfortable experience of "not-knowing" the pain and suffering that exists in the world (for those who had that luxury to begin with). It demonstrates that often one's greatest learning occurs in this place of discomfort and such learning requires fighting the impulse to return to the status quo. It also demonstrates the need for tools for negotiating reflections and emotions that emerge from intensive community engagement experiences. Beyond engagement in the community, engaging within is a critical component of creating just and effective partnerships. Laura Rendon reminds us that:

> Introspection, or deep involvement in the critical examination of one's beliefs, assumptions, and worldviews, is a second form of engagement. Faculty and students must be willing to confront their own fears and biases and the extent of their participation in maintaining the status quo. Self-reflexivity can serve as a means for faculty and students to probe more deeply into what they are learning and how the learning is transforming them. (2014, pp. 136–137)

This self-reflexivity can be promoted through classrooms that promote critical reflection activities. Critical reflection, as described by Ash and Clayon, "generates learning (articulating questions, confronting bias, examining causality, contrasting theory with practice, pointing to systemic issues), deepens learning (challenging simplistic conclusions, inviting alternative perspectives, asking "why" iteratively), and documents learning (producing tangible expressions of new understandings for evaluation)" (2009, pp. 27–28; Whitney and Clayton 2011). Critical reflection is the perfect tool for eliciting introspective awareness that goes below the surface, pushes us to our edge, and investigates any discomfort that arises in this process, in the classroom, or in the field. Research also shows that critical reflection and analysis through discussion and writing assignments can secure a stronger commitment to and belief in the student's ability to make a positive contribution while enhancing prosocial reasoning (Giles and Eyler 1994). Student reflections are augmented by the collective guidance and feedback from professors and community partners whose input affects student learning, skill development, and levels of commitment (Greene and Diehm 1995). Numerous evaluations of community engagement programs demonstrate that the most powerful education results from a combination of theoretical reading, active participation in the community, and involvement in a critical forum for reflection and analysis (Ash and Clayon 2009; Dewey 1938; Eyler and Giles 1999; Freire 2006; Greene and Diehm 1995; Illich 1971; Mabry 1998; Stanton et al. 1999).

As examined in the above example, contemplation of injustice as well as actions geared at its undoing may also result in challenging feelings of discomfort, even hopelessness and despair. Allowing students to acknowledge and feel these is an important learning process that gives them space to intentionally move into another phase of hopefulness. As veteran civic engagement scholar Thomas Ehrlich explains:

A key challenge is addressing students' frustration about the lack of change as a result of their civic service. Often the issues involved in civic work are so large that students begin to wonder "Is this really worth it? Are we really making a difference? Why am I really doing this?" These negative and doubting reactions can stop them from moving forward and staying committed to important work. These feelings that cause students to question or struggle, however, can also be some of life's greatest teaching tools, providing educators with opportunities to help students process their experiences and support them through these challenges, set backs, or even failures, so they can grow stronger and more committed.

Learning to experience the *joy* of engagement in civic, community, or political work and to gain *pleasure* from participation – as opposed to becoming discouraged by slow-moving change – is the larger opportunity that we have when these dark days come. As educators and leaders in civic engagement, we need to talk to students about these feelings before they emerge, while teaching and modeling taking pleasure and joy from being involved for the sake of being part of something greater than ourselves in order to foster a deeper, spiritual experience. (2009, p. 4)

Confronting hopelessness in a critically reflective and supportive environment can be helpful, as such reflections can organically move us towards imagining the changes we want to make. Community engagement partnerships then provide us with the vehicles to actually participate in such changes, which in turn can actually dissipate our despair and cultivate hope. Community engagement has been shown to bring great social awards through the connection, relationships, and mutual respect built with others, through the satisfaction of being a part of something greater than oneself and a cause you believe in (Verba et al. 1995). In fact, research shows direct links between purpose, connectedness, belonging, and hope: "engagement in collective civic action toward a common purpose increases connectedness among individuals in a community, and connections to fellow human beings satisfy a basic human need for belonging (Baumeister and Leary 1995)" (Flanagan and Bundick 2011, p. 23). As highlighted earlier, the act of community engagement can in and of itself nurture hope and healing for individuals and groups.

Research over the last three decades has found that community engagement has myriad effects on student development in the personal, cognitive, civic, professional, and academic realms.[5] More recently, scholars have found correlations between community engagement and improved wellbeing. In particular, they associate community engagement with students' development in terms of finding meaning, connection, and belonging with others in the world on issues of personal and social significance (Bringing Theory to Practice 2013; Finley 2012b; Flanagan and Bundick 2011; Harward 2012, 2016; Hurtado et al. 2012; Ryff and Keyes 1995; Swaner 2005). Beyond civic and social wellbeing, these researchers have found that community engagement positively influences the personal wellbeing of students. This is particularly crucial for students facing challenges to their mental health. The current generation of college students (Millenials) reports suffering from the most stress and the least relief of any other generation today (APA 2012). Securing positive mental health is a key component of holistic student success, since "mental health and well-being are complex constructs that encompass individuals' abilities to value their self-worth, realize their potential, cope with stress, work productively, relate positively with others, make healthy decisions, and contribute to community" (Swaner 2005, p. iv).

Students today face myriad economic and social challenges that exascerbate the stress of academia. A 2016 *Stress in America* survey showed that, of all generations, "younger adults are the most likely to say they have experienced some form of discrimination (75 percent of Millennials)," which we know is a critical cause of stress (APA 2016, p. 7). In addition, academic competition, intense social pressures (especially around sex, alcohol, and drugs), and identity development growing pains can make it difficult for college students to maintain a vibrant state of mental health. In fact, for an individual in college "the chances are almost one in two that he or she will become depressed to the point of being unable to function; one in two that he or she will have regular episodes of binge drinking (with the resulting significant risk of dangerous consequences such as sexual assault and car accidents); and one in ten that he or she will seriously consider suicide" (Swaner 2005, p. 1). However, the challenges and stresses of attending college may be mitigated by supportive environments that promote a sense of purpose and engagement through meaningful engagement with others:

> In studies of adolescents and young adults, volunteerism and collective action are also associated with various indicators of psycho-social well-being,

including self-efficacy, hope, and optimism (Uslaner 2002); collective efficacy and self-confidence (Astin and Sax 1998); sense of meaning (Astin et al. 1999); self-esteem (Thoits and Hewitt 2001); and satisfaction with one's daily activities (Pancer and Pratt 1999). Similarly, studies of service learning in high school and college settings find relationships with students' feelings of agency, efficacy, purpose and meaning in their life; their interpersonal skills; and their sense of living up to one's potential. (Astin et al. 2000; Markus et al. 1993; Youniss and Yates 1999; Flanagan and Bundick 2011, p. 22)

The link between wellbeing and civic engagement not only fortifies communities but also diminishes the likelihood of engaging in self-destructive behaviors, particularly among college students:

Participation in civic engagement has been associated with resistance to anti-social behavior, substance abuse, and disengagement from school (Finn and Checkoway 1998; Fogal 2004; Kelly 2009) [...] participation in CES or CA [community engagement service or community action] activities during the first year of college may decrease a student's likelihood for binge drinking and unhealthy alcohol use among first-year students. (Niotera et al. 2015, pp. 1 and 12)

Among its many impacts, community engagement can lead to deepening self-awareness and self-reflection, providing "opportunities for students to craft identities as moral individuals responsible both to self and to larger communities" (Swaner 2005, p. vi). Given the current epidemic of binge drinking, sexual violence, and mental illness on college campuses, curricular and co-curricular practices that actively reduce the factors leading to these problems are extremely important for institutions of higher education nationwide.

Research also shows that community engagement has longitudinal impacts on wellbeing that go well beyond the college years: "Results show that both college volunteering and service-learning have positive, indirect effects on several forms of well-being during adulthood, including personal growth, purpose in life, environmental mastery, and life satisfaction" (Flanagan and Bundick 2011, p. 22). Such experiences have been shown to lead to not only further volunteering as adults but also prosocial attitudes and values that are associated with wellbeing (ibid). A reciprocal cycle is generated such that greater wellbeing leads to more volunteering and more volunteering leads to further wellbeing (Thoits and Hewitt 2001).

Facilitating quality critical, contemplative community engagement begins with a commitment to an experiential pedagogical foundation centered on wellbeing, self-awareness, critical thinking, integrated learning, and relationship-building. Yet, the teaching and learning theories that ground this practice will make little difference if the engagement itself is not grounded in a social justice orientation. The following section examines the risks we face when community engagement programs work towards social service at the expense of social change and some concrete methods we can employ to shift these practices.

THE SOCIAL JUSTICE ORIENTATION OF CRITICAL, CONTEMPLATIVE COMMUNITY ENGAGEMENT

Despite the evidence that points to major gains amongst students who have participated in community engagement, numerous critiques against charity-oriented service models have arisen.[6] No matter how much they gain from the process nor how good their intentions are going in, students can end up doing more harm than good when entering a community with the notion that they are there to help, rescue, save the poor, needy, and marginalized with their gifts of formal education (read: superior knowledge), resources, and ways of being. The common refrain, 'I want to change the world,' implies that you know how to make positive changes and your belief in how to do so is right. This attitude fails to recognize the possibility that those people who you think need help may not want anything to do with your ideas about change, much less have you lead the charge. Students who are not conscious of these issues can perpetuate circumstances of marginalization and disempowerment when they become engaged with a community. These conditions are heightened when race and class dynamics put white or wealthy students in the roles of being service providers or researchers, while low-income communities or communities of color are positioned as recipients of service or objects of research.

The traditional notions of service implicit in a volunteer's quest to "help" marginalized communities reflect the underlying assumption of most service-providing institutions (including universities) that there are voids, deficits, or needs in communities (considered poor and less educated) that the institutions (considered richer and better educated) can fill. This paradigm is not meant to disempower communities, but it often does.

While a nurturing exchange can result from people engaging in palliative care, when services are repeatedly given to a group that is seen as vulnerable, marginalized, or powerless, the service itself, however well-intended, can end up perpetuating the position or view of the population as vulnerable, marginalized, and powerless. When efforts are not made to radically shift structural power dynamics in our society, a never-ending cycle of interlocking social and medical services becomes systematically exercised with marginalized communities, until it is established as the norm. Power is seized when this norm is such that only an outside agent (often coming from a different racial or class background or entrenched in a different value system) with more resources is seen as the "rescuer," able to save others from devastation. A power dynamic develops that turns outside service providers into stewards of care and insider community members into recipients and clients. This dynamic reflects thinly veiled assumption of superiority and inferiority rather than values of reciprocity and interconnectedness. This power dynamic is entangled in an economic system that benefits from the continued need for service. It benefits people whose status quo would be threatened if concerned citizens instead put their energies into organizing activities that would result in significant structural change.

McKnight (1995) and Kivel (2007) have expanded on this issue, unsettling many people engaged in social service work with their frank exploration of the harm caused by service interventions. They argue that well-intentioned people involved in social service can inadvertently perpetuate the oppressive ideologies and behaviors they allege to change. Their premise is that those who work in social service positions perpetuate injustice because systems of oppression are tied up in the ways service work is operationalized and embedded in hierarchical systems. The United States depends economically on some sectors of the national community (usually the poor or sick or oppressed) being in need so that other sectors (usually the middle class, healthy, and privileged) can find employment in servicing those needs. Little attention is paid to the intersections of race, class, and ethnicity that divide which groups are typically in need and which typically have the power to dole out the services.

The difference here is between working for social service, which provides relief, support, and palliative care for those suffering from the impacts of oppression, violence, and injustice, and working towards social change, which would undo the very structures and conditions of oppression, violence, and injustice that result in the need for these services. Kivel explains:

Although some groups are both working for social change and providing social services, there are many more groups providing social services that are not working for social change. In fact, many social service agencies may be intentionally or inadvertently working to maintain the status quo. After all, the non-profit industrial complex (NPIC) wouldn't exist without a lot of people in desperate straits. The NPIC provides jobs; it provides opportunities for professional development. It enables those who do the work to feel good about what we do and about our ability to help individuals survive in the system. It gives a patina of caring and concern to the ruling class which funds the work. While there is always the risk of not securing adequate funding, there is a greater risk that if we did something to really rock the boat and address the roots of the problems we would we lose whatever funding we've already managed to secure [...] The existence of these jobs serves to convince people that tremendous inequalities of wealth are natural and inevitable. Institutionalizing soup kitchens leads people to expect that inevitably there will be people without enough to eat; establishing permanent homeless shelters leads people to think that it is normal for there not to be enough affordable housing. (2007, p. 139)

Kivel's disconcertingly claim that organized social service industries are invariably tied to the inequitable distribution of power and wealth implicates anyone who finds employment as teachers, doctors, counselors, social workers, or non-profit service staff (myself included!). Examining the ways that service work ultimately upholds the very unequal structures workers hope to dismantle causes definitive discomfort. Yet from this awareness we can ascertain what in our lives and in our work will need to change in order to expose these contradictions and strategically organize coalition work across diverse organizations towards a collective shift in strategies and goals. The act of exploring how our social service systems may be part of the problem (by focusing all our time on attending immediate needs rather than addressing root conditions) may lead us to more creative and intentional visions for how to shift the systems relating to hierarchies of power, money, access, and distribution within which we currently operate.

In an effort then to create more social justice-oriented community engagement programs, we are tasked with examining to what degree community engagement is or is not actively linked to a restructuring of current hierarchies of power that sustain interlocking systems of domination. At the heart of every community-campus collaboration, we must examine if or how community engagement efforts have resulted in personal, institutional, social, and structural change. Without this commitment, we risk a lack of institutional accountability towards the ways in which institutions of higher education are implicated in systems of oppression, reproduce social hierarchies, and contribute to further distancing and misunderstanding between the campus and external communities (Razack 1998). These foundational quandaries related to service work are not easily solved, though keeping such provocations at the forefront of any community engagement effort will invariably influence its formation, methods, and goals. Luckily, candid conversations like these are beginning to shift the narrative within the dominant discourse on higher education's practices of community engagement (Verjee and Butterwick 2014).

There are many factors practitioners can consider in their efforts to create social justice-oriented community engagement programs and partnerships. Of the many studies that inform the topic of designing community engagement programs, I find Bonner Foundation's criteria for developing "high impact community engagement practices" (HICEP) to be the most well rounded and social justice focused. The Bonner Foundation promotes community engagement programs that emphasize the following qualities:

- *place* (place-based learning that incorporates community understanding, context, and assets and includes community voice in defining relationships and projects),
- *humility* (knowledge cocreation in which partners, students, and faculty share co-educator status),
- *integration* (of both co-curricular and curricular contexts and structures),
- *depth* (multi-year strategic agreements for capacity building),
- *development* (grounding in appropriate student and partner developmental needs, changing over time),
- *sequence* (scaffolded projects evolving over multiple semesters or calendar years),
- *teams* (involving multiple participants at different levels),
- *reflection* (structured and unstructured oral, written, and innovative formats),
- *mentors* (dialogue and coaching by partners, peers, and/or faculty),
- *learning* (collaborative and responsive teaching and learning opportunities),

- *capacity building* (designed to build the organization/agency over time),
- *evidence* (integration of evidence- based or proven program models), and
- *impact orientation* (identifiable outcomes and strategies for evaluation and measurement) (Hoy 2012, p. 6).

While not all engagement efforts will encompass all of these components, they are good to ones to work towards in creating a social justice-oriented community engagement program that will have long-term benefits for students and communities alike. Additional factors I find to be important include ensuring that students spend substantial time with the community partner organization and neighborhood, building solid reciprocal relationships with organization staff and community members, participating in community activities, collaborating in specific projects and research, reflecting on the intersections of practice and theory in a related course, and contributing in meaningful ways to the long-term, shared goals of social change that overturn oppressive systems.

Beyond configurations of off-campus partnerships, community engagement can be seen as a vehicle advancing social justice in the colleges themselves. Research indicates that community engagement experiences seem to actually decrease inequalities in student achievement:

> These kinds of educational experiences are especially powerful for students who may be the first in their family to attend college, and those who are historically underserved in postsecondary education... Research has shown persuasively that HIPs [high impact practices] improve the quality of students' experience, learning, retention, and success, particularly for underserved students (Kuh 2008). Moreover, HIPs are associated with outcomes such as improved graduation rates and narrowed achievement gaps between racial–ethnic groups. (Kinzie 2012, p. 13)

The degree to which community engagement programs forward social justice goals can also be elucidated by the thoughtfulness with which community-campus partnerships are developed. The following section outlines both potential landmines and lifelines in the creation of social justice-oriented community-campus partnerships.

PARTNERSHIP DEVELOPMENT WITHIN CRITICAL, CONTEMPLATIVE COMMUNITY ENGAGEMENT

The CCCE model involves developing equitable, effective, and reciprocal partnerships for social change. Such community-campus partnerships are cultivated based on mutual interests and needs related to the social issues present in the local community and the teaching, learning, and research goals of students, staff, and community partners. To move towards a more critical community engagement practice, it behooves campus constituents to look beyond traditional service-providing agencies and institutions to seek out more social justice, grassroots focused organizations. Where none exist, interested community members and campus members can develop them (refer to the Huerta del Valle example in Chap. 2). In other cases, partnerships with city institutions or conventional service providers invite opportunities to bring social justice-oriented critiques and ideas into these institutions, which can blossom into broader political and financial impacts. Alternatively, simply holding an event to connect local agencies, community leaders, and community members with faculty, staff, and students interested in community engagement can provide a platform for people to get to know each other and talk about their respective interests in social change. Such an event can lead to natural collaborations. Staff from community engagement centers (if they exist on campus) can help make these connections and provide curricular resources, student and faculty community engagement training, and community support. They may oversee logistics and facilitate partnership dynamics to support faculty and students in their direct work with communities. Relationships between local communities, organizations, institutions, associations, and individuals must be artfully facilitated with university faculty, students, or staff. Faculty members, students, or community partners often spearhead this work directly.

Regardless of who initiates and facilitates the building of the partnership, some key components of partnership-building must be attended to in the act of becoming proximate. These include the 'four Rs' of "relevance, respect, reciprocity, and reflection" (Butin 2014, p. viii). Other fundamental characteristics of trusting relationships are "benevolence, honesty, openness, reliability and competence" (Hoy and Tschannen-Moran 1999, cited in Noel 2014, p. 178). Miron and Moely (2006) encourage reciprocal actions between individuals or groups of individuals that contribute to a relationship or exchange that is two sided, mutually contingent, mutually rewarding, and wherein community partners have an equal voice.

Community partners should be involved in the design, implementation, and evaluation of the community engagement program and have positive interpersonal relations and good communication with campus partners. Dorado and Giles (2004) posit that there are typically three dominant behaviors/stages: learning (gaining familiarity with partners); aligning (reviewing/assessing partnership aims, goals, process, and outcomes); and nurturing (cultivating support on a committed path of engagement), and when we attend thoughtfully to each, the partnership outcomes are improved. Finally, Keith (1998) suggests that partnerships are most successful when they connect community service with community building; that is, partnerships that convey high levels of mutual respect and expectations, networks of support, the development of local capacities, relationship building across borders, an appreciation of the cultural and human capital and assets of each partner, a lack of disparity between partners' contributions, and a connection between service, democracy, and community building. When these qualities have been established in the relationship-building process, and time has been spent accompanying communities, then further engagement can take place around long-term partnership goals between the campus and community.

As the partnership begins to take shape, agreements about what the projects and student internships will entail usually follow. While pre-setting goals and roles can be helpful in generating expectations for many partnerships, there is also something to be said about allowing the goals to unfold once trust, understanding, and coherence have been built in the relationship. Or as my Peruvian mentor responded to me when I inquired what my work of accompaniment would entail, "*Vamos a hacer una amistad y ver a lo que el camino indica*"—we will make a friendship and see what the path indicates (J.I., *personal communication*, 2004). Some theorists in community engagement field describe this as an "activist–apprentice" approach, in which

> students enter the community as learners rather than as teachers, a shift that facilitates the defamiliarization that creates space for critical self-reflection[...] occupying the position of learner means that the goals and services of a collaboration between students and their community partners are not fully established beforehand (Schutz and Gere 1998, p. 145). [...] Shantz (2010) describes [this] as 'constructive anarchy,' or 'projects that provide examples of politics grounded in everyday resistance' (p. 1). (Bisignani 2014, pp. 101–102)

This is a far cry from the common service methodology utilized by many non-profits to administer "needs assessments" and then enter communities with fixed agendas to "fix" problems. Creating genuine relationships is the most important first step of any partnership in order for a solid enough sense of trust, shared understanding, and mutually beneficial aims to emerge that can guide the future of the work. As the partnership itself cements, conversations about explicit goals and roles can be fomented into more formal agreements (see Chap. 5).

Yet, even with thoughtful relationship-building, community-campus partnerships often confront tensions related to bringing groups with disparate life experiences together to learn from one another. I witnessed such an instance occurring with a student who had some trepidation about enrolling in my Inside-Out Prison Exchange course. Knowing that the "Special Needs Yard" where I held the class is populated with many people who have sex offenses on their records, this student was apprehensive about becoming proximate to this particular population, based on her own experience of sexual abuse. Yet, she had tutored incarcerated students in the other "General Population" yard of this same prison and had been transformed by that experience and wanted to move beyond the service-providing model of engagement into a peer-to-peer classroom environment. She told me after the class was over that although she had to tolerate initial discomfort, fear, and apprehension about being in this course, she ended up finding tremendous healing and growth. Because of the ongoing and meaningful conversations she engaged in with inside members of the class, she formed relationships with individuals on this yard embodying respect, caring, and mutual learning. She began to see and get to know each individual for the fullness of their humanity, rather than a presumed offense on their record (which she had no way of knowing for certain since neither the students nor I have any reason to learn about inside student's convictions). She said that it was the most healing experience she had around her own sexual abuse personally as well as a growing experience socio-politically when she realized how limited her work in the world would be if she only was willing to work with non-offenders. While individuals should always have a right to choose how and with whom they address such painful topics, I believe that healing and changing our interlocking systems of domination must include both targets and perpetrators, and through the willingness of this student to tolerate initial discomfort, she discovered deeper meaning in the notion that social justice work must include all of us, not just some of us.

Yet learning about "the other" and shattering assumptions, ignorance or fear about those we do not know or understand through the act of community engagement brings with it another set of concerns. In many cases, learning occurs for students of privilege at the expense of others in the community or in the classroom, those whose life experience with oppression is what opens their eyes. "I don't like to be in the room when someone is realizing I'm human," is how one bold, brilliant, and deeply pained queer woman of color explained it to me (R.C., *personal communication*, 2015). And while I have often been the first one to critique the potential harm that can come from community engagement efforts that lack respect, reciprocity, and deep relationships, I nonetheless felt like I was hit in the gut with this comment. At whose expense had my own students' learning occurred? Had we stopped to ask this in the classroom or in our many community partnerships? And even more to the point, at whose expense had and does my own learning occur? We are all actors in the community-campus partnership endeavor and the environments we create both in the classroom and in the field will determine the degree to which harm might and can occur. What may be eye-opening and stereotype-shattering realization for one may very well come at the dignity of another. While many "outside" students learn a great deal from their classes inside the prison, a concerning comment I hear regularly from them after their first class meeting with their new incarcerated class peers is, "I don't know what I was expecting, but those guys are human like anyone else." While this certainly is a realization that counters typical stereotypes projected onto people who are in prison and an important baseline to establish for a group that is about to integrate into a holistic class community for the semester, I worry greatly about the lack of full humanity that was not initially afforded or assumed in these first encounters and what harm that may have caused.

This reminds us that while student learning is the primary currency of institutions of higher education, we must be vigilant that it does not occur at the expense of the community. This relates to larger issues related to academic knowledge production, which has typically occurred within a system of higher education that divides the knowers (i.e., scientists, experts, intellectuals) from the known (i.e., community members seen as objects of study, not as sources of knowledge). One way to navigate these tensions is to see critical community engagement as turning the tables so that community members are seen not only as knowledge resources, but as esteemed teachers and mentors in their own right. As long as they give their consent to be educators (and it does not happen at their expense), community members can provide insightful analysis and leadership that supports the trajectory of each student's educational development as well as advancement in social change issues. Well-designed community-campus partnerships can alter biases about who holds the keys to knowledge in the society at large. The incarcerated students my undergraduates did not initially afford full humanity to are the same ones they report learning the most from in regards to concepts of state-sanctioned violence or the school-to-prison pipeline—more, they say, than from all the assigned theoretical readings that aim to explain the same things. Critically transforming the pedagogy of higher education to include marginalized voices as 'experts' in their own right not only pries open a previously exclusive trend of scholarship but also expands students' understanding of ways of knowing, being, and seeing the world. Revamping the traditions of knowledge production so that local knowledge is seen as a valid and intellectually rigorous source of learning significantly alters the social, cultural, and political landscape of knowledge production in the university. This in and of itself is a profound type of social change. Yet, as mentioned, we must be sure that its making does not occur at the expense of another's humanity. As such, faculty are charged to act as "ethical guides" to help students reflect on whether or not their growth and learning in community engagement efforts has resulted in any harm to the community (Vaccaro 2009).

Beyond these potential tensions within community-campus partnerships, there are others that can arise related to unequal power dynamics, differing timelines, and distinct end goals. For example, studies show that long-term educational and professional growth for community members is not typically an explicit goal of community-campus partnerships (Peterson et al. 2010). Thus, undergraduate student partners develop, but not always the communities with which they engage. While undergraduate students often acquire organizing, service, or research skills, access local knowledge and resources, get credit for classes, develop their careers, or are awarded grants for their work, they remain largely unaffected by the success or failure of the community to achieve its goals in the partnership. Furthermore, students' long and academically codified final papers for a service-learning or research classes are often of little use to the community agencies who need concise research reports that they can translate into community-organizing actions, service programs, policy statements, or grant proposals that would benefit the community. Finally, the limits of the semester calendar never fit neatly within the time table of community organizing or service providing, creating fall-out for long-term efforts of structural change (Peterson et al. 2010). Interrogating the tensions within community-campus partnerships holds both partners accountable for pushing the intentions, goals, projects, and long-term aims toward a greater emphasis on reciprocal benefits for all involved. Deeper levels of collaboration, power shifting, and organizing *within* the community-campus partnership is needed on multiple fronts.

One way to shift the power in community engagement partnerships is to consider who has the reins in deciding what the agenda is for community activist, research, or service efforts. When community members have the power to articulate what their needs are, what the remedies might be, and what resources might aid them, a bottom-up shift from *power over* to *power to* occurs.

Collective governance around the future directions of partnerships honors the knowledge and leadership of local members. This can occur by establishing on-campus institutional governance, for example, creating a standing committee that faculty, staff, students, and community partner representatives sit on to guide institutional community engagement policy, practices, and partnerships. Alternatively, it can occur amongst the community organizations themselves that collaborate with the college. Distinct community partners may come together to create a community board that will keep the college accountable to all the partners and find ways for community engagement partnerships to collaborate with each other in thematic areas.[7] Finally, collective governance can emerge within and guide the community-campus partnership itself. I have seen this unfold within two distinct partnerships, whose examples bring this concept to life.

The first example is the Inside-Out Prison Exchange Program's use of "think-tanks," which are composed of inside (incarcerated) and outside (non-incarcerated) students and faculty who meet regularly to make decisions about the aims of the partnership, from what kinds of classes should be taught inside, what procedures will be in place to ensure equitable access to classes for both inside and outside students, and what long-term goals the partnership would like to work on in regards to criminal justice. The think tank intentionally puts power in the hands of those seen as powerless to resist the hierarchical decision-making processes of the judicial and punitive systems within which this partnership operates. Working through bottom-up, participatory governance on efforts of liberatory education within a dehumanizing system does not alleviate the inherent contradiction that exists in the partnership, but it does cultivate hope that small yet powerful steps can be taken to dismantle the system from within. Hope is cultivated when community-campus decision-making groups work across differences in positionality, access, and life experience to make change happen even in the most unlikely of oppressive conditions.

The second example occurred in a process by which some students and I established a partnership with a local high school, resulting over time in substantial gains for students, community members, and the school itself. At the far eastern end of Los Angeles County, a few miles from where Pitzer College is located in Claremont, lies a public high school that has been entrenched in extremely high rates of violence, teenage pregnancy, and dismal graduation rates (Crime rates in Pomona 2017). While these problems have gotten better over time due to the community-driven efforts of a coalition of organizations, when the school approached me to build a partnership in 2007, there was little going on to support students caught in this reality. The partnership began with the high school peer counselor simply asking me: "Please send some of your college kids to our school. We have nothing here—no school clubs, no afterschool groups, no college mentors for my students to look up to. We just need people here to support these kids." I shared this with my "Social Change Practicum" course and two young women immediately wanted to get engaged. They went to the school and met with the teacher and the students in her peer counseling class. Attempting to become proximate as respectfully as they could to this new community, they entered with humility, no agenda, and energy directed at establishing meaningful relationships. Through conversations with the high school students, they learned quickly that most girls at the school had few role models or adults in whom they could confide (as their parents worked multiple jobs) and they just wanted a safe and secure place to come together and talk about the issues they faced. Together they came up with the idea to launch a support group for girls and the next week they postered fliers around the school announcing a new afterschool club, "Girl Talk."

The college interns expected about 25–30 high school students to come to the first meeting, but 60 girls showed up. Scrambling for more chairs and pizza, they finally got the group of cautious but eager students in a large circle. They explained that they were there to do what the students wanted; to support them in any way they felt they could be useful. To begin, they passed around index cards for everyone to write down the biggest concern they had in their life that they wanted to discuss in this group or find resources of support for. They intentionally did it this way so as to help everyone feel comfortable sharing personal problems and also to avoid mandatory reporting issues by maintaining anonymity. Of the 60 students present, 40 returned index cards; of the 40 cards collected, 29 indicated that the students faced issues of violence at the hands of their parents, boyfriends, gangs, or themselves. Other topics covered drugs, pregnancy, low self-esteem, depression, and isolation. My students quickly recognized both the extremity of suffering in the room and their own personal limitations for navigating interventions. This resulted in important conversations with me and the supervising high school teacher as well as with the college students directly about how to facilitate this group, resulting in numerous subsequent actions that guided the partnership's future.

My students proceeded by creating realistic expectations for what this group was and what they as student interns could offer. They were clear about their limitations when they discussed the fact that they were not trained therapists. What they could provide was an open-minded and open-hearted space for listening, supporting, witnessing, and respecting the narratives and experiences of everyone in the group. They agreed to research what resources existed in the community to support the young women in crisis, bring in guest speakers and workshop facilitators, and create a resource list of brochures, websites, and addresses the students to turn to when seeking direct assistance.[8]

In the 6 years since its inception, the "Girl Talk" program has grown more popular and spread its influence beyond the initial partnership. The group's founders were asked to present the program at a district-wide conference, which recruited teachers and counselors to replicate it at various schools throughout the district and extended into the creation of a young men's group. Basing the program on the assets within the school, independent of outside services, has made it more sustainable and community driven. The original college interns also trained other Pitzer students to carry on their roles once they graduated in order to surpass the academic limitations that usually hinder partnership sustainability. The next generation of college mentors expanded the effort by creating a Young Women's daylong conference on health and healing for mind, body, and spirit. It became such a success that it is now an annual, district-wide event with hundreds of young women from all of the middle and high schools in the area. Inspired by the original partnership, the two primary college leaders of this effort both went on to continue to work with marginalized youth in their communities and have both sought Masters degrees in Social Work.

I share this example because it demonstrates an effective shift from the typical scenario where service providers enter communities with fixed agendas focused on deficits and short-term relief to an emphasis on older peers bearing witness, offering support, and accompanying younger people through their suffering, connecting them to resources, and advocating for greater accountability on the part of the educational structure to address these needs across the board. Over the years, this program drew on the asset-based community development approach to support the community to build on its own strengths and networks in order to eliminate the need for outside services to build them up (McKnight 1995). This model can be followed by other programs which aim to partner with communities in identifying their own problems and meeting their own needs by building upon their own assets. Engaging in frank discussions about how to create such partnerships reduces the likelihood of over-dependency on outside partners (students, faculty, or service providers). The programs are then more likely to be sustained even if the university withdraws from the partnership later on.

While typical community engagement efforts usually occur within the short time frames of a few weeks to a few months (the length of a summer, spring, or winter break or a quarter, semester, or trimester), the above example demonstrates the need for long-term efforts to be kept at the forefront of any partnership. Potential partners should inquire if such short-term efforts are uprooting unjust social circumstances or simply making the unjust circumstances more tolerable. Long-term social change that gets to the root of an issue and creates structural, systemic, or political transformations is typically beyond the scope of single semester program. However, a move towards this direction might occur if some participants (i.e., faculty, staff, community partners, incoming college students) take on greater responsibility and commit to sustaining existing programs. Yet, to take most partnerships to the next level involves aligning community engagement collaborations with policy reform efforts. For example, Pitzer College and the high school's staff have yet to address why these young, low-income, Latina high school students face unrelenting amounts of suffering to begin with. While this example shows where the shift can occur in *how* we approach community partnerships, it also demonstrates the heavy-lifting that is necessary to shift towards securing long-term, systemic change on the issues presented in the partnership.

Another way to contextualize this is to recognize that distinct students and community partnerships will work on issues at different levels, depending on the capacity, time frame, and interests of those involved. Some may be more involved with efforts that bring people together for support, connection, and sustainability (of themselves and their efforts for change). Models of accompaniment and allyship such as the ones described in Chap. 2 are crucial here. Other community engagement efforts may concentrate more on direct action around the issues in society that are oppressive or destructive to individuals, communities, and the earth. Engagement efforts that halt destructive actions in local communities can be broken down into varying levels: (1) offering temporary but immediate relief services for those effected by destructive actions; (2) analyzing root conditions that have resulted in these destructive actions; and (3) creating alternative structures to operate within.

Joanna Macy's model, "The Great Turning," proposes three primary areas for action that correlate with epochal shifts to dominant narratives and structures:

(1) "Actions to slow the damage to Earth and its beings" such as researching and documenting problems; campaigning for laws that mitigate the effects of the problems, promotion of regulations, and their just enforcement; lobbying against policies that exacerbate the issues; whistle-blowing, boycotting, and protesting; conducting vigils and blockades; and service providing (such as shelters and food banks) (Macy and Brown 1998, pp. 17–18).

(2) "Analysis of structural causes and creation of structural alternatives" which includes understanding the dynamics, conditions, tacit agreements, and interlocking causes that have resulted in the problems we face and then creating alternatives that will sustain and support rather than deplete and oppress. This may occur, for example, through teach-ins, study groups, collaborative living arrangements and land trusts, restorative justice, community gardens, local currencies, renewable energy, new forms of education and health/wellness methods, local trading of skills, seeds and food, and community-based services (pp. 19–20).

(3) "Shift in perceptions of reality, both cognitively and spiritually" which involves exploration of alternative theories and practices, such as general living systems theory, deep ecology, liberation theology, engaged Buddhism, ecopsychology, or other insights and experiences that

"bring us home to each other and our mutual belonging in the living body of the Earth" (pp. 21–22).

Each of these three pathways of community engagement raise the consciousness of participating students around the underlying dynamics, interlocking causes, and unwitting participation in systems that perpetuate harm (p. 19). This can result in a strengthened sense of commitment to relationships and communities with which to make social change and new or regenerated practices or change models that provide alternatives to current systems. Macy urges us to look towards scientific breakthroughs and ancestral teachings to explore and put into action new models for society that support rather than harm our planet, community ties, and social structures. She also alerts us to the fact that we must also simultaneously engage "a cognitive evolution and spiritual awakening" since new ways of being in the world "cannot take root and survive without deeply ingrained values to sustain them" (p. 21). Thus, this shift in narrative is also a shift in consciousness.

CONCLUSION

This chapter presented the Critical, Contemplative Community Engagement model through examination of three primary areas: learning and teaching theories that ground the practice, principal factors to consider when crafting social justice-oriented community engagement programs, and the importance of cultivating ethical and reciprocal community-campus partnerships. When these three areas come into unison, they can cultivate strong and mutually beneficial programs that in turn advance shared goals and responsibilities for student learning, community impact, and the specific service, research, or organizing projects undertaken. The following set of questions should be considered by community members, community organizations, faculty, staff, and students in a shared and iterative manner to ensure that collaborative aims are grounded in the values of social justice examined in this chapter:

1. Is the partnership cultivated between college partners and the primary community partners within a framework that honors reciprocal, respectful, and ethical collaboration?
2. Is the community seen and treated as an equal partner (operating within an equitable exchange of knowledge, service, time, and resources) while also recognizing unequal power dynamics where they may exist?

3. How involved are local community members in co-navigating community-campus partnerships in the following areas:

    a. course curriculum and instruction (i.e., guest lectures, suggested readings, co-teaching so that students understand the social problems faced in that community)

    b. research, (i.e., role in co-creating, supporting, or overseeing research question, methods, implementation, analysis, distribution and application of results, authorship and ownership of research);

    c. funding, (i.e., role in fundraising or fund distribution for related infrastructure in terms of staff and organization capacity in order to oversee shared projects and the students involved); and

    d. policies (i.e., how community-campus service and research partnerships will be orchestrated, assessed, and hold each partner accountable to shared agreements for partnership, and how service or local social change efforts are linked to correlating social and public policy).

To bring these issues to life, Chap. 5 provides explicit praxis tools for practitioners that focus on partnership development considerations, community partnership and classroom activities, and student learning outcomes and community impacts. Collectively, these build a sense of connection, belonging, and accountability to nurture both contemplative and critical processes for student growth and community change.

Notes

1. Some of the leading networks and foundations include the Association of American Colleges and Universities, Bringing Theory to Practice, Center for Engaged Democracy, Imagining America, Community-Campus Partnerships for Health, Campus Compact, International Association For Research On Service Learning and Community Engagement, National Task Force on Civic Learning and Democratic Engagement, Coalition of Urban Metropolitan Universities; Bonner Foundation, Project Pericles, Carnegie Foundation for the Advancement of Teaching, Andrew W. Mellon Foundation, and Teagle Foundation, among others.
2. Portions of this chapter have been adapted from some of my previous publications: "Reviving and Revising the Civic Mission: A Radical Re-Imagining of 'Civic Engagement,'" *Metropolitan Universities*, vol. 25,

No. 3, March 2015; "Partnering With Youth Organizers to Prevent Violence: An Analysis of Relationships, Power and Change," *Progress in Community Health Partnerships: Research, Education, and Action,* Johns Hopkins University Press, vol. 4.3, pp. 235–242 (Fall 2010). With T. Dolan and S. Hanft; and "Engaged scholarship: reflections and research on the pedagogy of social change," *Teaching in Higher Education: Special Edition,* Vol. 14:5 pp. 541–552 (October, 2009).

3. See Berila (2016), Bernal et al. (2006), Bringing Theory to Practice (2013), Finley (2012b), Fernandes (2003), Flanagan and Bundick (2011), Ginwright (2001), Harward (2012), hooks (1994), Iyer (1991), Iverson and James (2014), Sweitzer and King (2014), Ryff and Keyes (1995), Bowman et al. (2010), Hurtado et al. (2012), Nicotera et al. (2015), Swaner (2005), Pasque (2008).

4. The quality of placement, for example, one that correlates with a student's interests and that is willing, able, and interested in supervising a student intern (Eyler and Giles 1999; Mabry 1998), as well as the duration and intensity of the engagement (Austin and Sax 1998; Mabry 1998) has been shown to have positive impact on student personal and interpersonal outcomes. An application of the engagement to academic content (and vice versa) has an impact on students, particularly learning outcomes (Eyler and Giles 1999).

5. The following scholarship relates to the impact of community engagement on these realms of student learning: Astin and Sax (1998), Boss (1994), Bowman et al. (2010), Bringing Theory to Practice (2013), Calderon (2007), Eyler and Giles (1999), Eyler et al. (1997), Gelmon et al. (1998), Gray et al. (1999), Hurtado et al. (2012), Jacoby (2003), Kendrick (1996), Kivel (2007), Lewis (2004), Kretzmann and McKnight (1993), Markus et al. (1993), Marullo and Edwards (2000), Mitchell (2008), Nicotera et al. (2015), Pasque (2008), Stanton (1990), Stanton et al. (1999), Strand et al. (2003), Strage (2004), Swaner (2005), Switzer and King (2014), The National Task Force on Civic Learning and Democratic Engagement (2012), Ward and Wolf-Wendel (2000).

6. For more on this topic, see Bacon (2002), Butin (2003), Blouin and Perry (2009), Cooks et al. (2004), Calderon (2007), Eyler and Giles (1999), Ferrari and Worrall (2000), Hess et al. (2007), Keith (2005), Kezar and Rhoads (2001), Lewis (2004), Mitchell (2008), Ward and Wolf-Wendel (2000). Also, to view in-depth evaluations that have emerged around the positive and negative effects of service learning on communities see Butin (2010), Iverson and James (2014), Ferrari and Worrall (2000), Gelmon et al. (1998), Jacoby (2003), Peterson (2009), Sandy (2007), Schmidt and Robby (2002), Vernon and Ward (1999).

7. Occidental College's Center for Community-based Learning has a good example of such a model, called the "Northeast Education Strategy Group"; see http://www.oxy.edu/center-community-based-learning/community-partners.

8. It is important to note that this situation also necessitated that I provided support for the college students in this placement in the form of training, guidance, and referrals to resources they could bring to the table, as well as discussions around their limitations and roles and their need to take care of themselves as they took care of others. They also worked thoughtfully with the supervising high school teacher to outline protocol for what to do if they were told that someone was in danger of hurting themselves or others or being hurt themselves.

REFERENCES

American Psychological Association. (2012). *Stress in America. Missing the healthcare connection.* Stress in America Survey.

American Psychological Association. (2016). *Stress in America: The impact of discrimination.* Stress in America Survey.

Ash, S. L., & Clayton, P. H. (2009). Generating, deepening, and documenting learning: The power of critical reflection in applied learning. *Journal of Applied Learning in Higher Education, 1,* 25–48.

Astin, A. W., & Sax, L. J. (1998). How undergraduates are affected by service participation. *Journal of College Student Development, 39,* 251–263.

Astin, A. W., Vogelgesang, L. J., Ikeda, E. K., & Yee, J. A. (2000). *How service learning affects students.* Los Angeles: Higher Education Research Institute, University of California.

Bacon, N. (2002). Differences in faculty and community partners' theories of learning. *Michigan Journal of Community Service Learning, 9*(1).

Baumeister, R. F., & Leary, M. R. (1995). The need to belong: Desire for interpersonal attachments as a fundamental human motivation. *Psychological Bulletin, 117,* 497.

Berila, B. (2016). *Integrating Mindfulness into Anti-Oppression Pedagogy.* New York, NY: Routledge.

Bernal, D. D., Elenes, C. A., Godinez, F. E., Villenas, S. (Eds.). (2006). *Chicana/Latina Education in Everyday Life: Feminista Perspectives on Pedagogy and Epistemology.* Albany: New York Press.

Bisignani, D. (2014). Transgressing intellectual boundaries begins with transgressing physical ones: Feminist community engagement as activist-apprentice pedagogy. In S. Iverson & J. James (Eds.), *Feminist community engagement: Achieving praxis* (pp. 93–111). New York, NY: Palgrave Macmillan.

Blouin, D. D., & Perry, E. M. (2009). Whom Does Service Learning Really Serve? Community-Based Organizations' Perspectives on Service Learning. *Teaching Sociology, 37*(2), 120–135.

Boss, J. A. (1994). The effect of community service work on the moral development of college ethics students. *Journal of Moral Education, 23*(2), 183–198.

Bowman, N., Brandenberger, J., Lapsley, D., Hill, P., & Quaranto, J. (2010). Serving in College, Flourishing in Adulthood: Does Community Engagement During the College Years Predict Adult Well-Being? *Applied Psychology: Health and Well Being, 2*(1), 14–34.

Boyer, E. (1994). The New American College. *Chronicle of Higher Education, A48*, 183–198.

Bringing Theory to Practice. (2013). *The well-being and flourishing of students: Considering well-being, and its connection to learning and civic engagement, as central to the mission of higher education.* Washington, DC: AAC&U.

Butin, D. (2010). *Service-learning in theory and practice: The future of community engagement in higher education.* New York, NY: Palgrave Macmillan.

Butin, D. W. (2003). Of What Use Is it? Multiple Conceptualizations of Service-Learning Within Education. *Teachers College Record, 105*(9), 1674–1692.

Butin, D. W. (Ed.). (2014). *Teaching social foundations of education: Contexts, theories, and issues.* New York, NY: Routledge.

Calderon, J. Z. (Ed.). (2007). *Race, poverty, and social justice: Multidisciplinary perspectives through service learning.* Sterling, VA: Stylus Publishing.

College, Pitzer. (2016). *Graduation requirements: Social responsibility praxis student learning outcomes and course criteria.* Claremont, CA: Pitzer College.

Cooks, L., Scharrer, E., & Castaneda Paredes, M. (2004). Toward a social approach to learning in community service learning. *Michigan Journal of Community Service Learning, 10*(2).

Cremin, L. A. (1970). *American education: The colonial experience, 1607–1783.* New York, NY: Harper & Row.

Crimes Rates in Pomona, CA. (2017). *City-data.com.* Retrieved February 27, 2017, from http://www.city-data.com/crime/crime-Pomona-California.html.

Dewey, J. (1938). *Experience and education.* The Kappa Delta Pi lecture series, no. 10.

Dorado, S., & Giles, D. E. (2004). Service-learning partnerships: Paths of engagement. *Michigan Journal of Community Service Learning, 9*, 25–37.

Ehrlich, T. (2009). *Engagement in civic work as spiritual development: An interview with Thomas Ehrlich* (pp. 1–5). Spirituality in Higher Education Newsletter.

Eyler, J., & Giles, D. E., Jr. (1999). *Where's the learning in service-learning?* San Francisco, CA: Jossey-Bass Publications.

Eyler, J., Giles, D. E., Jr., & Braxton, J. (1997). The impact of service-learning on college students. *Michigan Journal of Community Service Learning, 4,* 5–15.

Fernandes, L. (2003). *Transforming feminist practice; Non-violence, social justice and the possibilities of a spiritualized feminism.* San Francisco: Aunt Lute Books.

Ferrari, J. R., & Worrall, L. (2000). Assessments by community agencies: How 'the other side sees service-learning. *Michigan Journal of Community Service Learning, 7*(1).

Finley, A. (2012). The joy of learning: The impact of civic engagement on psychosocial well-being. *Diversity and Democracy, 3,* 8–10.

Flanagan, C., & Bundick, M. (2011). Civic engagement and psychosocial well-being in college students. *Liberal Education, 97*(2), 20–27. Spring.

Freire, P. (1970). *Pedagogy of the oppressed* (M. B. Ramos, Trans.). New York, NY: Continuum Publishing.

Freire, P. (2006). *Pedagogy of the oppressed* (30th anniversary ed.). New York, NY: Continuum Publishing.

Freire, P., & Shor, I. (1987). *A pedagogy for liberation: Dialogues on transforming education.* Westport, CT: Bergin & Garvey.

Gelmon, S. B., Holland, B. A., Seifer, S. D., Shinnamon, A., & Connors, K. (1998). Community-university partnerships for mutual learning. *Michigan Journal of Community Service Learning, 5,* 97–107.

Giles, D. E., & Eyler, J. (1994). The impact of a college community service laboratory on students' personal, social, and cognitive outcomes. *Journal of adolescence, 17*(4), 327.

Giles, D. E., Honnet, E., & Migliore, S. (1991). *Setting the agenda for effective research in combining service and learning in the 1990's.* Raleigh, NC: National Society of Experiential Education.

Gray, M. J., Ondaatje, E. H., & Zakaras, L. (1999). *Combining Service and Learning in Higher Education: Learn and Serve America, Higher Education.* Santa Monica, CA: RAND.

Greene, D., & Diehm, G. (1995). Educational and service outcomes of a service integration effort. *Michigan Journal of Community Service Learning, 2,* 54–62.

Harward, D. W. (2012). *Transforming undergraduate education: Theory that compels and practices that succeed.* Washington, DC: Rowman & Littlefield.

Harward, D. W. (Ed.). (2016). *Well-being and higher education: A strategy for change and the realization of education's greater purposes.* Washington, DC: Bringing Theory to Practice.

Hess, D. J., Lanig, H., & Vaughan, W. (2007). Educating for equity and social justice: A conceptual model for cultural engagement. *Multicultural Perspectives, 9*(1), 32–39.

hooks, b. (1994). *Teaching to transgress: Education as the practice of freedom.* New York, NY: Routledge.

hooks, b. (2003). *Teaching community: A pedagogy of hope*. New York, NY: Routledge.

hooks, b. (2016, April 20). *Dialogue featuring bell Hooks and Parker J. Palmer*. De Pere, WI: St. Norbert College.

Hoy, W. (2012). School characteristics that make a difference for the achievement of all students: A 40-year odyssey. *Journal of Educational Administration, 50* (1), 76–97.

Hoy, W. K., & Tschannen-Moran, M. (1999). Five faces of trust: An empirical confirmation in urban elementary schools. *Journal of School Leadership, 9*, 184–208.

Hurtado, S., Ruiz, A., & Whang, H. (2012). Advancing and assessing civic learning: New results from the Diverse Learning Environments survey. *Diversity & Democracy, 15*, 10–12.

Illich, I. (1971). *Deschooling society*. New York, NY: Harper and Row.

Iverson, S. V. D., & James, J. H. (2014). *Feminism and community engagement: An overview. In feminist community engagement: Achieving praxis* (pp. 9–27). Palgrave Macmillan US.

Iyer, R. N. (1991). *The essential writings of Mahatma Gandhi*. USA: Oxford University Press.

Jacoby, B. (Ed.). (2003). *Building partnerships for service-learning*. San Francisco: Wiley.

Keith, N. Z. (1998). Community service for community building: The school-based service corps as border crossers. *Michigan Journal of Community Service Learning, 4*, 86–96.

Keith, N. Z. (2005). Community service learning in the face of globalization: Rethinking theory and practice. *Michigan Journal of Community Service Learning 11*(2), 5–24.

Kendrick, J.R., Jr. (1996). Outcomes of service-learning in an introduction to sociology course. *Michigan Journal of Community Service Learning*, 72–81.

Kezar, A., & Rhoads, R. (2001). The dynamic tensions of service-learning in higher education: A philosophical perspective. *The Journal of Higher Education, 72*, 148–171.

Kinzie, J. (2012). High-impact Practices: Promoting Participation for All Students. *Diversity Democracy, 15*(3), 13–14.

Kivel, P. (2007). Social service or social change. In Incite (Ed.), *The revolution will not be funded: Beyond the non-profit industrial complex* (pp. 129–149). Cambridge, MA: South End Press.

Kretzmann, J. P., & McKnight, J. (1993). *Building communities from the inside out*. Evanston, IL: Center for Urban Affairs and Policy Research, Neighborhood Innovations Network.

Kuh, G. D. (2008). *High-impact educational practices: What they are, who has access to them, and why they matter*. Washington, DC: Association of American Colleges and Universities.

Lather, P. (1986). Research as praxis. *Harvard Educational Review, 56*(3), 257–278.

Lewis, T. L. (2004). Service learning for social change? Lessons from a liberal arts college. *Teaching Sociology, 32*(1), 94–108.

Mabry, J. B. (1998). Pedagogical variations in service-learning and student outcomes: How time, contact, and reflection matter. *Michigan Journal of Community Service Learning, 5*, 32–47.

Macy, J., & Brown, M. Y. (1998). *Coming back to life: Practices to reconnect our lives, our world*. Gabriola Island, BC: New Society Publishers.

Markus, G. B., Howard, J. P., & King, D. C. (1993). Integrating community service and classroom instruction enhances learning: Results from an experiment. *Educational Evaluation and Policy Analysis, 15*(4), 410–419.

Marullo, S., & Edwards, B. (2000). From charity to justice the potential of university-community collaboration for social change. *American Behavioral Scientist, 43*(5), 895–912.

McKnight, J. (1995). *The careless society: Community and its counterfeits*. New York, NY: Basic Books.

Miron, D., & Moely, B. E. (2006). Community agency voice and benefit in service-learning. *Michigan Journal of Community Service Learning, 12*(2), 27–37.

Mitchell, T. D. (2008). Traditional vs. critical service-learning: Engaging the literature to differentiate two models. *Michigan Journal of Community Service Learning, 14*(2).

Nicotera, N., Brewer, S., & Veeh, C. (2015). Civic activity and well-being among first-year college students. *The International Journal of Research on Service-Learning and Community Engagement, 3*(1).

Noel, J. (2014). *Developing sustainable community engagement by repositioning programs into communities*. In S. V. D. Iverson & J. H. James (Eds.), *Feminist community engagement: Achieving praxis* (pp. 175–191). Palgrave Macmillan US.

Oden, R. S., & Casey, T. A. (2007). Advancing service learning as a transformative method for social justice work. In J. Z. Calderon (Ed.), *Race, poverty, and social justice: Multidisciplinary perspectives through service learning* (pp. 3–22). Sterling, VA: Stylus Publishing.

Pancer, S. M., & Pratt, M. W. (1999). Social and family determinants of community service involvement in Canadian youth. In M. Yates & J. Youniss (Eds.), *Roots of civic identity: International perspectives on community service and activism in youth* (pp. 32–55). New York, NY: Cambridge University Press.

Pasque, P. A. (2008). Bridging civic engagement and mental health. In *Proceedings from the National Symposium for Civic Engagement and Mental Health*.

Peterson, T. H. (2009). Engaged scholarship: Reflections and research on the pedagogy of social change. *Teaching in Higher Education, 14*(5), 541–552.

Peterson, T. H. (2015). Reviving and Revising the Civic Mission: A Radical Re-Imagining of 'Civic Engagement'. *Metropolitan Universities, 25*(3).

Peterson, T. H., Dolan, T., & Hanft, S. (2010). Partnering with youth organizers to prevent violence: An analysis of relationships, power, and change. *Progress in Community Health Partnerships: Research, Education, and Action, 4*(3), 235–242.

Razack, S. (1998). *Looking white people in the eye: Gender, race, and culture in courtrooms and classrooms*. University of Toronto Press.

Rendón, L. (2014). *Sentipensante (Sensing/thinking): Educating for wholeness, social justice, and liberation*. Sterling, VA: Stylus.

Ryff, C. D., & Keyes, C. L. M. (1995). The structure of psychological well-being revisited. *Journal of Personality and Social Psychology, 69*(4), 719.

Sandy, M. (2007). *Community voices: A California campus compact study on partnerships*. Hayward: California Campus Compact.

Schmidt, A., & Robby, M. A. (2002). What's the value of ser- vice-learning to the community? *Michigan Journal of Community Service Learning, 9*(1), 27–33.

Schutz, A., & Gere, A. R. (1998). Service learning and English studies: Rethinking 'public' service. *College English, 60*(2), 129–149.

Shor, I. (1992). *Culture wars: School and society in the conservative restoration*. Chicago, IL: University of Chicago Press.

Stanton, T. K., Giles, D. E., & Cruz, N. I. (1999). *Service learning: A movement's pioneers reflect on its origins, practice, and future*. San Francsico, CA: Jossey-Bass.

Steinberg, S. R., & Kincheloe, J. L. (1998). *Students as researchers: Creating classrooms that matter*. London: Falmer Press.

Strage, A. (2004). Long-term academic benefits of service-learning: When and where do they manifest themselves? *College Student Journal, 38*(2), 257.

Strand, K. J., Cutforth, N., Stoecker, R., Marullo, S., & Donohue, P. (2003). *Community-based research and higher education: Principles and practices*. San Francisco, CA: Wiley.

Swaner, L. E. (2005). Educating for personal and social responsibility: A review of the literature. *Liberal Education, 91*(3), 14–21.

Sweitzer, H. K., & King, M. A. (2014). *The successful internship: personal, professional, and civic development in experiential learning* (4th ed.). Belmont, CA: Brooks/Cole Cengage.

The National Task Force on Civic Learning and Democratic Engagement. (2012). *A Crucible Moment: College Learning and Democracy's Future*. Washington, DC: Association of American Colleges and Universities.

Thoits, P. A., & Hewitt, L. N. (2001). Volunteer work and well-being. *Journal of Health and Social Behavior,* 115–131.

Vaccaro, A. (2009). Racial identity and the ethics of service learning as pedagogy. In S. Evans, C. Taylor, M. Dunlap & D. Miller (Eds.), *African Americans and community engagement in higher education* (pp. 119–134). Albany, NY: SUNY Press.

Verba, S., Schlozman, K. L., & Brady, H. E. (1995). *Voice and equality: Civic voluntarism in American politics.* Harvard University Press.

Verjee, B., & Butterwick, S. (2014). Conversations from within: Critical race feminism and the roots/routes of change. In S. Iverson & J. James (Eds.), *Feminist community engagement: Achieving praxis* (pp. 31–51). New York, NY: Palgrave Macmillan.

Vernon, A., & Ward, K. (1999). Campus and community partnerships: Assessing impacts and strengthening connections. *Michigan Journal of Community Service Learning, 6,* 30–37.

Ward, K., & Wolf-Wendel, L. (2000). Community-centered service learning moving from doing for to doing with. *American Behavioral Scientist, 43*(5), 767–780.

Westheimer, J., & Kahne, J. (2004). What kind of citizen? The politics of educating for democracy. *American Educational Research Journal, 41*(2), 237–269.

Whitney, B. C., & Clayton, P. H. (2011). Research on and through reflection in international service learning. *International Service Learning: Conceptual Frameworks and Research,* 145–187.

Praxis of Engagement

CHAPTER 5

Community Engagement Outcomes and Activities

Part II of this book applies the theories and methods examined thus far around self-awareness, wellbeing, social justice, and community-campus partnerships into tangible program models, evaluation designs, activities, and outcomes related to community engagement. This chapter introduces the praxis of critical, contemplative community engagement through effective activities for use in the classroom or during community-campus programs and the concrete student learning and community impact outcomes that can result.[1] Chapter 6 then presents an evaluation design for assessing community engagement course impacts on student learning. Finally, the concluding chapter proposes measures for weaving the concepts and strategies discussed throughout this book into the fabric of higher education institutions. All of the praxis tools presented in Part II have emerged from a mix of research, teaching, and application in the community engagement field. They have been informed by the findings of an action research evaluation of the impacts of community engagement, conducted at Pitzer College with students, faculty, staff, and community partners (Hicks 2009), a direct assessment effort of a local–global community engagement paired course program (Pitzer College 2010), and the findings from a rigorous review of literature in the field.[2]

The outcomes and activities presented in this chapter are organized around the four steps of social change that were introduced in Chap. 2: *becoming proximate, shifting the narrative, getting uncomfortable,* and *cultivating hope* (Stevenson 2016). Each of the four sections begins with partnership development considerations and classroom activities that can

© The Author(s) 2018   157
T. Hicks Peterson, *Student Development and Social Justice,*
https://doi.org/10.1007/978-3-319-57457-8_5

assist program designers, teachers, and community partners in developing critical, contemplative community engagement programs. These are followed by a list of possible student learning outcomes that are expected to result from participating in such programs. These learning outcomes would emerge from a mix of course readings, class discussions, critical reflections, and community projects and collaborations. Next are listed potential benefits to community members and agencies that partner with institutions of higher education in social justice-oriented community-campus partnerships. Finally, student reflections that demonstrate the impact of such programs are shared to further bring the concepts to life. It is not expected that every student, community partner or reader will participate in all of the activities suggested or that every collaboration will achieve all the outcomes presented in this chapter, but collectively these provide aspirations for all forms of Critical, Contemplative Community Engagement.[3]

Praxis: Becoming Proximate

Community Partnership Considerations

As community-campus partnerships crystalize, faculty, staff, students, and community members should work together to become clear about the roles, goals, logistics, and evaluation components of their community engagement collaboration. To concretize these aims, agreements reached are often recorded in a memorandum of understanding. This involves collectively creating a document that defines the concrete goals of the partnership, expectations, and responsibilities of all stakeholders to ensure that each party is accountable to upholding their shared agreements. Such a document should include stating

1. the assets, needs, and resources each partner brings to the table;
2. specific tasks or projects students and/or faculty will engage in;
3. community contributions pertaining to supervision, education, and orientation of students or collaborations with faculty or staff in terms of grant-writing, evaluation, etc.;
4. community involvement in education (guest teaching, co-teaching or co-enrolling), research, and service, as the community partner can or wants to;
5. university contributions to community needs (such as serving as advocates, co-researchers, or board members; providing access to

university resources like libraries, art and technology facilities, meetings spaces, etc.);
6. logistics and liability regarding clearance, insurance, transportation, and credits;
7. what mechanisms will be in place to ensure that all partners can regularly communicate and assess the effectiveness of partnership;
8. what mechanisms will be in place to ensure that all partners actively work to make changes as a result of assessment findings; and
9. a shared understanding of how larger structural/systemic/policy issues can be addressed beyond what specific projects the partnership focuses on.[4]

Classroom and Community Partnership Activities

Community Research Assignment
Assign students readings about the community, community organizations, and social change issue they will become involved with, both in the immediate context and in regards to the larger historic and systemic conditions that have led to the current circumstances.

Community Panel or Fieldtrip
Invite members of the community and community organizations to come represent themselves to students and faculty in the community engagement course, sharing their history and the assets, needs, and aims of the community. Sometimes a panel of representatives works best, other times visits to different sites in the community is more relevant. Afterward, invite students to create storymaps, asset maps, or GIS maps to visually map out the narratives, challenges, and resources of the community.

Icebreaker Activities
To create genuine conversation and opportunities change delve beyond surface narratives with a group that is first becoming proximate to each other, it is helpful to conduct icebreaker activities. These can be conducted among students towards the beginning of the semester or for community partners and students to do collaboratively, as the partnership develops. Two examples follow that help to build relationships by encouraging

participants to share information about themselves that reveals something of their personal experience.

Concentric Circles

Creating concentric circles (inner and outer circles that face each other), pairs are formed and partners are asked to each answer the prompted question, ensuring that each person gets a turn for 2 minutes and that each one practices active, contemplative listening when the other is talking. The facilitator should keep time and remind partners to change turns speaking at the 2 minutes mark. After both partners have shared for 2 minutes each, the outside circle moves one place to the left to create a new partner pair and a new question is asked. After some or all suggested questions are asked, facilitate a debrief about what participants learned, felt, and gained from this experience (highlighting the impact of the intentional, active listening component) and how it uncovered some of who they are and the aims of their coming together.

Suggested concentric circles prompts include the following:

1. What is the story of your name?
2. Where are you from (geographically, politically, culturally, spiritually)?
3. What communities do you belong to and which feels most important right now?
4. What price do you pay (and have others paid) for you to stand where you are today?
5. When was the first time you remember feeling excluded and/or misunderstood?
6. When was the first time you remember excluding someone or expressing a bias?
7. When have you advocated for yourself or someone else? What did you learn from that experience?
8. When have you failed yourself or someone else in the community? What did you learn from that experience?
9. What does the topic of this class (i.e., "social change") look like, sound like, and feel like?
10. Who/what does this class/partnership serve?
11. What are your hopes and fears around this community engagement endeavor?

"We are From" Group Poem[5]

1. Instruct participants to work individually to write a poem responding to the prompt: "*Where I'm from.*" Invite participants to relinquish nervousness around poetic cadence or spelling—anyone can do this! Encourage vivid imagery, bringing to life what it smells like, tastes like, feels like, looks like, or sounds like to be where they are from. Remind them that being specific and vulnerable helps us connect with our own experience and with each other. Ask participants to begin each line with "I am from…"

2. After 10 minutes of individual writing, return to the large group and ask each person to share their poem while everyone else actively listens and takes notes on any vivid imagery that struck them from someone else's poem.

3. Following each sharing of a poem, invite another participant to share one image or line that stayed with them from someone else's poem and why.

4. Ask each poet to circle their favorite line from their own poem.

5. Invite everyone to stand up and create a circle together wherein each person takes a turn and reads aloud their chosen one line from their poem, one after another, until everyone has shared a line of their poem.

6. Ask each person to read their one line again, but this time ask participants to change the first pronoun in their line from "I" to "We," so each line reads "We are from…" Each person's offered line should follow directly after the last one so it becomes one collective *"We Are From"* poem.

7. After the final version of the *"We Are From"* poem has been recited, follow up with a group debrief exploring both the process and the product of the activity and how participants understand the concepts and each other differently as a result of engaging in this form of individual and group expression.

8. Close the activity by reminding participants that this poem can only be created with this particular group of individuals, today. It binds the group together, even though personal experiences are distinct. Introduce the concept of "liberation arts" (see Chap. 3 and Watkins and Shulman 2008) and how the arts have always served as a vehicle for personal healing, collective empowerment, and community building.

Student Learning Outcomes

As the result of participation in a semester-long, critical, contemplative community engagement course, students should be able to demonstrate the following learning outcomes:

1. Students will be able to demonstrate the highest standards of professional and ethical conduct in relationship building in the community-campus partnership.
2. Students will be able to demonstrate critical and contemplative listening skills that help generate common ground for interactions with those from other positionalities while recognizing differences in dynamics of power, culture, values, and norms.
3. Students will be able to engage with diverse groups of people and perspectives which will foster their learning about existing assets, challenges, and aims of the community.
4. Students will be able to demonstrate skills, awareness, and commitment to cross-cultural communication, relationship building, and reciprocity that allows them to negotiate difference through a pluralistic orientation.
5. From the standpoint of their own and multiple cultural perspectives, students will be able to identify and describe local social justice issues and strategies that attempt to upturn them.
6. Students will be able to articulate a heightened sense of personal responsibility to community issues, differentiating between distinct paths towards engagement, such as accompaniment, advocacy, co-conspirators, service providers, and action researchers.
7. Through contemplation and self-reflection, students will become proximate to their internal experience, influencing self-awareness, self-care, and an embodied understanding of justice issues.

Community Impact Outcomes

As the result of participation in a semester-long, community-campus partnership for social change, community members and/or community partner agencies should be able to demonstrate the following impact outcomes:

1. Community members and agencies will be able to engage in reciprocal, respectful, and ethical community-campus partnership that is specific to and will benefit the community.
2. Community members and agencies will gain an opportunity to practice supervision, mentorship, knowledge exchange, and collaboration with students and faculty.
3. Community members and agencies will gain exposure to other cultures and communities, expanded world views, and academic skills, such as writing, research, public speaking, art, language, and/or critical thinking.
4. Community-based research projects will follow appropriate ethical standards, such as informed consent, mutual benefits, and collaboration in designing, conducting, sharing, and/or applying end products of the shared research effort.
5. Community members and agencies will gain an opportunity to cultivate empowerment, self-development, and interpersonal relationship development within the context of the community and academy.
6. Community members and agencies will be able to contribute to applied research and the production of knowledge for related disciplines and/or social change efforts.
7. Community wellbeing will be expanded and increased as a result of connection, meaning, purpose, and unity through collective change-making process.

Student Reflection on Becoming Proximate

This reflection is from an incarcerated student in an Inside-Out Prison Exchange course:

I came to class feeling a bit skeptical and nervous. Skeptical about being judged by the outside [non-incarcerated] students, and nervous because I wasn't really sure what the class would be like. I felt a bit more at ease once we set the ground rules about how we would conduct ourselves in class. The ice breakers were very effective. It forced us to open up and engage with the outside students. The "[story of your] name" ice breaker gave us a common connection. We all have a name, we all have a story to tell about our name, or lack of–as we found out today. The "[concentric] circles" ice breaker was even more effective in bringing our guards down and letting us interact with one another. The choice of questions asked by the professor left no room for shyness. It made us think, and once again opened us up to connecting, this time through our differences. Some of the questions equally confused both inside and outside students. The interaction was fantastic, my brain is still zooming. I believe it was a very effective class. We built a completely free community within the confines of a prison. It was utterly healing to my spiritual self and psyche. I was no longer a prisoner in the system, but a student of a prestigious college. My preconceived notion of judgment was completely off kilter. The outside students were very respectful, warm, open, and embracing. I cannot wait for the next class and to see what the semester will bring. If I was to be asked "what did class look, sound, and feel like?' I'd reply 'Bright eyes expounding on topics uncommonly heard around these rigid systematic grounds. It felt like freedom.'[6]

PRAXIS: SHIFTING THE NARRATIVE

Community Partnership Considerations

In order to effect change in the hierarchies of knowledge that continue to divide our society, we can look to our community partnerships to reconfigure power mapping in community-campus partnerships. Shifting the narrative around knowledge production involves shifting the power dynamics by

1. co-teaching courses with community members in order to bring important but often overlooked knowledge and experience to the topic of the course;
2. co-enrolling community members in the community engagement course in order to provide access to academic knowledge for those usually excluded from these realms and to include their perspectives and knowledges in these realms. Ideally, all enrolled would receive equal credits for their involvement;
3. holding community engagement classes in the communities in which they partner in order to physically become more proximate to and integrated with the local community; and
4. bringing scholars to locations in the community where specific knowledge is sought and expertise can benefit community members.

Classroom and Community Partnership Activities

Social Change Autobiography
Assign students to write a paper to critically reflect on their own positionality, values, beliefs, biases, and personal experiences that inform their understanding and interest in the social change issues pertinent to this partnership.

Researching Root Conditions of Injustice
Assign students to find diverse artifacts (social media, texts, films, historical archives, interviews, public policies) that speak to fundamental structural/systemic/legislative issues that surround the community issue that the community-campus partnership wishes to impact.

Researching Historic Social Change Efforts
Assign students an ethnographic interviewing project, connecting with those they have already built relationships in the community or others that may know about local challenges and achievements. This might include elders, city officials, clergy, teachers, community organizers, or service providers. Questions might include asking for instances where folks came together to imagine changes they could make to improve quality of life, places where community came together to garner skills and support to reach their goals, instances where they attempted to shift the narrative and failed and what they learned in that process, as well as instances where they surmounted obstacles to collectively mobilize on a community-driven issue.

Multiple Paths of Engagement
Consider diverse levels of engagement that courses can offer students (direct service providing, grassroots community organizing, advocacy campaigns, writing letters to an elected official lobbying policy change) and provide resources for various routes of engagement.

Trauma of Injustice: Assumptions and Principles
To shift the narratives we hold about trauma and social justice (and the relationship between the two), it is important to provide basic assumptions and principles of both for participants to refer to throughout readings and discussions on the topic. Below are listed some core social justice assumptions and principles of a trauma-informed justice practice. These can

be shared at the beginning of the semester or used as prompts to facilitate dialogue in workshops with community partners.

Social Justice 101: Basic Assumptions (DiAngelo and Sensoy 2012)

- All people are individuals, but they are also members of social groups.
- These social groups are valued unequally in society and social groups that are valued more highly have greater access to the resources of a society.
- Social injustice is real, exists today, and results in unequal access to resources between groups of people—these inequalities and unequal access (and the subsequent violence to body and spirit that results) are historically, culturally, socially, and politically entrenched in a variety of systems, policies, and common practices.
- Those who claim to be for social justice must be engaged in self-reflection about their own socialization into these groups (their 'positionality') and must strategically act from that awareness in ways that challenge social injustice on personal, interpersonal, and institutional levels.
- This action requires a commitment to an ongoing and lifelong process.

Principles of a Trauma-Informed Justice Practice (Peterson and Khouri 2015)

- We see injustice as a collective trauma that impacts everyone, even those benefitting from it.
- We stand for collective self-regulation which places equally the dignity, personal empowerment, and survival needs of everyone.
- We understand that effective communication is a cornerstone of this movement, and we use our tools to speak in a grounded way that honors the humanity of everyone involved.
- We recognize that a healthy expression of outrage is our right and to speak truth to power is our duty.
- We learn from those who have come before us, remembering that though unjust structures seem impenetrable and unbearable, "the arc of the universe moves towards justice" and countless others have successfully eradicated hatred and justice through active resistance that is informed by critical analysis, non-violent communication, and compassion.

- A world without trauma begins with a world without justice. We must first learn how to cope with and respond to existing trauma and injustice in healthy, functional, and empowered ways while also seeking new ways to build a world that is not built on the unmet needs of others.
- We see community as the foundation and the goal of this movement. It takes community support to make change and a just society is one where everyone feels included, valued, supported, and loved. This is the Collective Community that we vision in our future.

Student Learning Outcomes

As the result of participation in a semester-long, critical, contemplative community engagement course, students should be able to demonstrate the following learning outcomes:

1. Students will be able to identify and describe social (in)justice issues and their root causes (e.g., structural, political, social, economic, and environmental conditions) that have resulted in the need for community engagement.
2. Students will be able to identify and describe the ethical and political implications of injustice, such as social problems, social stratification, the interdependence and intersection of systems of oppression, interpersonal and structural discrimination, and unequal distribution and access to power and resources (including natural resources).
3. Students will be able to demonstrate raised critical consciousness about the way they see themselves in relation to knowledge and power in society and the way they act in school and daily life to reproduce or to transform social conditions.
4. Students will be able to engage in a reciprocal application of learning of tools and theories to/from field and class, and demonstrate integrative learning (from various sources), shifting understanding of knowledge production and participation in both academic and public life.
5. Students will demonstrate heightened sense of purposefulness, self-realization, and moral and ethical reasoning.

Community Impact Outcomes

As the result of participation in a semester-long, community-campus partnership for social change, community members and/or community partner agencies should be able to demonstrate the following impact outcomes:

1. Community members will develop an increased sense of personal value and political power as a result of being seen as knowledge producer, research contributor, and/or community educator, both in the community and in the academy.
2. Disrupting exclusive or cloistered academic spaces, partnerships will gain increased levels of access to resources, such as the college libraries, meeting spaces, dining halls, art supplies, and classrooms as well as greater exposure to and connection with the college, in general, and fellow activists and students, in particular.
3. Disrupting practices that are exploitative, deficit-based, or hierarchical, these critical community-campus partnerships and their projects will recognize and build on existing assets of the community, follow   community-driven   agendas,   and   confront community-identified problems.
4. Community members and agencies will increase development of self-expression, exercising of rights, participation in advocacy, and civic engagement themselves.
5. Community agencies will develop energy and ideas with college partners that inspire change in programs and approaches to the communities they serve.

Student Reflection on Shifting the Narrative

This reflection is from a student in a community engagement local–global paired course:

> I think it is possible to create changes in other communities, but it is necessary to have the correct mental approach when engaging in any sort of service. The first step must be to stop thinking of it as another community, and begin seeing how you are a part of the same community. My favorite quotation from the class comes from the syllabus. The quotation is from Lila

Watson, an aboriginal woman. She said, 'If you have come to help me, you are wasting your time. But if you have come because your liberation is bound up with mine, then let us walk together.' This quotation is particularly meaningful to me because I am always wary when people go into another community to 'help' them. The word 'help' implies the superiority of the helper, and the inferiority of the one being helped. If you want to create change in another community, you must realize that they are not really a different community. We are all tied together, as citizens of the world. To change another community, we must realize that their wellbeing is connected to our wellbeing.[7]

Praxis: Getting Uncomfortable

Community Partnership Considerations

It is critical to interrogate how community engagement efforts conducted through community-campus partnerships might themselves maintain or advance unequal systems, yet such interrogation can elicit discomfort. Evaluating social change progress of the partnership is a topic that should be integrated into classroom discussions, community discussions, and year-end partnership evaluations, using prompts such as the following:

1. Are students critically analyzing the existing structural inequalities that have forwarded the need of outsiders entering into a community to conduct services?
2. How might they perpetuate the divide by participating in such hierarchical relationships?
3. How can we ensure that it is not solely the student, faculty, and/or service providers that gain greater capacity and success from this community-campus partnership but also the community members who directly face the brunt of oppression?
4. Are larger goals of community building and social change kept at the forefront of the work or lost in the time constraints of the university's academic calendar or desire to do only immediately gratifying service providing?
5. Are there any ways in which students, faculty, or the partnership itself inadvertently causes harm in the community?

Classroom and Community Partnership Activities

Communication Agreements[8]

One way to create a safe enough space for people to navigate discomfort successfully for learning and growth to occur is to begin both the semester's class and the partnership itself by creating community agreements. "Community agreements," also known as "communication agreements" or "ground rules for communication," are a collectively made list of qualities people want to cultivate that will make a space conducive for respectful and effective communication. Although best created by eliciting ideas from the group, below is a sample of key elements of community agreements that can help make participants feel included, protected, and supported:

1. *Respect Others:* You will hear ideas that may be new or different to you, and opinions with which you may disagree. As you participate and interact, try to take in new information without judgment and to keep an open mind. Make sure that your words and body language reflect a respectful attitude toward others. Engage contemplative listening, which means being open, present, and mindful of what is being said, responding thoughtfully rather than reacting mindlessly.

2. *Speak From the "I":* Speak from your own personal experiences and do not judge the thoughts or experiences of others. Use I-statements such as "I feel..." or "In my experience..." Avoid "You should" statements and generalizations of any kind.

3. *Respect Confidentiality:* Please make sure that everything said in the room stays in the room. When sharing personal anecdotes, make sure to avoid using the real names of other people. Do not sensationalize someone's private experience by sharing their narrative without their consent.

4. *Share "Air Time":* While you are encouraged to express your ideas and opinions, do not monopolize the group's time. Help create a safe space in which everyone can speak. No one, however, is obligated to speak. Move into the conversation (if you tend to stay more on the sidelines) and move back from the conversation (if you tend to take up more room in group dialogues). Recognize how one's positionality often impacts how much air time they tend to take.

5. *No Rescuing or Advising:* While we want to support each person as well as speak out when we hear something we think is "wrong," we need to respect that we aren't here to advise or save anyone. Ask engaging questions and call people up, not out.

Personal Pain and Healing Activity

Acknowledging personal pain and discomfort is a critical step in the process of generating self-love and compassion—which, as has already been discussed at length, is necessary for generating a love ethic and solidarity within community work. The following activity aims to bridge inner conflict and self-love so that we may be more attuned to and compassionate with ourselves and others. Alert students that this activity may initially elicit discomfort but will also bring them back home to the embodiment of self-love.

1. Ask students to go around in a circle and share a personal reflection about anything in their lives that is inhibiting their well-being—this may include stress and anxiety felt from academic pressures, emotional challenges of relationships, and/or anger around experiences of injustice on campus.
2. After all have shared, ask students to write down the "self-talk" they experience within when feelings of pain or anxiety arise in regards to these situations.
3. Invite students then to check in with their embodied state—where they may feel the pain in their bodies—and encourage them to take a deep breath, ground their bodies, and sit mindfully with any resulting pain.
4. Then ask students to recall a picture of themselves as children, one that depicts a time where they felt joyful or empowered. As people visualize this image of their younger selves, ask them to acknowledge the radiance and wisdom the child possesses.
5. Ask students now to sit with this different sensation and breath into it —acknowledging and honoring that radiance by taking more breaths and seeing if they can actually embody it. Ask if students can sense a shift in the energy of the room, as collectively the group begins to move from unsettledness to a heartfelt awareness or calling back of a lost self.

6. Ask students to mindfully return from this visualization and begin a conversation about the ways in which our innocent sense of self can be dampened by a socialization process that teaches us to be less vulnerable and honest and more cynical and self-conscious. Ask students to then examine the "self-talk" list they created earlier, which often times includes highly critical things they tend to say to themselves about the suffering they face; the harsh critic's voice within that taunts, with exaggerated ridicule, the endless nature of one's flaws or fears. Ask students, "Would you ever say those things to the little child in that picture?"

7. Invite an open discussion for folks to share if or how the tenderness and love they once felt about themselves had been replaced with self-deprecation, low self-esteem, or emotional distress. Encourage them to consider why we tend to be our own worst enemy and the societal influences that inform such habits. Invite students to imagine how we can collectively commit to eradicating abusive self-talk from our daily lives, increase practices of self-love and where these actions might intersect with community building and social change.

8. Invite students to create a new "self-talk" list that shares a conversation with their inner child—perhaps this includes a message from one's older self to one's inner child about self-love or hope or capacity for resilience. Perhaps, it is actually a message from the inner child to the older self about our true nature or the radiance we hold. If students feel comfortable, invite them to share aloud the new self-talk statements they've created in order to embody and affirm them in the embrace of the class community.

9. At the end of the activity, ask each student to bring a picture of themselves as a child so that the class can honor that little person we all still carry within and become accountable to each other to take better care of and reconnect with the beauty within ourselves which we once felt so easily. Close by asking students if they can imagine approaching each other, as well as people they don't know or maybe even like, with the open-hearted tenderness they would show their inner child. Ask them to imagine how this shift might change interactions and methods within social change movements.[9]

Student Learning Outcomes

As the result of participation in a semester-long, critical, contemplative community engagement course, students should be able to demonstrate the following learning outcomes:

1. Students will be able to critically analyze how their own assumptions, biases, privilege, or marginalization inform their understanding/worldview of social (in)justice issues and how their positionality impacts their community engagement.
2. Students will be able to identify, describe, and locate themselves in the hegemonic structures and practices that further social injustice and oppression or acts of liberation.
3. Students will be able to identify, describe, and critically analyze the potential pitfalls of community-campus partnerships.
4. Students will be able to identify their motives for community engagement and explore any related personal woundedness that may impact engagement.
5. Students will be able to begin to recognize how patterns of oppression in society may have insinuated themselves into their bodies, minds, and spirits and learn to sit with, eventually transform, the discomfort that results, reflecting contemplatively on habits of reaction and opportunities for healing.

Community Impact Outcomes

As the result of participation in a semester-long, community-campus partnership for social change, community members and/or community partner agencies should be able to demonstrate the following impact outcomes:

1. Community members and agencies will confront students, faculty, and staff that may not respect, understand, or connect well with the community and the issues the partnership is based on, and by necessity, will increase problem-solving, communication, and project management skills.
2. Community members and agencies will confront the stress and trauma of injustice and, through community engagement

collaborative projects, will increase community-building and problem-solving skills.

3. Community members and agencies will confront complex power and relationship dynamics in community projects and community-campus partnerships and will increase community-building and problem-solving skills to deal with them.

4. Community members and agencies will heighten critical consciousness in confronting unsettling aspects of making radical change and refusing to be buffer zones.

5. Community members and agencies will confront the stress that comes from managing collaborative projects (i.e., grants, workload, volunteer vs paid staff) and learn strategies for handling such changes collectively and sustainably.

Student Reflection on Getting Uncomfortable

This reflection is from a Pitzer student in an Inside-Out Prison Exchange course:

> When taking me to church every Sunday, my babysitter, Ceci would introduce me as her daughter. I would wear the dress she made me and sit in Sunday school speaking Spanish with the other children. The Spanish Ceci taught me has been a blessing, breaking many communication barriers. Though only recently have I begun to think more about the nuances of my relationship with her, and our two families' relationships. Did I merely perceive membership in Ceci's community? Could she ever have membership in mine? Have I ever genuinely had multiple memberships? Is such a state possible? My whiteness, my socioeconomic status, my gender and my sexual orientation colors every experience that I have; it does not shift so fluidly as my context.

Praxis: Cultivating Hope

Community Partnership Considerations

Hope can be cultivated when individuals come together to create mutually beneficial relationships around shared goals for empowerment, undergirded by a sense of autonomy and agency to set the rules of their own engagement. A fruitful activity for students, faculty, staff, and community members to engage in during the nascent stages of a partnership would be to create a brainstorm of what partnership characteristics are most important to them and what those would look like in action. To help inspire or complement such a list, participants can refer to those qualities discussed in Chap. 4 that researchers have found to be most important, such as "relevance, respect, reciprocity, and reflection" (Butin 2014, p. viii) and "benevolence, honesty, openness, reliability and competence" (Hoy and Tschannen-Moran 1999, cited in Noel 2014, p. 178).

Partners may also wish to examine the three stages of partnership development (as outlined by Dorado and Giles 2004), with special attention to prompts that investigate what these actions will look like on the ground level of their own community-campus collaborations:

Stage 1: Learning (gaining familiarity with partners): How will this occur? Where? With whom?

Stage 2: Aligning (reviewing/assessing partnership aims, goals, process, and outcomes): How often will this occur? With whom? How will the group uphold accountability for each partner?

Stage 3: Nurturing (cultivating support on a committed path of engagement): What concrete practices will communities and campuses forward to nurture this collaboration? What feels supportive to each?

Classroom and Community Partnership Activities

Ginwright (2015) defines collective hope as a series of maneuvers that bond, inspire, and uplift communities. Some of these may include connecting with others over common lived experiences, building on inherent community assets, cultivating radical imaginings of what the future could look like, garnering skills and support to reach goals, and mobilizing successfully on a community-driven issue. The following are ideas that help reach, or make visible, these lofty aims.

Tangible Outcomes: A Projects-Based Class Assignment
Assign students a project-based "action project" wherein they take their theoretical frameworks from class, together with their knowledge of and experience in the local community, to formulate some action that will be

tangible and beneficial to the community. Examples might include organizing an event, lobbying on behalf of an issue, crafting a grant proposal to
fund a community organization, creating a new website or other online
media for community partners, or making a documentary about community members. Walking away with some tangible evidence of progress helps
keep momentum and motivation in the long-term process of slow-moving
change.

Liberation Arts: Theatre Activities to Cultivate Hope
Inserting art practices into theoretical discussions helps students embody
and connect to concepts beyond an intellectual grasp, allowing them to see
the issue and each other from a different perspective. Artistic collaborations
in the classroom and in workshops with community partners are also
valuable tools to provide emotional release, self-discovery, communication,
and connection. As discussed in Chap. 3, art-making has long been seen as
an act of self-expression, personal expression, spiritual expression, and
political expression, creating a vehicle for healing and social change. "The
need to establish harmony, if only to afford respite from tension, is as
fundamental a human need as the need to create. The two are intertwined"
(Hall 1997a, b, p. 25).
    The following are lesson plans based on "Theatre of the Oppressed"
activities as presented by Arvind Singhall in his article, "Empowering the
Oppressed Through Participatory Theatre" (2004). These can be used for
direct implementation in a community engagement classroom or
campus-community workshop. This is taken from my "Healing Arts and
Social Change" Inside-Out Prison Exchange course but the concepts used
(healing and social change) can be replaced by the primary areas in focus
for any class or partnership:
    General Premise:

Imagination + Bodies + Words = Theatre;

Community + Hope + Collective Will = Social Change

Create two groups, one assigned to do *Image Theatre* and one assigned
to do *Forum Theatre* and give the following instructions:

Image Theatre: Participants create a non-verbal physical image as a
group, using poses, expressions, and/or props that indicate the Prevailing
Reality Image of "Oppression," another one that presents the Ideal Image

of "Social Change" and then a final one representing the Transitional image (what it looks like to get from one to the next). *Forum Theatre:* "Begin with an enactment of a scene in which a protagonist (played by an actor) tries, unsuccessfully, to overcome oppression relevant to this particular audience. The 'joker' (MC) then invites 'spectactors' [audience members who will become actors and jump in the scene to improvise a solution] to replace the protagonist at any point in the scene where they believe an alternative action could lead to a solution. Anyone can propose a solution but it must be done on stage. The scene is replayed numerous times with different interventions from different 'spectactors.' This results in dialogue about the oppression, an examination of alternatives, and a rehearsal for real solutions" (Singhal 2004, p. 148). Participants must first decide on the problem/oppression they wish to show in a "scene" and who will play what parts (including the joker)—all need a role and need to be prepared to invite the spectactors on stage to enact different solutions and to facilitate the post-show discussion.

Each group presents their respective image theatre and forum theatre pieces, with a post-performance group debrief after each one, which explores both the process and the product of the activity and how participants feel and understand the concepts and each other differently as a result of engaging in this embodied, artistic, and multiple-perspectives lens.

Celebrating Accomplishments: A Community Event
When a community-driven issue has been successfully fought for and accomplished, marking this achievement with a community celebration in which the informal leaders of the community are honored by the formal leaders affirms community power, knowledge, and connection, cultivating inspiration and hope for the next challenge that awaits.

Student Learning Outcomes

As the result of participation in a semester-long, critical, contemplative community engagement course, students should be able to demonstrate the following learning outcomes:

1. Students will develop social agency and the moral and political courage to take risks to achieve a greater public good.

2. Students will be able to use hands-on experiences to explore strategies to remove barriers to equality and/or inclusiveness and build community.
3. Students will be able to ascertain interdependence with, responsibility to, and inspiration from community partners.
4. Students will be able to identify key components to promoting wellbeing, healing, hope, motivation, and political agency, such as meaningful connections to culture, self, others, and a shared sense of purpose, meaning, and vision for change.
5. Students will be able to demonstrate practices of mindfulness and self-care as a way to navigate personal and collective pain.

Community Impact Outcomes

As the result of participation in a semester-long, community-campus partnership for social change, community members and/or community partner agencies should be able to demonstrate the following impact outcomes:

1. Community members increase sense of belonging, connection, and responsibility to others—others that share similar lived experiences and others who are different but to whom they see as interconnected.
2. Community members experience an increased esteem of education, inspiration, hope, and sense of being valued from an academic perspective.
3. Community members experience greater commitment, endurance, courage, and hope as a result of achieving some community change goal or connection to larger social change movement.
4. Communities exemplify transformative change and healing through the ways they operate their community-building programs and initiatives, thus embodying and forwarding the values of peace, love, and justice upon which social movements are based.
5. Communities increase practices for community care and wellbeing by bearing witness to each other's suffering and fears, as well as supporting the development of each other's strengths and hopes.

Student Reflection on Cultivating Hope

This reflection is from an incarcerated student in an Inside-Out Prison Exchange course:

Social change must be in the forefront of the works. The only way I see that to be possible, is to unite as a whole: black and white, man and woman, rich and poor, Christian and Jew. The American people must stop being selfish in their own endeavors and begin to be selfless toward others. They must not allow the media and politicians to shadow their insight on what's right and what's wrong and be true to their selves no matter what storm that might bring. Acting on our beliefs will forever impact the future of America, but reacting in our beliefs will only condition history.

A great deal of excellence comes from this inside-out prison exchange program, but like everything else in life that's just one point of view. The program is the birth of something so extraordinary and allows society to view prisoners from a different perspective. It leads to second chances and causes a ripple effect throughout the prison system. The program is not only intellectually educational but mentally and emotionally educational as well [...] Bringing these styles of education into the prison system won't necessarily dismantle the prison system, but it most definitely continues to dismantle my institutionalization.

In conclusion, hope is contagious. In the beginning of this essay I explained my sympathy for the young students of Pitzer. After reviewing my work I've come to realize that perhaps that feeling of sympathy is actually a feeling of envy. Yes, I worry that one day their enthusiasm, hopes, and drive will be crushed by the weight of reality, but that's only because I lost sight of hope. I found writing my analysis to be very difficult and conflicting because the outside students shined light upon the darkest side of my soul allowing me to once again have hope. I stand by my theory that this nation, or world for that matter, will not settle its differences any time soon, if at all, but that does not mean we shouldn't try. This program, however, has opened my heart and my mind to a hopeful future. I understand that a theory or praxis isn't necessarily created or shared with the expectations to change the world in a day, however, I look forward to a day when it will be.

At the end of the day, truth will consistently change as we continue to grow. Definitions of justice, peace, community, social healing and change, righteousness, etc. will continue to vary depending on the individual and his/her life experiences. What matters is that we never lose hope, never stop fighting for what we believe in, and always be open to change.

NOTES

1. The student learning outcomes dispersed between the four sections of this chapter are adaptations of Pitzer College's graduation requirements: "social responsibility praxis," "social justice theory," and "intercultural understanding" student learning outcomes (Pitzer College 2016a, b, c), most of which I co-created. An earlier version of many of the "social responsibility praxis" and "social justice theory" student learning outcomes originally emerged from findings of the action research project I conducted with Pitzer students, faculty, staff, and community partners (Hicks 2009) and a review of literature in the field (listed in the following footnote). They were then collaboratively edited and revised by faculty and administrative colleagues in preparation for a direct assessment project we undertook in 2010 (see Chap. 6). The learning outcomes were once again updated and adapted with two faculty colleagues, Melinda Herrold-Menzies and Halford Fairchild, through our work on the Graduation Requirements task force subcommittee at Pitzer, 2013–2016. The outcomes went through additional, minor revisions once they were presented to the faculty and student governance committees at Pitzer and the final version was voted into policy in 2016. All of Pitzer's approved student learning outcomes for social responsibility praxis, social justice theory, and intercultural understanding, along with correlating course criteria, can be found in Appendix III.

2. This included, among others, the works of Astin and Sax (1998), Bacon (2002), Boss (1994), Bowman et al. (2010), Bringing Theory to Practice (2013); Harward (2016), Calderon (2007), Cruz and Giles (2000), Dorado and Giles (2004), Eyler and Giles (1999), Eyler et al. (1997), Ferrari and Worrall (2000), Finley (2012), Gelmon et al. (1998), Gray et al. (1998), Harward (2012, 2016), Hurtado et al. (2012), Jacoby (2003), Jorge (2003), Kendrick (1996), Kivel (2007), Lewis (2004), Kretzmann and McKnight (1993), Markus et al. (1993), Marullo and Edwards (2000), Mitchell (2008), Miron and Moely (2006), Nicotera et al. (2015), Pasque (2008), Sandy (2007), Schmidt and Robby (2002), Cotton and Stanton (1990), Stanton et al. (1998), Stoecker (2005), Strand et al. (2003), Strage (2004), Swaner (2005), Sweitzer and King (2014), The National Task Force on Civic Learning and Democratic Engagement (2012), Vernon and Ward (1999), and Ward and Wolf-Wendel (2000).

3. Unless otherwise indicated, all the activities and critical reflection prompts in this chapter are ones I have created and facilitated in the community engagement classes I have taught at Pitzer since 2006.

4. Adapted in part from Pitzer College Community Engagement Center MOU template, 2016.

5. I originally encountered the primary prompt for this activity ("where I'm from") in the curriculum of a long-standing poetry program that Pitzer students facilitate at a local juvenile detention center. Given how fraught the question "Where you from?" is when posed to youth on the streets who may be from opposing neighborhoods or gangs, this activity aimed to re-cast the question as one that can elicit self-expression about one's background and community. I further adapted it by bringing in the group poem components (steps 3–8).

6. I am grateful to each of the students in this and the next chapter that have allowed me to share their insightful reflections. The activities mentioned in this student excerpt: ground rules (for communication), the name game, concentric circles, and "what did class look, sound, and feel like?" are all exercises provided in this chapter for practitioners to incorporate into their own community-campus partnerships or classes.

7. This quote was originally introduced in Chap. 2, end note iv, and is actually accredited not to Lila Watson as the student suggests, but to the Aboriginal activists group, Queensland, 1970s.

8. This activity is an adapted version of "Establishing a Safe Learning Environment," (Anti-Defamation League 2017). The final communication guideline (#5) was adapted from the circle of trust communication rules explored in the chapter "Deep Speaks to Deep" in *A Hidden Wholeness: The journey towards an undivided life* (Palmer 2009).

9. This activity melds together two similar activities that occurred in two of my classes. One version of this activity was offered by Margo Okazawa-Rey, during a visit to my Pitzer class, "Healing ourselves and healing our communities." Margo is an original member of the Combahee River Collective and co-author of *Activist Scholarship: Antiracism, Feminism, and Social Change* (Sudbury and Okazawa-Rey 2015). Another version of this activity was facilitated by Terry Sivers during a student-led workshop in the local men's prison, California Rehabilitation Center, which occurred during my course "Community-based education and social change" through Claremont Graduate University, where Terry is a doctoral student.

References

Anti-Defamation League. (2017). *Establishing a safe learning environment.* The Anti-Defamation League's Curricular Resources. Retrieved March 1, 2017, from https://www.adl.org/education/resources/tools-and-strategies/establishing-a-safe-learning-environment.

Astin, A. W., & Sax, L. J. (1998). How undergraduates are affected by service participation. *Journal of College Student Development, 39,* 251–263.

Bacon, N. (2002). Differences in faculty and community partners' theories of learning. *Michigan Journal of Community Service Learning*, 9(1).

Boss, J. A. (1994). The effect of community service work on the moral development of college ethics students. *Journal of Moral Education*, 23(2), 183–198.

Bowman, N., Brandenberger, J., Lapsley, D., Hill, P., & Quaranto, J. (2010). Serving in College, Flourishing in Adulthood: Does Community Engagement During the College Years Predict Adult Well-Being?. *Applied Psychology: Health and Well Being*, 2(1), 14–34.

Bringing Theory to Practice. (2013). *The well-being and flourishing of students: Considering well-being, and its connection to learning and civic engagement, as central to the mission of higher education*. Washington, DC: AAC&U.

Butin, D. W. (Ed.). (2014). *Teaching social foundations of education: Contexts, theories, and issues*. New York, NY: Routledge.

Calderon, J. Z. (Ed.). (2007). *Race, poverty, and social justice: Multidisciplinary perspectives through service learning*. Sterling, VA: Stylus Publishing.

Cotton, D. & Stanton, T. K. (1990). Joining campus and community through service learning. *New Directions for Student Services, 50*, 101–110.

Cruz, N., & Giles, D. E. (2000). Where's the community in service-learning? *Michigan Journal of Community Service Learning*, 28–34.

DiAngelo, R., & Sensoy, O. (2012). *Is everyone really equal? An introduction to key concepts in social justice education*. New York, NY: Teachers College Press.

Dorado, S., & Giles, D. E. (2004). Service-learning partnerships: Paths of engagement. *Michigan Journal of Community Service Learning, 9*, 25–37.

Eyler, J., & Giles, D. (1999). *Where's the Learning in Service-Learning?*. San Francisco: CA: Jossey-Bass Publications.

Eyler, J., Giles, D. E., Jr., & Braxton, J. (1997). The impact of service-learning on college students. *Michigan Journal of Community Service Learning, 4*, 5–15.

Ferrari, J. R., & Worrall, L. (2000). Assessments by community agencies: How 'the other side sees service-learning. *Michigan Journal of Community Service Learning, 7*(1).

Finley, A. (2012). *Making Progress? What We Know about the Achievement of Liberal Education Outcomes*. Washington, DC: AA&U.

Gelmon, S. B., Holland, B. A., Seifer, S. D., Shinnamon, A., & Connors, K. (1998). Community-university partnerships for mutual learning. *Michigan Journal of Community Service Learning, 5*, 97–107.

Ginwright, S. (2015). *Hope and healing in urban education: How urban activists and teachers are reclaiming matters of the heart*. New York, NY: Routledge.

Hall, N. (1997a). Creativity and incarceration: The purpose of art in a prison culture. In D. Gussak & E. Virshup (Eds.), *Drawing time: Art therapy in prisons and other correctional settings* (pp. 25–41). Chicago, IL: Magnolia Street Publishers.

Hall, S. (1997b). *Representation: Cultural representations and signifying practices* (Vol. 2). Thousand Oaks, CA: Sage.

Harward, D. W. (2012). *Civic Provocations.* Washington, DC.: Bringing Theory to Practice.

Harward, D. W. (Ed.). (2016). *Well-Being and Higher Education: A Strategy for Change and the Realization of Education's Greater Purposes.* Washington, D.C.: Bringing Theory to Practice.

Hicks, T. (2009). *Engaged scholarship and education: A case study on the pedagogy of social change.* Unpublished Dissertation, Claremont Claremont Graduate University, Claremont, CA.

Hoy, W. K., & Tschannen-Moran, M. (1999). Five faces of trust: An empirical confirmation in urban elementary schools. *Journal of School Leadership, 9,* 184–208.

Hurtado, S., Ruiz, A., & Whang, H. (2012). Advancing and assessing civic learning: New results from the Diverse Learning Environments survey. *Diversity & Democracy, 15,* 10–12.

Jacoby, B. (Ed.). (2003). *Building partnerships for service-learning.* San Francisco: Wiley.

Jorge, E. (2003). Outcomes for community partners in an unmediated service-learning program. *Michigan Journal of Community Service Learning, 10,* 28–38.

Kendrick, J.R., Jr. (1996). Outcomes of service-learning in an introduction to sociology course. *Michigan Journal of Community Service Learning,* 72–81.

Kivel, P. (2007). Social service or social change. In Incite (Ed.), *The revolution will not be funded: Beyond the non-profit industrial complex* (pp. 129–149). Cambridge, MA: South End Press.

Kretzmann, J. P., & McKnight, J. (1993). *Building communities from the inside out.* Evanston, IL: Center for Urban Affairs and Policy Research, Neighborhood Innovations Network.

Lewis, T. L. (2004). Service learning for social change? Lessons from a liberal arts college. *Teaching Sociology, 32*(1), 94–108.

Markus, G. B., Howard, J. P., & King, D. C. (1993). Integrating community service and classroom instruction enhances learning: Results from an experiment. *Educational Evaluation and Policy Analysis, 15*(4), 410–419.

Marullo, S., & Edwards, B. (2000). From charity to justice the potential of university-community collaboration for social change. *American Behavioral Scientist, 43*(5), 895–912.

Miron, D., & Moely, B. E. (2006). Community agency voice and benefit in service-learning. *Michigan Journal of Community Service Learning, 12*(2), 27–37.

Mitchell, T. D. (2008). Traditional vs. critical service-learning: Engaging the literature to differentiate two models. *Michigan Journal of Community Service Learning, 14*(2).

Nicotera, N., Brewer, S., & Veeh, C. (2015). Civic activity and well-being among first-year college students. *The International Journal of Research on Service-Learning and Community Engagement, 3*(1).

Noel, J. (2014). *Developing sustainable community engagement by repositioning programs into communities.* In S. V. D. Iverson & J. H. James (Eds.), *Feminist community engagement: Achieving praxis* (pp. 175–191). Palgrave Macmillan US.

Palmer, P. J. (2009). *A hidden wholeness: The journey toward an undivided life.* San Francisco, CA: Wiley.

Pasque, P. A. (2008). Bridging civic engagement and mental health. In *Proceedings from the National Symposium for Civic Engagement and Mental Health.*

Peterson, T. H. & Khouri, H. (2015). *The trauma of injustice.* Online Course, Off the Mat and Into the World.

Pitzer College. (2010). Educational effectiveness review. *Pitzer College Report for Western Association of Schools and Colleges (WASC).* Retrieved March 7, 2016, from, http://pitweb.pitzer.edu/institutional-research/wasc-accreditation/.

Pitzer College. (2016a). *Graduation requirements: Social responsibility praxis student learning outcomes and course criteria.* Claremont, CA: Pitzer College.

Pitzer College. (2016b). *Graduation requirements: Social justice theory student learning outcomes and course criteria.* Claremont, CA: Pitzer College.

Pitzer College. (2016c). *Graduation requirements: Local-global intercultural understanding student learning outcomes and course criteria.* Claremont, CA: Pitzer College.

Sandy, M. (2007). *Community voices: A California campus compact study on partnerships.* Hayward, CA: California Campus Compact.

Schmidt, A., & Robby, M. A. (2002). What's the value of service learning to the community?. *Michigan Journal of Community Service Learning, 9*(1), 27–33.

Singhal, A. (2004). *Entertainment-education through participatory theater: Freirean strategies for empowering the oppressed. Entertainment-education and social change: History, research, and practice* (pp. 377–398).

Stanton, T. K., Giles, D. E., & Cruz, N. I. (1998). *Service learning: A movement's pioneers reflect on its origins, practice, and future.* San Francisco: Jossey Bass.

Stevenson, B. (2016, March 29). American injustice: Mercy, humanity and making a difference. In *Criminal Justice Symposium.* Claremont, CA: Pomona College.

Stoecker, R. (2005). *Research methods for community change: A project-based approach* (2nd ed.). Thousand Oaks, CA: Sage.

Strage, A. (2004). Long-term academic benefits of service-learning: When and where do they manifest themselves? *College Student Journal, 38*(2), 257.

Strand, K. J., Cutforth, N., Stoecker, R., Marullo, S., & Donohue, P. (2003). *Community-based research and higher education: Principles and practices.* San Francisco, CA: Wiley.

Sudbury, J., & Okazawa-Rey, M. (2015). *Activist scholarship: Antiracism, feminism, and social change.* New York, NY: Routledge.

Swaner, L. E. (2005). Educating for personal and social responsibility: A review of the literature. *Liberal Education, 91*(3), 14–21.

Sweitzer, H. K., & King, M. A. (2014). *The successful internship: personal, professional, and civic development in experiential learning,* (4th ed.). Belmont, CA: Brooks/Cole Cengage.

The National Task Force on Civic Learning and Democratic Engagement. (2012). *A Crucible Moment: College Learning and Democracy's Future.* Washington, DC: Association of American Colleges and Universities.

Vernon, A., & Ward, K. (1999). Campus and community partnerships: Assessing impacts and strengthening connections. *Michigan Journal of Community Service Learning, 6,* 30–37.

Ward, K., & Wolf-Wendel, L. (2000). Community-centered service learning moving from doing for to doing with. *American Behavioral Scientist, 43*(5), 767–780.

Watkins, M., & Shulman, H. (2008). *Towards psychologies of liberation.* New York, NY: Palgrave Macmillan.

CHAPTER 6

Evaluation Case Study: "Healing Ourselves, Healing Our Communities"

This chapter provides a concrete roadmap for practitioners interested in curriculum and evaluation designs exemplifying the Critical, Contemplative Community Engagement model. This case study brings to life the theoretical frameworks and pedagogical approaches discussed in Part I of this book and an evaluation project aimed at verifying student learning therein. The "Healing ourselves, healing our communities" program consisted of a set of two courses surrounding healing and social change that were taught in the USA and Mexico over linked Spring and Summer school sessions. The program is evaluated here in order to

1. expand notions of community engagement to include both local and global involvement;
2. extend dialogues around community engagement to include partnerships that focus on indigenous knowledge systems and healing traditions; and
3. disrupt traditional notions of student engagement beyond the academic and civic realms to include theoretical and experiential learning processes that enhance personal, emotional, and spiritual growth.

Using a direct assessment approach, the rubric used for the program evaluation successfully captured student development in three areas: self-knowledge, intercultural understanding, and local–global connections. While challenges remain concerning how to accurately and holistically

© The Author(s) 2018   187
T. Hicks Peterson, *Student Development and Social Justice*,
https://doi.org/10.1007/978-3-319-57457-8_6

evaluate nuanced and subjective personal and intellectual growth that occur over time, the case study presented here provides a useful template for practitioners interested in designing curricula and assessment methods that embody the ethos of critical, contemplative community engagement.

Overview of the Local–Global Paired Course Program

To strengthen the link between distinct local and global community-based learning initiatives, Pitzer college created the "local–global paired course program" in which a semester seminar course explores a particular theme with community partners in the college's surrounding communities, followed by studying and engaging with the same topic in a location abroad during the summer. When Pitzer college administrators first proposed this idea to funders, they drew on the charge given by Martha Nussbaum in her article on "Liberal Education and Global Community":

> The idea of liberal education is more important than ever in our interdependent world. An education based on the idea of an inclusive global citizenship and on the possibilities of the compassionate imagination has the potential to transcend divisions created by distance, cultural difference, and mistrust. Developing the ideal further and thinking about how to modify it in light of our times is one of the most exciting and urgent tasks we can undertake as educators and citizens. (1994, p. 1)

Pitzer College leaders felt that it was incumbent upon higher education institutions to build an international consciousness into traditional fields of study by bringing students interested in the "foreign" into a dialogue with "the other" in their own communities. By helping students see how the local is already profoundly interconnected with the "foreign" and "the other" in their homelands, colleges and universities could help society's new generation of leaders understand how to make diversity an asset for communities rather than a threat to unity. This was the curricular rationale given for the creation of the school's "Institute for Global and Local Action and Study" and the local–global paired course program.[1]

I had the opportunity to develop one of the first of these paired course programs at Pitzer. I chose to explore the link between personal development and social justice through the lens of indigenous knowledge and mindful engagement, two areas usually neglected in typical community engagement programs. The result was a two-course program titled "Healing ourselves, healing our communities" that brought theory and practice to life through community-campus partnerships with indigenous communities in both the USA and Mexico. This paired course program emphasized the importance of learning about and exercising mindful approaches to working for peace and justice for activist students who are often highly invested in being agents of change but still grappling with their own personal development and experiences of woundedness. It also aimed to ethically guide students who were interested in translating their desires for change into action, especially when engaging with communities culturally, racially, or economically distinct from their own.

The paired courses drew on social change theories, well being practices, and critical pedagogical approaches that have been covered in Chaps. 2 and 3 of this book. They were also couched in epistemological, cosmological, and cultural frameworks of indigenous knowledge (discussed briefly in Chap. 2). As I don't in any way claim authority to represent indigenous knowledge, students were introduced to fundamental principles of indigenous knowledge systems through theoretical readings while primarily teachings about them were carried out by guest lecturers and by indigenous elders with whom we partnered in the community. Through these teachings, they learned about how practices of mutual nurturing between and among human and non-human beings is the basis for the belief that we exist in an interconnected community, where relationships between land, animals, family, and community are one and the same. These relationships are exemplified through language, the words and phrases that espouse the interbeing of land, community, self, heart, and body (Armstrong 2006). These relationships also indicate a process of reciprocal dialogue, that is, communing and communicating between the senses. These ideas and related practices informed a large part of the course content, as they related to students' exploration into strategies for healing, transformation, and wellbeing of individuals and communities. They also influenced the way the courses were structured, the teaching methods, and the experiential learning that occurred while partnering with native communities locally and abroad.

The primary learning outcomes of this paired course program included engaging a praxis of social responsibility and intercultural understanding, developing an awareness of self, capacity, and positionality in community engagement efforts, and garnering the ability to critically analyze and situate local circumstances within broader, global contexts. The works of diverse scholars from such fields as cultural studies, globalization studies, indigenous studies, and feminist theory were assigned to explore theories that bridge individual wellbeing and self-realization with community wellbeing and social change. The course examined issues such as knowledge production and alternative epistemologies, decolonization and cultural affirmation of indigenous cultural traditions, environmental sustainability, and practices of engaged mindfulness and conscious activism.

The initial seminar course was offered during the spring semester of 2010 to a diverse group of fifteen students at Pitzer College. Seven of these students were then chosen to attend the month-long summer program in Mexico.[2] The spring semester course was held on the Pitzer campus, with students engaged in the community by participating in collaborative projects and being mentored by members of the Costanoan Rusmen Carmel/Ohlone and Gabrieleno/Tongva nations. The Ohlone and Tongva are two tribal nations of urban Indians living in and around the major metropolitan county of Los Angeles in which Pitzer is located. The related summer course was co-developed in partnership with a grassroots, community-based organization that facilitates indigenous Mexican healing practices for personal and community development, located in a semi-rural, small town near Cuernavaca, in Central Mexico.[3]

Through assigned reading, in-class discussions, lectures, guest speakers, experiential activities, and community engagement in both courses, students learned about and practiced strategies for individual and collective transformation. Community engagement ethics were rigorously explored and practiced weekly in a practicum in the community and in online forums encouraging critical reflection. Students wrote numerous personal reflections and critical analysis papers on their own journey of self-awareness and healing, community knowledge, and community-building strategies within the context of existing theoretical frameworks around personal development and social change. Final papers required that students weave together theoretical underpinnings of both personal and community development with their own experiences of community engagement and self-realization; these were later analyzed closely as part of a direct assessment project.

Overview of the Local Community Engagement Course

The spring course set the groundwork and themes as well as an intentionality and coherence among learning outcomes that were carried out in both components of the paired-course program. The community engagement component of the spring course connected students with local Ohlone and Tongva elders for regular meetings, workshops, and community outreach projects. Each student committed 4 hours a week outside of class to working on specific projects and partnership-building. As a result of accompanying and establishing mentoring relationships with elders, students were invited to participate in educational workshops around native craft-making, trainings in native domestic violence advocacy, fetal alcohol syndrome, and an indigenous girls' self-esteem program. Through informal meetings and gatherings in the homes of native elders or at the tribal office, students were able to learn respectively about Ohlone and Tongva history, traditions, stories, and cultural values. In addition to fieldtrips to model traditional native villages and native educational centers, students were welcomed as participants at tribal functions such as pow wows, ceremonial dances, ancestor walks, sweat lodges, women's healing circles, and inter-tribal ceremonial gatherings. Through these experiential activities, students increased their intercultural understanding and learned about ways of knowing, being, and healing from two distinct but interconnected local tribal traditions (the Ohlone and Tongva).

In the spirit of reciprocity, Pitzer students volunteered their time, tools, and resources to various classes, events, fundraisers, and workshops hosted by local native partners. They secured and prepared land at Pitzer College and renewed a donated plot of land in nearby Pomona for an organic farm and garden for use by tribal members. They co-coordinated and co-facilitated a mentoring group between college students and native youth. They assisted in recording tribal events to be used in the tribe's fundraising, outreach, and archival purposes. They wrote and secured mini-grants to support some of the aforementioned programs. They created and maintained social media interfaces (i.e., Facebook pages, blogs, email distributions) to connect college students with tribal partners and the general public. Finally, they assisted with the outreach and organizing efforts of Pitzer College's annual Native Youth to College program, a Native American film festival, and a Native-academic community partnerships conference.[4] Whereas most of the students were only engaged in the tribal communities and the resulting projects while they were attending the spring seminar course, some of the students joined a small network of faculty, staff, and students to work for subsequent years on these and other projects related to our multifaceted community partnership with these two local tribes.

The assigned theoretical texts and community practicums introduced students to native epistemological perspectives on individuality and community, pain and healing, language, rights, governance, relationships to land, and the interconnection of the physical, mental, spiritual, and emotional bodies. Infusing different ways of knowing into the classroom and community engagement settings promoted a paradigm shift around students' notions of epistemology and ontology and turned the students into active participants in decolonizing the academy. This intentional pedagogical and theoretical framing of the course is supported by many native scholars and non-native academic allies who wish to challenge the dominant colonial narratives that persist in the academy and reconsider the ways we think about, teach, and demonstrate the values of indigenous knowledge production and authorship in the academy.[5]

Overview of the Community Engagement Course Abroad

Continuing the study of native approaches to healing and social change begun in the local, spring semester component of the program, a month-long, two-course credit summer abroad program took place in Central Mexico. It provided a brief, though intensive exploration of indigenous Mexican cosmologies and healing and community wellbeing practices. The summer program was conceived, taught, and coordinated in collaboration with a local healer, a native to the area whose long-standing relationships with community members enabled students to engage with local host families and guest lecturers and provided opportunities for service learning and cultural projects.[6] Students learned by studying conventional scholarly texts, attending academic lectures, and participating in workshops held by spiritual leaders, oral storytelling events, and experiencing sweat lodges, energetic massage, herbal remedies, meditation, and singing. Fieldtrips to local sacred sites and ancient ruins within the state of Morelos provided other contexts for learning, as did residing with host families in the neighborhood and attending daily intensive Spanish language classes. While the community engagement component of this course was limited by the 4-week timeframe of the program, students devoted 6 hours per week to one of two local community service learning partnerships: a *convivencia* (orphanage for abandoned or abused children) and a local alternative healing spa and treatment center.

Course content focused on a variety of Mexican philosophies surrounding illness and wellness, the interconnection of mind–body–spirit, and the ancient knowledge systems that drive energetic, botanic, and meditative practices of healing. Through an exploration of both theory and practice, students gained exposure to indigenous Mexican beliefs around life and death, spirituality, gender, justice, and peacemaking. The summer course explored presuppositions of indigenous and non-indigenous philosophies, metaphysics, and the ethics that affect the value systems and decision-making processes related to ecology, health, food, community building, economic sustainability, and human/treaty rights. They also learned about the global contexts of local knowledge and culture and to recognize the impacts of global restructuring on indigenous communities. Students were taught perspectives and skills for critically analyzing and dialoging about the roles, tensions, and praxis of indigenous healing practices within a global context. The critical reflection and experiential learning activities supported students in becoming aware of their own wellbeing and self-realization processes. The paired-course structure, specific readings, discussions, and writing prompts encouraged them to make connections between what they learned in the local spring course with their experiences and studies in the summer abroad program.

ASSESSMENT: HOW TO EVALUATE *THAT* KIND OF LEARNING

Beyond providing a local–global community engagement program template, this chapter also aims to provide scholar practitioners and administrators a glimpse of the process and product of evaluating such a program. Student learning in the areas of student and community wellbeing, social responsibility, intercultural understanding, and the connection between local and global impacts of community engagement are becoming increasingly important outcomes for institutions interested in such high-impact practices. Assessing the actual student learning that occurs in such courses presents unusual challenges, however, because the outcomes are often highly subjective and nuanced, and may not be readily apparent immediately following the close of the learning experience, but rather emerge over time. Furthermore, when courses involve marginalized and alternative knowledge producers in community-based learning on topics that engage students' personal, emotional, and even spiritual growth, the students' holistic academic and personal development is sometimes difficult to demonstrate, much less evaluate. It is especially difficult to do so when looking beyond evidence that merely *asserts* that learning outcomes have been achieved to evidence that actually *demonstrates* it. Such a process of evaluation is best achieved utilizing a multi-pronged approach that includes student reflections (self-reporting) and direct assessment of student written work. The assessment processes used for this paired-course program are provided here to contribute to the field of community engagement, adding to the fine work of other scholars and teachers that have created meaningful learning and growth opportunities for students, measurable learning outcomes, and effective strategies of assessment.[7] In this section, I introduce the approaches to assessment used, including the potentially transferable rubrics created to assess student learning, and discuss the overall outcomes achieved by students in this local–global paired course program.

Developing Student Learning Outcomes and Assessment Rubrics

Designing learning outcomes for this particular set of courses which would capture the nuances of experiential, critical education and measure self-awareness, self-realization, a deepening of community knowledge and relationships, and an understanding of indigenous cosmologies and epistemological frameworks, all within the scaffolding of globalization, proved to be a fascinating challenge. The conversations with assessment collaborators that were born while trying to craft meaningful learning outcomes, as well as pinpoint how evaluators would conclude when a student had demonstrated that learning in their written work, revealed that evaluation itself is a true blend of art and science. Ideas gleaned from existing evaluation tools and the findings of expert evaluators in the field proved helpful.[8] These contributed to the creation of an initial list of key outcomes for engaged learning (Hicks 2009). This list was then transformed into an assessment rubric specific to the paired-course evaluation.[9] The methodology, tools, and iterations of the rubric (based on emergent discoveries by the inter-raters) are explored here.

The aim to create a non-reductionist method of assessing learning and student development resulted in the creation of the following course learning outcomes:

- self-knowledge (defined as reflexivity and awareness of capacities, skills, and perspectives as well as an awareness of one's positionality, biases, and values);
- intercultural understanding (including the ability to appreciate and cross-cultural boundaries and engage diverse perspectives to examine social issues in the theoretical and practical); and

- local–global connections (including the ability to compare, contrast, identify, and analyze points of intersection between local and global perspectives on course topic and situate local circumstances within a broader, global context).

While not explicitly a part of the final rubric used in this assessment, the following were additional student learning outcomes taught to in this course:

- community knowledge (recognizing the needs and strengths of a community, as defined through the lens and experience of that community);
- interpersonal competency (demonstrating leadership, teamwork, and problem-solving skills, as well as rigorous professional and ethical conduct);
- social responsibility (attaining a heightened sense of personal responsibility to community issues); and
- the praxis of critical community engagement (applying community lessons to understand theory and vice versa).

I attempted to follow the promising practice for effective evaluation developed by Ash and Clayton which "begins with the identification of desired learning outcomes. It then proceeds with the expression of learning goals in terms of assessable learning objectives and continues to the design and implementation of teaching and learning strategies (such as reflection) aligned with those objectives, all the while developing assessment strategies that are well-matched to the objectives and to the teaching and learning strategies and that can be used to inform future revisions of either or both" (2009, p. 29). Once the student learning outcomes and critical reflection learning strategies were established, the rubric was created as a tool to analyze to what degree students achieved these outcomes and the direct assessment design was outlined. The original learning outcomes and the final assessment rubric are listed in Tables 6.1 and 6.2.

Direct Assessment Focus: Final Critical Reflection Papers

As documented in their written work, students gained from combined processes of reading academic texts, engaging in lectures, in-class discussions, experiential activities, and reflecting on the partnership-building and community engagement collaborations they participated in locally and

Table 6.1   Student learning outcomes and evidence of learning

Learning objectives	Learning outcomes	Evidence of learning
Self-knowledge	Students will reflect on, evaluate, and critique their experiences in depth. Students will demonstrate an awareness of their own perceptions, biases, assumptions, issues of power, privilege, and positionality. Students will exhibit development in sense of self, capacity, and moral reasoning	• Pre- and post-internship student surveys
Community knowledge	Students will recognize and practice service ethics in a weekly practicum, including how to negotiate issues of responsibility, respect, and reciprocity as they relate to participation with local community mentors and organizations. Through this community engagement, students will become more aware of local knowledge, assets, and cultures	• Course evaluations • Student proposals and subsequent community-based action projects • Weekly journal reflections • Final papers • Final presentations • Assessment by community partners • Community partner site interview debrief notes • Student focus groups
Interpersonal competency	Students will demonstrate leadership, teamwork, problem-solving and communication skills, as well as rigorous professional and ethical conduct in classroom and community settings.	
Intercultural understanding	Students will appreciate different cultures, cross-cultural boundaries, and have close connections with community members. Students will use effective strategies to communicate across cultures and engage diverse perspectives to examine social issues in the theoretical and practical.	
Local–global connections	Students will be able to compare, contrast, and analyze points of intersection between local and global perspectives on course topics. Students will be able to critically	

(continued)

Table 6.1 (continued)

Learning objectives	Learning outcomes	Evidence of learning
Social responsibility	analyze and situate local circumstances within a broader, global context (i.e., politically, culturally, socially, historically) Students will demonstrate a heightened sense of personal responsibility to community issues and an awareness of systematic and historical roots of the conditions affecting local communities. Students will demonstrate an understanding of and commitment to personal ethics and values of community engagement	

abroad. Every week students participated in both written and verbal forms of reflection in order to assess the impacts of their cultural immersion and community engagement experiences. The critical reflection assignments in this class exemplified the components of "High Quality Reflection" introduced by Eyler et al. in that they were "continuous (ongoing); connected (with assignments and activities related to and building on one another and including explicit integration with learning goals and academic material); challenging (including in terms of the expectation that students take responsibility for their own learning); and contextualized (to the community setting and broader public issues and to the students' own particular roles)" (qtd in Ash and Clayton 2009, p. 35). In addition to weekly reflection and critical analysis essays, student crafted final papers that wove personal reflections with critical/theoretical analysis. These papers were the primary focus of direct assessment.

The instructions for both spring and summer final papers asked students to utilize theoretical frameworks from the course and their own personal reflections to craft a manifesto for healing as social change, incorporating a reflection on their own state of consciousness as it relates to healing practices; positionality as it relates to bias, assumptions, and social responsibility; and sense of self and capacity within local community partnerships and projects. Additionally, the summer program asked students to specifically explore the philosophical and practical aspects of at least two

Table 6.2   Rubric for assessing student learning in local–global paired courses

Learning outcome	Level of achievement			
	Initial 1	Emerging 2	Developed 3	Highly developed 4
Self-knowledge	Cannot evaluate one's experiences in the field. Only reiterates observations in narrative form and does not reflect on them	Has the ability to reflect on one's experiences in the field, but is not deeply aware of values, beliefs, and attitudes one holds and how these impact the ways in which one sees and acts with others	Can reflect on one's experiences and also critique one's interactions with others. Shares personal thoughts and beliefs about own experiences and is aware of one's personal biases and/or privileges	Can reflect on, evaluate, and critique one's experiences in depth. Demonstrates an awareness of own perceptions, biases, assumptions; issues of power, privilege, and positionality. Exhibits development in sense of self, capacity, and moral reasoning
Intercultural understanding	Does not appreciate or empathize with different cultures, ways of being, or viewpoints. Lacks direct contact with community	Has empathy and appreciation for other cultures. However, still lacks the ability to effectively interact and connect with other cultures/community members	Displays knowledge of one's biases, assumptions, and perceptions *in relating to other cultures.* Has established a working relationship with some community members and is just beginning to understand effective strategies to	Appreciates different cultures, can cross cultural boundaries, and has close connections with community members. Uses effective strategies to communicate across cultures and engage diverse perspectives to examine social issues in the

(continued)

Table 6.2 (continued)

Learning outcome	Level of achievement			
	Initial 1	Emerging 2	Developed 3	Highly developed 4
Local–global connections	Lacks the ability to describe local and global perspectives on course topic	Has the ability to describe local and global perspectives on course topic but lacks skills to compare, contrast, or find intersections within them. Cannot situate local circumstances within broader, global context	communicate across cultures Has the ability to compare and contrast but not find points of intersection between local and global perspectives on course topic. Ability to situate local circumstances within broader, global context but does not provide in-depth analysis	theoretical and practical Demonstrates integration of conceptual knowledge and personal experience in order to compare, contrast, identify, and analyze points of intersection between local and global perspectives on course topic. Ability to critically analyze and situate local circumstances within broader, global context (i.e., politically, culturally, socially, historically)

traditional Mexican healing traditions and epistemology; demonstrate an understanding of different Mexican cultural practices, cultural communication strategies, and social issues; compare, contrast, and analyze points of intersection between local and global perspectives on the course topics; and situate the local circumstances surrounding indigenous knowledge and healing in Mexico within a broader, global context.

Methodology

The direct assessment conducted around this course was guided by the rubric (Table 6.2). It involved close readings of student final papers from both courses to assess and compare their performance at the end of the spring and the summer courses, and to ascertain the degree to which their writing reflected the achievement of anticipated learning outcomes. This qualitative evaluation design also included a review of self-reported reflections by students and community members (including in-take and out-take surveys, course evaluations, community input, and student focus groups) regarding perceptions of growth, learning, and impact that resulted from the courses. Analyzing this data did not take priority in the evaluation project at the time so the assessment concentrated solely on the findings of the direct assessment of students' written work from both sets of courses.

The singular focus on direct assessment was a result of Pitzer College's previous accreditation review, which found that past evidence of successful learning had been based entirely on indirect data (self-reporting) as opposed to direct assessments of demonstrations of learning as evidenced in student writing. Pitzer's reviewers indicated that self-reported evaluation data were less worthy evidence of students successfully achieving stated learning outcomes and thus, in preparation for the follow-up accreditation visit, the administration decided to focus on direct assessment exclusively, highlighting some of the school's innovative curricular offerings (i.e., the new local–global paired course program) that emphasized foundational values and programs (social responsibility/community engagement and study abroad).[10] As such, administrators from the dean of faculty's office (the associate dean and the assistant director of academic curriculum), along with members of both the Study Abroad and Community Engagement Centers (the directors and assistant directors of each), were given the task of evaluating final papers from both courses. Already the Director of the Community Engagement Center and the faculty member who taught the paired course, I took on a third role as a member of the evaluation team.

The three-part process for doing this assessment began with a critical examination of the direct assessment rubric for completeness and usefulness, an evaluation of one student's spring semester term paper for the purpose of establishing a baseline and inter-rater reliability, and a final evaluation of spring and summer student final papers for the purpose of assessing achievement of student learning outcomes and growth from the baseline. The first part entailed discussing each learning outcome to be assessed and the ways in which the rubric indicated the level of achievement of each outcome. The gradations for marking increasing levels of achievement went from "1" representing only "initial" achievement of the learning outcome, to "2" for "emerging" level, to "3" for "developed" achievement, to "4" representing "highly developed" achievement. An earlier version of the learning rubric (Table 6.1) did not contain such gradations of achievement, but only noted if outcomes had been completely or not at all achieved. This proved harder to use for assessments because students rarely completely achieve or completely fail to achieve any of the outcomes, but more typically achieve them to varying degrees. This problem has been noted by other evaluation teams, such as Ash and Clayton, who explain: "The creation of a rubric that expresses varying levels of quality or mastery, from novice to expert or from under-developed to excellent, can be extremely helpful in guiding this [assessment] process" (2009, p. 38). Thus, our team used began by changing the rubric so that it contained gradations of achievement. We also narrowed the list of student learning outcomes from the six taught in the course (see Table 6.1) to a condensed version of three (Table 6.2) so that the assessment process would be more manageable given our existing evaluation capacity.

Each member of the local–global assessment team received the seven final analysis papers from the spring semester course for the first part of a two-part norming process. First, the team members conducted an initial pilot evaluation in order to secure inter-rater reliability by having each evaluator read the same sample paper and rate it based upon their assessment of the student's level of achievement for the three learning objectives. The team then discussed their ratings assessment for the student, with an explicit emphasis on establishing a common understanding of the rubric and its application to student papers. Overall, there was a very strong consensus about the rating results and the team felt satisfied that norming was occurring amongst the inter-raters' approaches to the evaluation.

For the second stage of the norming process, individual evaluators then read each paper and scored students on their achievement of each learning outcome, based on how their written work communicated their levels of understanding on the agreed-upon scales and the application of the rubric. Once all spring papers were evaluated, the team came together to discuss each paper, their ratings, and to verify that they were each approaching the evaluation rubric with a shared understanding. Further discussion ensued in the actual process of sharing scores (utilizing examples from student papers to ensure inter-rater reliability). In the discussion after the evaluation scores were compiled, the team members found that their individual ratings, with regard to the first two objectives, self-knowledge, and intercultural understanding, were remarkably similar. Some significant disparities in rating on the third category ("local–global connections") led to a comprehensive discussion on whether students should be rated on their conceptual analysis of the connections between the global and the local or based upon their experiential understanding of the relationship. The team agreed that for students to attain a high level of achievement (i.e., "developed" or "highly developed") for this objective, they must be able to demonstrate that they could integrate the conceptual knowledge they gained through taking the course with the more experiential elements that resulted from their hands-on engagement with the host culture. Articulating the integration of the conceptual and the experiential led to a team consensus on how to rate the local–global learning objective and further ensured inter-rater reliability and norming across the board. This particular experience in the norming process was beneficial even beyond ascertaining inter-rater reliability. We found that the process demanded that we reflect on and challenge what it is we meant by (and how our students could demonstrate) "local–global connections." This critical reflective process in the arena of assessment rightly echoed the kind of critical reflection and questioning process we espouse in our critical pedagogy approaches.

In the final step of the direct assessment process, final "scores" were determined by averaging individual evaluator scores for each student, and then the students as a group, resulting in a final set of baseline data from the spring course papers. After the second component (the summer abroad course) was finished and the paired-course program was effectively complete, the team returned to assess the final papers of the same seven students from their second (abroad) course. Again, final "scores" were determined by averaging individual evaluator scores for each student, and then the students as a group, thus securing a set of growth scores from the summer course. This three-part process produced a cohesive and targeted approach to direct assessment which maintained focus on assessing student achievement of learning outcomes in meaningful ways that could contribute to future discussions of curriculum and program implementation.

Direct Assessment Findings

Results of the direct assessment of the final papers from the spring 2010 course found that out of possible four points (described above), students averaged a score of 2.64 in the category of "self-knowledge" (meaning that the average finding of the evaluators showed that the students achieved this objective somewhere between the categories of "emerging" and "developing" levels of understanding, leaning toward the latter). For the category of intercultural understanding, students averaged a score of 2.30, and for the local–global connections, they averaged a score of 1.5 (which made sense, given that they had not yet been exposed to the "global" study abroad component of the course).

In assessing the seven final papers from the summer (abroad) course, the group noticed a marked improvement in student scores, not only in the third "local–global" objective, but also in the other two as well. The students overall demonstrated growth in all categories: in the category of "self-knowledge" students moved from an average score of 2.64 in the spring evaluation to an average score of 3.21 after the summer course; in the category of "intercultural understanding," they moved from an average score of 2.30 to 2.64; and in the category of "local–global connections," students demonstrated the greatest growth as they moved from an average score of 1.5 to 3.21 (see Table 6.3). The findings reveal that initial learning occurred for all students in the first course pertaining to all three assessed areas of self-knowledge, intercultural understanding, and local–global connections. The assessment also found that the summer component of the local–global paired course did, in fact, produce significant growth and proved to be an additive learning experience, not simply for students' understanding of the link between the local and global, but in all categories of the two courses' learning objectives.

The students in the paired course program demonstrated learning in all areas of the assessment rubric, but in particular in the areas of self-knowledge (which was shown to have the highest marks of

Table 6.3 Direct assessment final scores of local–global course

Student learning outcomes	Spring assessment scores	Summer assessment scores
Self-knowledge	2.64	3.21
Intercultural understanding	2.30	2.64
Local–global connections	1.5	3.21

achievement after both the spring and the summer programs). With so many variables present, it is impossible to draw definitive conclusions about the causality of this finding, but there are some general deductions I would venture to make about why this is the case. In both courses, students engaged in a regular, critical practice of reflection, in which they demonstrated a growing awareness of self and acknowledging the knowledge, truth, and values they held which they believed to be universal. The theme of the course concentrated a great deal on the cultivation of self-knowledge. In class discussions, weekly writing activities, and through course readings, students began to recognize and challenge their own perceptions, biases, assumptions, and positions of power and privilege. The readings and lectures also explored in depth the epistemological paradigm in which most of the students had been raised and educated. They offered opportunities to consider other perspectives and ontologies. The course repeatedly invited them to investigate how their own personal practices of ethics, compassion, and peace or violence (within their own bodies, families, and peer groups) correlated with how those topics play out in interpersonal and structural ways in society. Given the amount of attention this set of courses gave to theories and practices of self-development, it makes sense that the "self-knowledge" category demonstrated the greatest level of achievement. While it is nonetheless impressive for first year students to achieve at this high level, it could indicate a propensity for already self-possessed students to self-select into the course.

While it is difficult to present the ways in which students demonstrated their attainment of the learning objectives through small excerpts from their papers (because more often than not, this demonstration occurred cumulatively throughout the entire paper or set of papers), a few examples from student papers that exemplify the aims of each learning outcome are shared here to provide a space for student voices. In one instance, a student wrote:

> I came into this class with previous practice in and knowledge about some of the topics covered, but my background and the culture in which I have been raised has nevertheless informed my experience. Despite my exposure to ideas outside of the dominate hegemony, and though my intentions have been good, conventional ideology infiltrated my subconscious, shaping the words I used, the values and the scales by which I measure things.

Another student reflected on her personal experience in the community partnership with one of our local Native American tribal partners. This extract demonstrates her ability to reflect on her own worldview and implicit assumptions about progress:

> Of Beath's seven attributes for guiding social change, I found attribute seven, 'being joyful without attachment to goals' to be the most relevant to my experience with the tribe.[11] It took some time to adjust to my internship with the tribe. At times, I found the meetings exhausting because of the lack of organization. Often it seemed that issues would be addressed, however we would move to the next issue before completely resolving it. I find truth in the attribute of "being joyful without attachment to goals" because now, looking back at the internship experience, although not all of my goals were achieved, so much was accomplished that I feel extremely joyful. I recognize that 'progress' is seen differently depending on the cultural perspective and that I should not be frustrated, but instead, handle these differences with an open mind. [...] Detaching myself from my initial goals and looking at the garden project with a critical perspective, I am overjoyed with the outcome. Although the project did not always follow the agenda I found effective, it created its own agenda, which has ultimately been extremely successful. Recognizing these differences became incredibly important when deciding the diverse strategies to implement when 'healing ourselves and our communities.'

While there are more complex ways the student could extrapolate how cultural, racial, and ethnic background influences worldview and specific notions of time, space, progress, and partnership work, her awareness and emerging analysis demonstrate development within not only the self-knowledge but also the intercultural understanding learning outcome. Demonstration of learning within the intercultural understanding outcome was replicated by another student who wrote, "I realized that I had been measuring ideas using a value system created outside of the context of the cultures that generated those ideas." This understanding was also sought through praxis (illuminated both by the theoretical frameworks in course readings and the experiential learning and critical reflections within internships), enabling these students to recognize how integral intercultural understanding is when working within a community–campus partnership.

While there was demonstrated achievement in the intercultural understanding learning objective in both the spring and summer course assessments, it is not terribly surprising that the students did not appear to grow a great deal more by the end of the summer program. This may be attributed to the fact that deep learning and practice of intercultural understanding takes longer than a semester or summer program to achieve (or articulate), especially considering the disparity that existed between the cultural experience of the students (six middle- to upper-class white women, and one middle-class Latina woman, all of whom were approximately 18 years old) and the community members with whom we partnered (working class Mexican and indigenous youth and elders). The fact that they rated between the "emerging" and "developing" levels of achievement for this outcome (instead of within the "initial" level of gradation) at least demonstrates that the course was successful in moving them along this continuum to some degree (unless, again, they were already at that level when they entered the course, which this assessment did not investigate). I believe that greater growth in this learning outcome is best attained over time, when students participate in ongoing relationships and opportunities to practice ethical relationship building across cultural divides and expand their knowledge of diverse perspectives in examining social issues in the theoretical and practical. Greater training and teaching towards the complexities of "intercultural understanding" could very well also be needed. Follow-up interviews exploring this topic in greater depth could aid in developing better and expanded lesson plans around this topic.

In regards to the final learning objective, "local–global connections," students demonstrated a significant leap in their achievement from spring to summer (from 1.5 to 3.21). This is most likely attributed to the depth of reading, discussion, and writing they participated in during the summer program on the topics of globalization and analyzing the impact of global restructuring on Mexican indigenous healing traditions. It may also be attributed to the intentional framework of the paired-course program, which was meant to lay the groundwork for students to make meaningful theoretical and practical connections between their local and global community engagement fieldwork and coursework.

As a result of the summer abroad program, students deepened their understanding of indigenous Mexican cosmology and practices for healing, as well as how to frame these within discussions of globalization, development, and social change. Furthermore, they demonstrated understanding of the ability to impact global change on a local level, as this student explains:

We must recognize that we do not need to add to pollution by traveling across the world to fight capitalism and its ripple effects. With record levels of violence and poverty, food insecurity, environmental destruction, and racism in our own community, it is apparent that there are plenty of outlets surrounding us in which to engage positively. Responding to our local circumstances with the knowledge of our global impact allows us to build power-to for our communities and empowers others to tear down fences in their locality. Because while fences divide us, make us feel alone, and disconnect us from the Earth and compassion; awareness, activism, and healing is a bridge slowly being built that will reconnect each of us to the rest of humanity, and humanity with the Earth.

The statistically significant increase in all measurements indicates that the linkage across the set of paired courses allowed students to experience strong growth in all categories of the learning outcomes rubric. The summative evaluation of all student papers revealed that they grew significantly in a short period of time, especially in their ability to reflect on their own psychosocial wellbeing, further work they needed to do in their own paths of self-care and personal development, and how these related to their perceived sense of purposefulness in community building and social change. I close this section with a final excerpt from a student paper, demonstrating not only the student's achievement within the learning outcomes framework but also illustrating many of the principal aims of the paired course program:

> Understanding the gaps in our knowledge, the cavities in our consciousness, and the social and economic divides that manifest as a result is necessary to the survival of humanity. We must recognize where fences are built within ourselves and on the land, segregating and marginalizing others. We can then begin to do the work of healing ourselves, and of healing our communities. To learn about the effects of our travels, the impacts of our market consumption, to realize the limits of our knowledge and to begin to respect different ways of knowing, is to begin this healing process.

LIMITATIONS, OPPORTUNITIES, AND LESSONS LEARNED

Just as I hope students use critical reflection assignments as a means of deepening their learning and gaining insight about where the process and outcomes of community engagement can be strengthened, I believe that it is important for me as a teacher and evaluator to engage in a similar process of reflection. As Ash and Clayton describe it, "the designer of applied learning opportunities is best understood as a reflective practitioner herself —one who engages in the same critical reflection that she expects from her students—thereby improving her thinking and action relative to the work of generating, deepening, and documenting student learning in applied learning" (2009, p. 28). As such, this last section will focus on the limitations of and lessons learned from this experience, changes that can inform future curricular and assessment endeavors, and critical questions that remain.

Assessing student learning in community engagement is a challenging task, especially in a course that encourages experiential learning and growth on topics intimately related to a student's personal, moral, and spiritual transformation. Furthermore, measuring how well students grasp the epistemological frameworks that link indigenous knowledge systems, critical pedagogy, and interdisciplinarity, while also evaluating how students transitioned from theoretical understandings to developing a sense of agency in their engagement, requires a sophisticated assessment strategy. Despite the wariness of the accreditation review team to rely on self-reporting data, I feel that triangulation of evaluation data would strengthen the findings of this assessment. This would include an examination of ethnographic evaluation mechanisms, such as formal in-field participant observation and input from community partners on student growth, as well as mixed methods indicators, such as students' journal writing throughout semester and results from student pre- and post-course surveys. This additional raw data did in fact exist, but neither was it given priority during this assessment effort nor did the capacity for evaluating and analyzing exist (evaluation capacity addressed below). A more comprehensive evaluation could be done in the future if support for such efforts became available, but without these additional data and relying on a small sample size, demonstrating growth by evaluating only two sets of written work by a total of seven students weakens the validity of the study findings.

Other issues that may weaken the validity of the direct assessment findings include the inability to determine which aspects of the learning outcomes were ones the students already entered the class fully aware of. I find myself in a similar position as Daniel Shapiro (2012), who noted in his study that "because assignments were not structured for detecting changes in student attitudes, beliefs, and knowledge over the course of the semester, this study was not able to distinguish what knowledge and skills students had before entering the course from what students learned from the course and their service-learning experiences" (p. 54). In addition, even though through the direct assessment of student writing we could often witness the depth a student's understanding of the concepts of the course and general reflection on self-awareness and personal actions, there were many occasions when the students' writings seemed to *assert* that they had learned a great deal rather than *demonstrate* it. This points to the issue of "praxis gap." Students may understand and even be able to articulate a concept, but they do not always demonstrate in their writing if or how they are able to apply it. I am doubtful that reading papers alone allows us to fully verify students' abilities to engage in praxis. Given that praxis itself involves putting theory into action, assessing it would also need to occur in action. I believe that integrating other methods and evidence of learning would address this gap and provide additional validity to the findings.

To make a comprehensive study possible requires rethinking the priorities and responsibilities of the evaluation and community engagement center staff and faculty so that such capacity exists. This would involve complex negotiations and possible re-structuring of college time, resources, and energy towards assessment work. Given that Pitzer's singular "office of institutional research" staff evaluator had recently vacated her position, it was incumbent on my colleagues and I to design and conduct the evaluation in its entirety, though none of us are professional or expert evaluators. Having practitioners who lack evaluation expertise conduct program evaluations is typical within academia (Gelmon et al. 2001), but it can lead to problems with design and execution (as some readers may find in the case presented here). For example, while the direct assessment of final papers was appropriate in measuring the absolute outcomes in the rubric, in retrospect I can see that some of the general course learning outcomes were value-added outcomes, which require pre–post-test assessment. These important lessons were learned from the evaluation process. Nevertheless, I do feel overall that the experience and knowledge each evaluator brought to the table from their years of experience as administrators, teachers, and participants in community engagement programs and evaluations was substantial enough to result in a productive and informative direct assessment model. Providing greater support and resources for assessment on college campuses is a rapidly growing trend (Kuh et al. 2014).[12]

Another insight that resulted from this assessment is that learning in this kind of course is often the kind of growth that emerges over time, once students have had space to ruminate on the impact on their lived experiences. The student learning outcomes measured here are important, but perhaps just the beginning of a longer road toward comprehensive evaluation. As Polin and Keene (2010, p. 30) similarly observe, "meaningful assessment must include the longitudinal; we know that many important impacts are developmental and realized long after the class is over. We also are aware there is significant interest in and a perceived need for expanding this area, as noted by scholars in the field (Sax et al. 1999; Denson et al. 2005; Eyler 2000; Kiely 2005)." Some of the greatest indicators of student learning that I feel most confident about came from one-on-one conversations I had with students several years after they participated in the program and had had significant time and distance in which to digest and integrate the paired-course experience into their daily lives. In particular, I was impressed by how they articulated the impact of that experience in their applications for graduate school and post-baccalaureate fellowships such as the Fulbright and Watson awards. Their reflections in these application essays eloquently demonstrated the many ways this one first year local–global experience had taken root in both their value systems and academic and career aspirations. The takeaway for me in this process has pointed to the essential value of evaluating learning over time (over the course of the semester *and* over the course of student's college careers, if not beyond).

A significant hurdle negotiated in the evaluation effort relates to the broader issue of attempting to quantify deeply qualitative experiences. It was noted in the methodology section the challenge presented by the very subjective and nuanced ways in which students articulated (and demonstrated) their learning and the ways each evaluator negotiated the standard/definition of each outcome. Unpacking these nuances and potential areas for diverse demonstrations and interpretations proved critical to making the evaluation effort as streamlined and coherent as possible, but also underscored the impossibility of totally eradicating the reality that some range of diverse interpretation exists in shared qualitative analysis. This also raises the question if standards for assessing validity and inter-rater reliability that have been lifted from quantitative evaluation protocols can simply be adopted for qualitative evaluation, given the fundamental differences in the nature of the data (data collection, analysis, and sample size, in particular). Simply put, there is a heuristic importance in qualitative assessment that does not conform to all quantitative notions of validity. Other qualitative researchers and evaluators have also contended with how the nuanced, subjective, and qualitative nature of growth on personal, political, academic, and civic areas must be taken into consideration when developing standards for inter-rater reliability and validity scales (Bickman and Rog 2008; Bringing Theory to Practice 2013; Creswell 2013; Denzin and Lincoln 2011; Keyes 2002; Steinberg and Kincheloe 1998; Strand et al. 2003). In this study, we attempted to address the question of norming by conducting a pilot assessment wherein all evaluators rated the first paper and discussed their scores and their approach to their scoring framework to build an interpretation consensus. This initial discussion continued amongst evaluators throughout the assessment process and helped establish a shared understanding of the approach to and interpretation of the qualitative outcomes they assessed.

This use of critical conversations amongst evaluators to inform the assessment process falls into the "social approach to community service learning," as characterized by Cooks et al. (2004), which provides "a foundation for raising questions that place communication as central to learning and situate CSL [community service learning] projects in their social, political, and moral context" (as qtd in Shapiro 2012, p. 53). This context shaped the learning outcomes as they were being developed and informed the interpretation and assessment of them in student writing. Communication of this kind resulted in a critical learning experience for the evaluators, just as communication and context amongst the students, faculty, and community partners who developed the community engagement partnership served to inform learning for all involved. Context also extends to the "ethnographic sensibility" necessary in qualitative assessment so that the assessment effort accurately captures the unique learning and growth that occurs in experiential programs; Polin and Keene remind us that "we can move toward an ethnographic sensibility by framing the questions that drive assessment in a way that recognizes students as complex social actors and allows for the exploration of their lived experiences and sense making" (2010, p. 29).

My involvement (as both teacher and evaluator of the program) may be a red flag to some readers, in that significant time spent with the students in the classroom, in the field, and abroad invariably had an impact on my reading and evaluation of student work. In response to this potential critique, I point to the claim of Polin and Keene that this background knowledge and relationship provides an ethnographic context that can enrich rather than taint the evaluation process:

> The importance of context cannot be overstated. Critiques of collecting stories as data, or of using student journals and/or critical incident reports, are that the results are not generalizable or comparable, and that it is difficult to understand the complete context from which these stories are drawn (Gelmon, Holland, Driscoll, Spring, and Kerrigan, 2001). While this could be true for external evaluators who are not immersed in the communities in which they are doing research, or for those who don't know their students well, this is not the case for those of us involved in sustained, developmental, cohort-based programs employing a relational approach to teaching, where practitioners come to know their students' context to a much greater degree than we might otherwise (Mitchell, Visconti, Keene, and Battistoni, in press). In these situations, practitioner evaluators are in a position to immerse themselves as participant observers in the communities in which they are gathering data. (2010, p. 24)

Employing a relational approach to teaching and having spent a lot of time in the field with my students, I was afforded insight from my own participant observations, reflexive conversations with community partners, students, guest teachers, and other program assistants that offered an informal triangulation from which to verify the findings that emerged in the reading of student papers. As is the practice for most feminist researchers and teachers (Bernal et al. 2006; Hooks 1994; Lather 1986; Madison 2011; Mamidipudi and Gajjala 2008; Riessman 2005; Sudbury and Okazawa-Rey 2015; Tellez 2005; Wolf 1992), I continually practiced a reflective and reflexive practice regarding any bias I held about these students whom I knew so well. To avoid my assessments being either overly empathic or overly critical, I relied on the norming process. Evaluating the same papers as my team and finding my scores to be in line with theirs assured me that the ethnographic and relational approach was a beneficial rather than problematic factor in the analysis process.

CONCLUSION

This case study provides a template for curricular development and evaluation design that brings the concepts of this book directly into practice for those who teach or administer community engagement programs. The local–global paired course model integrates the theoretical frameworks (e.g., asset-based community development, critical pedagogy, indigenous knowledge, healing justice) that were explored in Chap. 2 of this book with the pedagogical approaches (including self-reflection and contemplative and healing practices) examined in Chap. 3 and the community–campus partnership development guidelines and class room activities presented in Chaps. 4 and 5. Bringing to this a unique evaluation design and assessment rubrics for capturing student learning further contributes to readers' abilities to apply the main concepts of this book in practice. While obviously this program was unique in its small size, funding support, rich resources in terms of knowledgeable and willing community and college partners, and specific approach to evaluation (through direct assessment of student writing), I believe the heart of this project is one that may resonate with a growing number of engaged scholars, evaluators, and teachers interested in linking self-development and community engagement in local–global contexts.

NOTES

1. This description of the curricular rationale for the local–global paired course program was originally written as part of the College's grant proposal.
2. The seven students chosen to participate in the summer course were all completing their first year of college, which was one of the criteria of the Mellon grant that supported the local–global paired course program (this was seen as a strategy to address sophomore retention issues).
3. Although the students in this 2010 program would only be engaged in these communities for a short time, I had been developing relationships with these community partners and co-educators in Claremont since 2008 and those in Mexico since 2006. I had worked actively with these community partners over the years to sustain trust, honesty, flexibility, and shared intentions in our collaborations, following the qualities of community–campus partnership development outlined in Chap. 4. Our previous work together established the necessary rapport and friendship that would allow for critical, contemplative community engagement to occur in the short time frame of the paired course program.
4. The Pitzer College-Western University annual Native Youth to College program emerged at the beginning stages of our Native community–campus partnerships in 2008, as a result of direct charges by our two elder advisors, RobertJohn Knapp and Tony Cerda, to "get our kids to college!" Within months, Pitzer alum and Community Engagement Center staff member, Scott Scoggins, had crafted a program, under their guidance, and raised funds

from our dean of faculty to put on the first program. This program is a 2-week-long residential experience for 20–25 Native youth and 5 Native mentors from across the country who spend equal time in affirming native traditions and preparing students mentally, emotionally, academically, and logistically for getting into college. Building on another decolonizing/intercultural practice that occurs year long, locally selected "Elders in Residence" share history, traditions, stories, plant medicine, and cultural values in ceremony, lectures, and outings to local cultural sites. The program also includes an intensive creative writing workshop series (preparing students to write their personal essay for college applications), an intensive college application workshop (engaging students in drafting their Common App template), a community health sciences lecture series (providing access to medical researchers and practitioners in the field), as well as multi-day fieldtrips to local Native villages to learn crafts, history, myths, songs, and ceremonial traditions from participating local tribes. Student evaluations over the 9 years of this program have been consistently positive, reporting both strong academic learning and cultural affirmation, and a sense of support to continue "walking in two worlds" so that going to college does not necessitate losing one's cultural lens, roots, and knowledge base (Ball 2004; Gruenewald 2003). The other programs are not annual but have taken place at Pitzer when funding and coordination allows: three distinct Native American film festivals and speakers series took place at Pitzer in 2008, 2009, and 2011, screening films by, about, and for native peoples, which were chosen, introduced, and facilitated in post-screening discussions by local tribal youth and scholars in partnership with Pitzer College students and faculty. Additionally, Pitzer hosted three different Tribal Nations-Academic Community Partnerships Conferences, which took place in 2010, 2011, and 2013, with presentations from Native and non-Native scholars and students on issues relating to native science, indigenous knowledge systems, and community–campus partnerships.

5. Literature that supports these claims and practices include Alfred 2005; Alfred and Corntassel 2005; Apffel-Marglin and PRATEC 1998; Barnhardt and Kawagley 2005; Cajete 2000; Delgado and Gomez 2003; Kirkness and Barnhardt 1991; Mankiller 2004; Moore 2006; Prakash 1999; Semali and Kincheloe 1999; Shiva 1993; Smith 1999; Steinman 2011; and Wilson 2008.

6. This summer program could not have been possible (nor such a success) without the fine work of my collaborator, friend, and colleague, Judith Estela Roman. As a curandera (healer), lawyer, peace studies scholar, and community organizer, she has had tremendous impact on the lives of many and we were very fortunate to have her partnership and collaboration in this effort.

7. See Ash and Clayton 2009; Driscoll et al. 1998; Eyler et al. 1997; Eyler et al. 2001; Ferrari and Worrall 2000; Galura et al. 2004; Gelmon et al.

1998; Glass et al. 2011; Gray et al. 1999; Honnet and Poulsen 1989; Markus et al. 1993; Miron and Moely 2006; Myers-Lipton 1998; Polin and Keene 2010; Sandy 2007; Sax and Astin 1997; Shapiro 2012; Shavelson 2007; Strage 2004; Strand et al. 2003; Vernon and Ward 1999.

8. A long line of practitioners have wrestled with these evaluation challenges ever since service learning first gained popularity in the late 1980s, then was catapulted forward by the charge given through the Wingspread Conference to foment evaluation efforts (Gelmon et al. 2001). I drew on the following resources: AAC&U Liberal Education and America's Promise 2012; Bacon 2002; Boyte and Farr 1997; Costa and Kallick 2000; Eyler and Giles 1996; Eyler et al. 2001; Giles et al. 1991; Markus et al. 1993; National Survey on Student Engagement 2008; Oden and Casey 2007; Overbaugh and Schultz 2012; Ryff and Keyes 1995; Tufts College 2012).

9. The creation of these rubrics and assessment activities were part of my doctoral research (Hicks 2009) and informed by Pitzer's WASC (accreditation) review which encouraged more direct assessment of student learning, especially in the areas of local/global action and study. The original student learning outcomes rubric, Table 6.1, is a synthesized version of a longer list I created of learning outcomes, inspired by my own research findings (Hicks 2009) as well as a review of the literature on student learning outcomes in service learning/community engagement. In the fashion of action research, I introduced this list and received considerable feedback and editing from my colleague, Sandra Mayo, Tricia Morgan, and, later, other members of our evaluation team for this project, all of which resulted in an improved and more refined rubric. For the second rubric concentrating on the local–global course program specifically, another round of (minor) revisions occurred with the input of my study abroad colleagues, Michael Ballagh and Mike Donahue and (then) associate dean, Kerry Walk and (then) assistant director of academic curriculum, Katrina Sitar (resulting in Table 6.2). I thank all of these colleagues, as well as graduate assistant, Nancy Arguirre, for their keen feedback during this process and I thank the authors of the many reports and articles whose ideas in part contributed to the original list, as listed in the previous endnote.

10. This assessment project was written about in Pitzer's *Effectiveness Review Report for WASC* (2010).

11. The student is referring to Beath 2005.

12. Indeed, this has already begun happening at Pitzer College, which has bolstered support and staff for the office of institutional research and academic assessment, due in large part to the recommendations of the most recent accreditation review.

REFERENCES

Alfred, T. (2005). *Wasáse: Indigenous Pathways of Action and Freedom.* Peterborough, ON: Broadview Press.

Alfred, T., & Corntassel, J. (2005). Being Indigenous: Resurgences against Contemporary Colonialism. *Government and Opposition, 40,* 597–614.

Apffel-Marglin, F., & PRATEC. (1998). *The spirit of regeneration: Andean culture confronting western notions of development.* New York: Zed Books.

Armstrong, J. (2006). Community: Sharing one skin. In J. Mander & V. Tauli-Corpuz (Eds.), *Paradigm wars: Indigenous peoples' resistance to globalization.* San Francisco: Sierra Club Books.

Ash, S. L., & Clayton, P. H. (2009). Generating, deepening, and documenting learning: The power of critical reflection in applied learning. *Journal of Applied Learning in Higher Education., 1,* 25–48.

Association of American Colleges and Universities. (2012). *Liberal education and America's promise. An introduction to LEAP.* Retrieved December 18, 2012 from http://www.aacu.org/LEAP/index.cfm.

Bacon, N. (2002). Differences in faculty and community partners' theories of learning. *Michigan Journal of Community Service Learning, 9*(1).

Barnhardt, R., & Kawagley, A. O. (2005). Indigenous knowledge systems and Alaska Native ways of knowing. *Anthropology & education quarterly, 36*(1), 8–23.

Bickman, L., & Rog, D. J. (Eds.), (2008). *The Sage handbook of applied social research methods.* Thousand Oaks, CA: Sage Publications.

Boyte, H. D., & Farr, H. (1997). The work of citizenship and the problem of service-learning. In R. Battistoni & W. Hudson (Eds.), *Experiencing citizenship: Concepts and models of service-learning in political science* (pp. 35–48). Stylus: Sterling VA.

Bringing Theory to Practice. (2013). *The well-being and flourishing of students: Considering well-being, and its connection to learning and civic engagement, as central to the mission of higher education.* Washington, D.C: AAC&U.

Cajete, G. (2000). *Native science: Natural laws of interdependence.* Santa Fe, NM: Clear Light Publishers.

Cooks, L., Scharrer, E., & Castaneda Paredes, M. (2004). Toward a social approach to learning in community service learning. *Michigan Journal of Community Service Learning, 10*(2).

Costa, A. L., & Kallick, B. (2000). *Discovering & exploring habits of mind. A developmental series.* Alexandria, VA: Association for Supervision and Curriculum Development.

Creswell, J. W. (2013). *Qualitative inquiry and research design: Choosing among five approaches.* Thousand Oaks, CA: Sage.

Delgado, F. & Gomez. F. (2003). *Knowledge and belief systems in Latin America.* In B. Haverkort, K. V. Hooft, & W. Hiemstra, (Eds.), *Ancient roots, new shoots, endogenous development in practice.* London: Zed Books.

Denson, N., Vogelgesang, L., & Saenz, V. (2005). *Can service learning and a college climate of service lead to increased political engagement after college.* UCLA: Higher Education Research Institute.

Denzin, N. K. & Lincoln, Y. S. (2011). *The sage handbook of qualitative research.* Sage.

Eyler, J., Giles, D. E., & Schmiede, A. (1996). *A practitioner's guide to reflection in service-learning: Student voices & reflections.* Nashville, TN: Vanderbilt University.

Eyler, J., Giles, D. E., Jr., & Braxton, J. (1997). The impact of service-learning on college students. *Michigan Journal of Community Service Learning, 4,* 5–15.

Eyler, J. S. (2000). What do we most need to know about the impact of service-learning on student learning? *Michigan Journal of Community Service Learning,* 11–17.

Eyler, J., Giles, D. E., Jr., Stenson, C. M., & Gray, C. J. (2001). *At a glance: What we know about the effects of service-learning on college students, faculty, institutions and communities, 1993–2000* (3rd ed.). Nashville, TN: Vanderbilt University.

Ferrari, J. R. & Worrall, L. (2000). Assessments by community agencies: How 'the other side sees service-learning. *Michigan Journal of Community Service. Learning, 7*(1).

Galura, J., Pasque, P. A., Schoem, D., & Howard, J. (2004). *Engaging the whole of service-learning, diversity, and learning communities.* Ann Arbor, MI: OCSL Press.

Gelmon, S. B., Holland, B. A., Seifer, S. D., Shinnamon, A., & Connors, K. (1998). Community-university partnerships for mutual learning. *Michigan Journal of Community Service Learning, 5,* 97–107.

Gelmon, S. B., Holland, B., Driscoll, A., Spring, A., & Kerrigan, S. (2001). *Assessing service-learning and civic engagement: Principles and techniques.* Boston, MA: Campus Compact.

Giles, D. E., Honnet, E., & Migliore, S. (1991). *Setting the agenda for effective research in combining service and learning in the 1990's.* Raleigh, NC: National Society of Experiential Education.

Glass, C. R., Doberneck, D. M., & Schweitzer, J. H. (2011). Unpacking faculty engagement: The types of activities faculty members report as publicly engaged scholarship during promotion and tenure. *Journal of Higher Education Outreach and Engagement, 15*(1), 7–30.

Gray, M. J., Ondaatje, E. H., & Zakaras, L. (1999). *Combining service and learning in higher education: Learn and serve America, higher education.* Santa Monica, CA: RAND.

Hicks, T. (2009). *Engaged scholarship and education: A case study on the pedagogy of social change.* Unpublished Dissertation. Claremont, CA: Claremont Claremont Graduate University.

Honnet, E. P., & Poulsen, S. J. (1989). *A wingspread special report.* Racine, WI: The Johnson Foundation.

hooks, b. (1994). *Teaching to transgress: Education as the practice of freedom.* New York, NY: Routledge.

Keyes, C. L. (2002). The mental health continuum: From languishing to flourishing in life. *Journal of health and social behavior,* 207–222.

Kiely, R. (2005). A transformative learning model for service-learning: A longitudinal case study. *Michigan Journal of Community Service Learning, 12*(1).

Kirkness, V. J. & Barnhardt, R. (1991). First nations and higher education: The four R's-respect, relevance, reciprocity, responsibility. *Journal of American Indian Education,* 1–15.

Kuh, G. D., Jankowski, N., Ikenberry, S. O., & Kinzie, J. (2014). *Knowing what students know and can do: The current state of student learning outcomes assessment in US colleges and universities.* Urbana, IL: University of Illinois and Indiana University, National Institute for Learning Outcomes Assessment (NILOA).

Lather, P. (1986). Research as praxis. *Harvard educational review, 56*(3), 257–278.

Longley, M. J. et al. 1998. *Assessing the impact of service learning: A workbook of strategies and methods.* Center for Academic Excellence. Portland, OR: Portland State University.

Madison, D. S. (2011). *Critical ethnography: Method, ethics, and performance.* Thousand Oaks: Sage.

Mamidipudi, A., & Gajjala, R. (2008). Juxtaposing handloom weaving and modernity: building theory through praxis. *Development in Practice, 18*(2), 235–244.

Mankiller, W. (2004). *Every day is a good day: Reflections by contemporary indigenous women.* Golden, CO: Fulcrum Publishing.

Markus, G. B., Howard, J. P., & King, D. C. (1993). Integrating community service and classroom instruction enhances learning: Results from an experiment. *Educational evaluation and policy analysis, 15*(4), 410–419.

Miron, D., & Moely, B. E. (2006). Community agency voice and benefit in service-learning. *Michigan Journal of Community Service Learning, 12*(2), 27–37.

Moore, M. (Ed.). (2006). *Eating fire, tasting blood: Anthology of the American Indian holocaust.* New York: Thunder Mouth Press.

Myers-Lipton, S. J. (1998). Effect of a comprehensive service-learning program on college students' civic responsibility. *Teaching Sociology,* 243–258.

National Survey on Student Engagement. (2008). *Promoting engagement for all students: The imperative to look within, 2008 results.* Retrieved December 20,

2012 from http://nsse.iub.edu/NSSE_2008_Results/docs/withhold/NSSE2008_Results_revised_11-14-2008.pdf.

Oden, R. S., & Casey, T. A. (2007). Advancing service learning as a transformative method for social justice work. In J. Z. Calderon (Ed.), *Race, poverty, and social justice: Multidisciplinary perspectives through service learning* (pp. 3–22). Sterling, VA: Stylus Publishing.

Overbaugh, R. C. & Schultz, L. (2012). *Bloom's taxonomy.* Retrieved August 7, 2016 from http://www.odu.edu/educ/roverbau/Bloom/blooms_taxonomy.htm.

Pitzer College. (2010). *Educational Effectiveness Review.* Pitzer college report for Western association of schools and colleges (WASC). Retrieved March 7, 2016 from http://pitweb.pitzer.edu/institutional-research/wasc-accreditation/.

Polin, D. K., & Keene, A. S. (2010). Bringing an ethnographic sensibility to service-learning assessment. *Michigan Journal of Community Service Learning, 16*(2), 22–37.

Prakash, M. S. (1999). Indigenous knowledge systems—Ecological literacy through initiation into people's science. In L. M. Semali & J. L. Kincheloe (Eds.), *What is indigenous knowledge? Voices from the academy* (pp. 157–178). New York: Falmer press.

Riessman, C. K. (2005). Exporting ethics: A narrative about narrative research in South India. *Health, 9*(4), 473–490.

Ryff, C. D., & Keyes, C. L. M. (1995). The structure of psychological well-being revisited. *Journal of Personality and Social Psychology, 69*(4), 719.

Sandy, M. (2007). *Community voices: A California campus compact study on partnerships.* Hayward, CA: California Campus Compact.

Sax, L. J., Astin, A. W., & Avalos, J. (1999). Long-term effects of volunteerism during the undergraduate years. *The review of higher education, 22*(2), 187–202.

Sax, L. (1997). The benefits of service: Evidence from undergraduates. *Educational record,* 25.

Semali, L., & Kincheloe, J. L. (1999). *What is indigenous knowledge?: Voices from the academy.* New York, NY: Routledge.

Shapiro, D. F. (2012). Collaborative faculty assessment of service-learning student work to improve student and faculty learning and course design. *Michigan Journal of Community Service Learning, 19*(1), 44–58.

Shavelson, R. J., Schneider, C. G. & Shulman, L. S. (2007). *A brief history of student learning assessment: How we got where we are and a proposal for where to go next.* Association of American Colleges and Universities.

Shiva, V. (1993). *Monocultures of the mind: Perspectives on biodiversity and biotechonology.* London: Zed.

Smith, L. T. (1999). *Decolonizing methodologies: Research and indigenous peoples.* London: Zed books.

Steinberg, S. R., & Kincheloe, J. L. (1998). *Students as researchers: Creating classrooms that matter*. London: Falmer Press.

Steinman, E. (2011). "Making space": Lessons from collaborations with tribal nations. *Michigan Journal of Community Service Learning, 18*(1), 5–19.

Strage, A. (2004). Long-term academic benefits of service-learning: When and where do they manifest themselves?. *College Student Journal, 38*(2), 257.

Strand, K. J., Cutforth, N., Stoecker, R., Marullo, S., & Donohue, P. (2003). *Community-based research and higher education: Principles and practices*. San Francisco, CA: Wiley.

Sudbury, J., & Okazawa-Rey, M. (2015). *Activist scholarship: Antiracism, feminism, and social change*. New York, NY: Routledge.

Téllez, M. (2005). Doing research at the borderlands: Notes from a Chicana feminist ethnographer. *Chicana/Latina Studies*, 46–70.

Tufts College, Medford, MA. (2012). *Tisch college of citizenship and public service. Student civic learning outcomes*. Received December 18, 2012 from http://activecitizen.tufts.edu/wp-content/uploads/learning_outcomes_13.pdf.

Vernon, A., & Ward, K. (1999). Campus and community partnerships: Assessing impacts and strengthening connections. *Michigan Journal of Community Service Learning, 6*, 30–37.

Villenas, S., Godinez, F., Delgado Bernal, D., & Elenes, A. (2006). *Chicana/Latina education in everyday life: Feminista perspectives on pedagogy and epistemology*. New York, NY: SUNY Press.

Wilson, S. (2008). *Research is ceremony: Indigenous research methods*. Black Point: Fernwood Publishing.

Wolf, M. (1992). *A thrice-told tale: Feminism, postmodernism, and ethnographic responsibility*. San Jose, CA: Stanford University Press.

CHAPTER 7

Transforming Our Ourselves, Transforming Institutions

From theoretical frameworks to mindfulness practices, from hands-on classroom activities to practical evaluation designs, this book has traversed myriad dimensions of the Critical, Contemplative Community Engagement model. Practitioners of community engagement will hopefully walk away from reading this book with new or sharpened tools to help their classrooms and communities more thoughtfully *know peace and know justice*. Using social justice-oriented community engagement approaches may also enable them to more effectively, ethically, and sustainably do the work to *create peace and justice*, not only in the world at large, but just as importantly in their own lives and in the various communities they partake in. The actions that activists, accompanists, and accomplices take against injustice create greater senses of agency, connection, healing, and hope. As such, the goals and purposes of social movements are broadened to include not simply major wins in policy or culture wars, but intimate gains in the quality of life, sense of wellbeing, self-realization, and shared healing that can result for those involved in them.

To personally and collectively, politically and spiritually, embody this way of knowing peace and justice requires that we intentionally exchange complacency and despair with hope and compassion. Just as we are required to show up at the frontlines of our shared struggles, we must also prioritize practices of grounding and healing ourselves and our communities. The most challenging demand yet is to look hard at the biases, hatred, violence, and ignorance that we find intolerable in others as mirrors for where we hold these things within ourselves. It is here that we can

© The Author(s) 2018   221
T. Hicks Peterson, *Student Development and Social Justice*,
https://doi.org/10.1007/978-3-319-57457-8_7

become more accountable to the next generation's demands to create more inclusive and healing spaces, behaviors, policies, and practices. It is also our responsibility to provide young people with the tools— including intellectual and political understanding, self-awareness, and hope —needed to take society to the next stage of peace and justice. Along with academic achievement, colleges and universities are thus charged with supporting the moral, civic, and emotional development of our young people. Community engagement practices provide a critical pathway for addressing student development and wellbeing, which are fundamental values of higher education. As Swaner explains, this notion is gaining traction in colleges and universities nationwide:

> Most institutions, upon re-examining their mission statements, find that their goals address not only intellectual aims, but also the whole development of students as well as the realization of their full potential – both of which encompass students' mental health and well-being. Institutions also identify goals related to students' becoming productive, responsible members of the larger communities to which they will belong – which likewise pertain to students' civic development. It is against this backdrop that the question arises of how *engaged learning*, a central facet of curricular reform in higher education, may be related to both of these goals. (2005, p. 2)

While there are some key scholars investigating the relevance of student development and wellbeing to intellectual skill-building and community engagement (Villenas et al. 2006; Finley 2012; Flanagan and Bundick 2011; Ginwright 2001; Harward 2012; Hooks 2003; Owens Ryff and Keyes 1995; Swaner 2005), ways of teaching and assessing these outcomes require further exploration. My research finds that we need more nuanced tools of evaluation for assessing subtle shifts in the beliefs, values, perceptions, self-identity, pur-posefulness, and sense of responsibility related to the personal and social changes that occur during community engagement experiences. Some quantitative standardized scales have emerged to assess student "flourishing" (e.g., Keyes 2009) and qualitative evaluation tools are also being developed (Finley and McNair 2013). However, we are still just in the beginning phases of comprehensively tackling assessment of student wellbeing in the academic community service learning context (Finley 2013). We also need further assessments on how service-learning outcomes differ depending on the posi-tionality of the student (Simons et al. 2011; McNair and Finley 2013; Harper et al. 2005; Machtmes et al. 2009).

Beyond increasing assessment efforts, institutions of higher education must become clearer about the kinds of engagement they encourage and what sorts of community outcomes they seek to support. Westheimer and Kahne articulate three categories that usually come to the fore when people working in higher education ask the question, "What kind of citizen do we need to support an effective democratic society?" These include (1) the "personally responsible citizen" who acts responsibly within the community by paying taxes, obeying laws, and volunteering to lend a hand in times of crisis; (2) the "participatory citizen" who is an active member of community organizations and organizes community efforts to care for those in need; and (3) the "justice-oriented citizen" who critically assesses social, political, and economic structures to see beyond surface causes and seeks out areas of injustice to address (2004, p. 2). Essentially, Westheimer and Kahne ask whether schools are creating programs to nurture the first form of citizenship that "contributes food to a food drive," the second form that "helps to organize a food drive," or the third form that "explores why people are hungry and acts to solve root causes" (ibid.). Hopefully, this book's examination of the limitations of charity models of community engagement and the benefits of establishing social justice-oriented community engagement models has given readers a foundation upon which to stimulate institutional discussions around such priorities and goals. Institutional decisions about what kind of community engagement model should be promoted will influence student learning, the outcomes of community partnerships, and attempts at social change.

While evaluating the impact of community engagement on the communities themselves has burgeoned over the last 20 years,[1] institutions of higher education still do not treat community outcomes as important as student learning. Community partners and the impacts on communities are still not given as much oversight, assessment, funding, or overall attention. That community engagement is still seen primarily as an avenue for student learning rather than benefit for the community is a potentially harmful reality of this practice.

We must emphasize that the notion of "social responsibility" does not apply solely to students but to the institutions of higher education themselves. The original aims of higher education to support holistic student development, democratic participation, and the public good can all be bolstered by dedicating college and university resources to community engagement. Given that nearly all institutions of higher education articulate the importance of contributing to civic responsibility in their original charters, school administrators can draw on institutional mission statements as evidence of the value of integrating community-based teaching, learning, and scholarship in all facets of college life (Peterson 2015). I believe that once institutions of higher education are seen as civic actors themselves, ones that have a civic responsibility to the communities in which they are embedded, they will then more distinctly value the community engagement work of their students, faculty, and staff.

COMMUNITY ENGAGEMENT IN INSTITUTIONAL POLICY AND PRACTICE

Taking such a commitment seriously means recognizing and embedding community engagement in every facet of college life. More often than not, these efforts become siloed in certain departments or community engagement centers rather than seen as integral parts of the identity of the college. We need to weave community engagement into the educational objectives, requirements, and classroom curricula across all disciplines as well as in student affairs programs and advancement campaigns throughout the college. Essentially, we need to move community engagement from the "Center" to the "center" of each institution of higher education (Harwood 2012). Service-learning pioneer, Nadinne Cruz, has long advised to integrate community engagement into every strategic plan of every department (Cruz 2009). It should not be an activity that only receives a smattering of staff attention or institutional funding in distinct classes here or there. Rather, it should be integrated into an institution's values and practices such that it seeps into every facet of its functioning. The infrastructure (i.e., resources, expertise, and capacity) to implement these practices must also be made available.

More concretely valuing and institutionalizing community engagement in colleges and universities will play out differently for the different constituents therein. For students, this could mean recognizing the value of community engagement activities in their transcripts, requiring community engagement courses for graduation, making community engagement a component of majors or minors or theme of first year seminars, or developing a community engagement certificate. For staff, this could mean providing sufficient employees and resources to create, manage, oversee, support, fundraise, and assess the work of community engagement that occurs between the school and the community. For faculty, it would definitely mean recognizing the value of community engagement activities in hiring, tenure, and promotion reviews. If community engagement is not stated and practiced as an institutional priority in hiring, faculty who believe in and want to integrate this form of pedagogy and scholarship will not be encouraged to apply for positions at the institution and those who are already there will not be rewarded for that work once up for review. If policy language for faculty reviews does not concretely highlight the value and importance of engaged/public/activist scholarship and teaching, faculty will not feel encouraged or supported in incorporating these approaches into their classes, scholarship, and service.

Given the criticality of this last point, an in-depth exploration is provided for how institutions of higher education can move beyond recognizing the "extra" work involved for faculty who teach community-engaged courses or do community-engaged scholarship to examining the different ways a community engagement approach will impact the nature, timeline, disciplinary boundaries, and outputs of said scholarship. This involves a cultural shift around the priorities of faculty output. The current common understanding is that "untenured faculty are more likely to receive promotion for publishing in peer-reviewed journals than for showing an active commitment to addressing community problems (Freeman and Richards 1996)" (Calleson et al. 2005, p. 1). Leaders in the field, Sherril Gelmon, Catherine Jordon, and Sarena Seifer, summarize the principle challenges to recognizing community-engaged scholarship in higher education:

> While scholarly journals are critical for communication with academic audiences, they are poor vehicles for communicating with practitioners, policymakers, community leaders and the public. Effective CES [community-engaged scholarship] demands that the scholar produce diverse forms of scholarship in innovative formats, such as documentaries, websites, briefs, or manuals- for non-academic audiences and uses. But work presented in those formats may not be recognized as serious scholarship by academic peers.

> The work of community-engaged scholars can be undervalued in a number of other ways as well. Sometimes other faculty, academic administrators, and committee members or external reviewers in the promotion and tenure processes assume that the rigor of community-engaged work suffers as a result of what are considered best practices in community engagement, such as shared decision-making. Sometimes community-engaged scholars are questioned about the amount of time they spend in the community during

partnership formation, which can require a lengthy process of building relationships and trust. (2013, p. 59)

Advocating for the inclusion of community engagement efforts as valued components of a college education (both for students and for faculty) goes against the more traditional realm of academia. It invariably requires all constituents to be involved in strategic discussions and concerted efforts to make institutional changes. Renegotiating priorities and the terms of required outputs must be wrestled with first in dialogue amongst practitioners and power holders (faculty and administrators) in order for change to occur in the policy and practice of faculty assessment. Such conversations must directly address how flexible, nuanced, and progressive these bodies are willing to be in how they define and measure the impact of scholarship, how they are planning to recognize and evaluate diverse outputs and forms of scholarship, and how willing they are to embrace the transdisciplinary, shared authorship typical of community engagement scholarship (Ellison and Eatman 2008; Glassick et al. 1997; Cavallaro 2016).

Given that each campus will, according to its own culture, climate, mission, and priorities, grapple differently with how best to define and support community-engaged scholarship and teaching, there is no one perfect policy that will change everything. In the opening essay of a recent issue of the *Journal of Metropolitan Universities* that was dedicated entirely to the subject of engaged scholarship, editor Claire Cavallaro insisted that multiple facets had to be explored in the process of institutionalizing engaged scholarship, including:

> the ways that institutions define engaged scholarship and differentiate it from (or integrate it into) the review of teaching, service, and conventional forms of scholarship; how engaged scholarship is presented and evaluated, including the extent to which it results in "traditional" outputs and who is defined as "peers" in peer review; challenges encountered and strategies that have been successful in achieving institutional change; and the outcomes and consequences, in terms of impact on institutional performance, academic culture, or impacts on faculty, students, and communities. (2016, p. 3)

I believe that a cultural shift around this issue is just as important as the endpoint of policy development. Policy matters less when stakeholders are not interested in practicing it. To arrive at a cohesive, inclusive, and valued understanding of engaged scholarship and teaching and alter evaluation policies and campus culture accordingly requires broad organizational change. Given the slow-moving pace of change for institutions of higher education, this can feel like an impossible challenge. Parker Palmer, who has worked both inside academia and community-building initiatives, speaks eloquently of the need to relinquish our defeatism at the seemingly immovable nature of academia. Indeed, to change our institutions, he encourages utilizing a movement model which "abandons the logic of organizations in order to gather the power necessary to rewrite the logic of organizations" (Palmer 1992, p. 12). He insists that such change must start small and intimately in order to gain traction collectively and result in significant, sustainable change organizationally. Thus, cultivating wellbeing and justice from the inside out is not just relevant to students and the communities they partner with, but also to faculty and administrators as they work to construct institutions that will advance goals of increasing knowledge for personal and public good with integrity and purpose.

The model for educational reform that Parker Palmer suggests begins not on the level of policy or organizational reform but directly with individual faculty who find it no longer tenable to live "a divided life." Simply put, a divided life makes individuals choose to adhere to professional expectations that do not align with the components of their vocation that make them feel purposeful, whole, and engaged. As Palmer explains:

> For these teachers, the decision is really quite simple: Caring about teaching and about students brings them health as persons, and to collaborate in a denial of that fact is to collaborate in a diminishment of their own lives. They refuse any longer to act outwardly in contradiction to something they know inwardly to be true that teaching, and teaching well, is a source of identity for them. They understand that this refusal may evoke the wrath of the gods of the professions, who are often threatened when we reach for personal wholeness. But still, they persist.

Choosing to stop leading a divided life is an intimate decision. Each individual must wrestle with their own sense of integrity that guides their pedagogical and scholarly approaches. However, it gains momentum when individuals make this shift together and build collective power in the process:

Faculty who have decided to live "divided no more" are often unaware of each other's existence so weak are the communal structures of the academy, and so diffident are intellectuals about sharing such "private" matters. It is difficult for faculty to seek each other out for mutual support. But it is clear from all great movements that mutual support is vital if the inner decision is to be sustained and if the movement is to take its next crucial steps toward gathering power.

Where support groups do exist, they assume a simple form and function. Six or eight faculty from a variety of departments agree to meet on a regular but manageable schedule (say, once every 2 weeks) simply to talk about [community-engaged] teaching. (The mix of departments is important because of the political vulnerability faculty often feel within their own guild halls.) They talk about what they teach, how they teach, what works and what doesn't, and most important of all the joys and pains of being a teacher. The conversations are informal, confidential, and, above all, candid. (p. 13)

Rich understandings of what we mean by engaged teaching and scholarship, or perhaps more accurately the many things that community engagement can mean across many fields and pedagogical approaches, emerge from these conversations. It is a place where people give voice to the kinds of support and rewards they need to be able to do this work well.

Finding personal support first in such a community of practice is tantamount to having the energy and power to seek broader institutional support. In these intimate supportive spaces, individuals come to see that the personal challenges they face in order to feel whole, supported, and undivided are actually socially shared and politically constructed. These challenges are sustained by structural powers and historical constructs around the "accepted" aims of teaching, learning, and research. This circles back to the activist mantra that emerged from the Feminist movement: "the personal is political." The personal must shift into public demands so a movement for change can be mobilized:

As support groups develop, individuals learn to translate their private concerns into public issues, and they grow in their ability to give voice to these issues in public and compelling ways. To put it more precisely, support groups help people discover that their problems are not "private" at all, but have been occasioned by public conditions and therefore require public remedies. (p. 14)

I have taken part in many such conversations over the years, some intimate and voluntary and others as part of formal committee meetings and strategic planning sessions, but only recently have I seen these conversations come to fruition in major policy and cultural changes. Starting in 2009 at Pitzer College, I gathered a small group of new and veteran community-engaged teachers and scholars in a regularly held support group (the "Community Engagement Faculty Network") to discuss practices, hopes, disappointments, and dreams for how to engage more effectively in community engagement teaching, service, and scholarship and how our school could better support us. Those conversations organically evolved into an effort to mobilize our personal concerns into public demands requiring public remedies. Iterations of this original support group went on to co-author white papers and proposals around the value of the work of engaged scholarship and teaching. As members of this academic community, we saw community engagement as a priority for the university that would have broader political, social, and community meaning and impact if implemented. These discussions and the resulting advocacy on the part of a growing group of faculty members eventually mobilized a number of significant changes to school policies.

Pitzer altered the conventional reward systems so that engaged and public scholarship and teaching is now distinctly valued and recognized in promotion and tenure review policies. Simultaneous to this effort, a small faculty task force also conducted an in-depth evaluation of and change to our student graduation requirements so that they now include two required social justice and community engagement courses, and two intercultural understanding (local and global) courses, all of which are held to a rigorous set of criteria and student learning outcomes. We also made a series of changes to better integrate the values of community engagement into our courses and programs on campus. We hired a long-time community partner, who is a local community organizer and educator, as a visiting professor who teaches community-organizing and "radical" civic engagement classes and integrated into the institution's long-term strategic plan the promise to create a community-organizing institute within the college's community engagement center. We increased college access programming with underrepresented first-generation students in the area (a 2-week residential program aimed specifically at Native American youth and a semester-long program aimed specifically at women in recovery). We trained numerous Pitzer students and local community members in a variety of courses in qualitative research methodology so that research projects could be co-driven by community members (from research design to data collection, analysis, and authorship), thus actualizing collaborative, reciprocal, and power-sharing ideals.[2] We transformed our mandatory ethics training and orientations for student who engage in local communities (through courses, work study, or as volunteers) to flag larger structural issues of inequality in the communities and our relationships with them, and the issues students need to be mindful of as they navigate their participation, reflect on their positionality, and consider how they can prevent inadvertently causing harm. Additionally, we put more focus on ways to link grassroots or service participation in communities with efforts that will effect public policy or structural change (for example, by offering workshops to help students cultivate skills for more effective messaging, organizing, and activism, implementing a "letter to an elected official" policy writing competition, and a rigorous, student-led voter registration effort).[3]

This shift from individual commitment to institutional commitment took many years and did not occur without strife or upending patience. Some of these changes have been swift and significant, while others are small and still lagging. But true to Palmer's model of living an undivided life and engaging a movement model of change, such changes reinforce the notion that the self-actualizing of our social and political visions is a crucial first step for collective and organization change. Those interested not only in the processes for making such changes, but also in the actual products that they yield are referred to Appendices III and IV, where I provide Pitzer's revised tenure and review and graduation requirement policies demonstrating how the college now recognizes and values the work of community-based teaching, research, and service.

Such is the nature of academia that the repercussions of most institutional transformations take a long time to translate into positive benefits to local communities. Nevertheless, the concrete changes listed above exemplify some of what can be done to bridge short-term, service-oriented collaborations into long-term, social justice efforts for power shifting and social change. By changing our institutions and establishing social justice-oriented student learning and community impact goals, we can disarm some of the hidden landmines of service-learning programs and build community partnerships based on shared visions and power.

LIMITATIONS AND OPPORTUNITIES

This book has attempted to operate on many levels: exploring individual identity and sense of purpose as it relates to impacting broader change, and the very real need to embody peacefulness and wellbeing within before attempting to advance it in the world. It has also aimed to provide concrete strategies and models for making that change in the world, ones that invest in a community's own assets, relationships, and ability to grow amid and through differences, despair, and devastation. Furthermore, the book has aimed to bring the entirety of this effort into the work of colleges and universities, as both a tool and responsibility of education itself. Weaving together these multiple topics, theoretical frameworks, and disciplines brings a necessary (and otherwise lacking) integrated analysis to the field, though perhaps at the cost of a more nuanced, in-depth exploration of each individual topic. I see the interdependence of each of these facets clearly. I also see that each one is deserving of its own book so that readers could take a deep dive into all the theories, contested ground, and intersecting analysis that exist around these distinct and linked topics.

While the case can be made for the book's reach being too broad, it can also be made that it is too narrow—with the focus of much of this research being on the impacts of community engagement in this one college, within just a few programs, and a few surrounding communities. While statistically significant and ethnically diverse samples were drawn of faculty, staff, students, and community members in this study, and the range of literature was far-reaching, the qualitative component still focuses in on a single place —a suburban, private, progressive, liberal arts college located next to a major metropolis, in one of the country's most liberal states. The abroad components of this work also focus singularly on Latin America (Peru and Mexico), and with distinct native and mestizo semi-rural communities therein. Thus, those whose political, geographic, educational, and cultural locations differ greatly from those highlighted here may find certain ideas or programs to be non-generalizable. I recognize this limitation yet hope that while the execution of what I propose here must necessarily be customized to each setting for each reader, the concepts themselves may be transferable and meaningful across a broad range of constituents and regions.

Every educational conference and activist gathering I attend these days seems to mention (in their own distinct vernacular) the themes of how we can promote both peace and justice in today's volatile political climate. It is exciting to see fervent activists embrace the concept of compassion and conventional academics embrace concerns of the community. I believe that an opening is emerging for those interested in pursuing the lines of inquiry I have proposed here to create spaces in their schools, policies, and communities for these dialogues, and to develop more fully the values of critical, contemplative engagement. Moving beyond institutions of higher education, these concepts can blossom and transform community-based organizations, foundations, businesses, and city government. When these entities partner with grassroots efforts and alternative structures aimed at radical healing and social change, having the power to make broad-based shifts to society becomes imaginable!

In the face of current injustices that seem to mount daily, we must commit ourselves to tangible and immediate pathways for engagement with, and care of, our communities and ourselves. We must link our efforts at personal transformation with collective healing and social transformation, and in so doing elevate the broader political and national conversations that are shaping the future of our world. Peace and justice are not created by someone else out there; they are generated by each of us, each day, from right where we stand.

Notes

1. Bacon 2002; Bringing Theory to Practice 2013; Calderon 2007; Cruz and Giles 2000; Dorado and Giles 2004; Gelmon et al. 1998; Jacoby 2003; Jorge 2003; Ferrari and Worrall 2000; Kretzmann and McKnight 1993; Marullo and Edwards 2000; Miron and Moely 2006; Partnership Forum 2008; Sandy 2007; Schmidt and Robby 2002; Stoecker 2005; Strand et al. 2003; Vernon and Ward 1999
2. To see the full scope of one such collaborative community-based research and organizing partnership, see Peterson et al. 2010.
3. This has occurred in collaboration with Project Pericles and their programs; Debating for Democracy On the Road; Debating for Democracy Letter to an Elected Official, and Student Choices, Student Voices voter registration campaign. For more about these programs, go to: www.projectpericles.org.

REFERENCES

Bacon, N. (2002). Differences in faculty and community partners' theories of learning. *Michigan Journal of Community Service Learning, 9*(1).

Bringing Theory to Practice. (2013). *The well-being and flourishing of students: Considering well-being, and its connection to learning and civic engagement, as central to the mission of higher education.* Washington, D.C: AAC&U.

Calderon, J. Z. (Ed.). (2007). *Race, poverty, and social justice: Multidisciplinary perspectives through service learning.* Sterling, VA: Stylus Publishing.

Calleson, D. C., Kauper-Brown, J., & Seifer, S. D. (2005). *Community-engaged scholarship toolkit.* Seattle, WA: Community-campus partnerships for health.

Cavallaro, C. C. (2016). Recognizing engaged scholarship in faculty reward structures: Challenges and progress. *Metropolitan Universities Journal, 2.*

Cruz, N. (2009). *Personal communication.* Claremont, CA.: Pitzer College.

Cruz, N. & Giles, D. E. (2000). Where's the community in service-learning? *Michigan Journal of Community Service Learning,* 28–34.

Dorado, S., & Giles, D. E. (2004). Service-learning partnerships: Paths of engagement. *Michigan Journal of Community Service Learning, 9,* 25–37.

Ellison, J., & Eatman, T. (2008). *Scholarship in public: Knowledge creation and tenure policy in the engaged university.* Syracuse, NY: Imagining America.

Ferrari, J. R. & Worrall, L. (2000). Assessments by community agencies: How the other side sees service-learning. *Michigan Journal of Community Service. Learning, 7*(1).

Finley, A. (2012). *Making progress? What we know about the achievement of liberal education outcomes.* Washington, DC: AA&U.

Finley, A. (2013). Assessing well-being as a function of learning well. The well-being and flourishing of students: Considering well-being, and its connection to learning and civic engagement, as central to the mission of higher education' in Bringing Theory to Practice. *The well-being and flourishing of students: Considering well-being, and its connection to learning and civic engagement, as central to the mission of higher education* (p. 7). Washington, D. C: AAC&U.

Finley, A., & McNair, T. (2013). *Assessing underserved students' engagement in high impact practices.* Washington, DC: AAC&U.

Flanagan, C., & Bundick, M. (2011). Civic engagement and psychosocial well-being in college students. *Liberal Education, Spring, 97*(2), 20–27.

Freeman, D., & Richards, J. C. (1996). *Teacher learning in language teaching.* Cambridge, MA: Cambridge University Press.

Gelmon, S. B., Holland, B. A., Seifer, S. D., Shinnamon, A., & Connors, K. (1998). Community-university partnerships for mutual learning. *Michigan Journal of Community Service Learning, 5,* 97–107.

Ginwright, S. (2001). Critical Resistance: American Racism and African American Youth. *Youth Development Journal, 3.*

Glassick, C. E., Huber, M. T., & Maeroff, G. I. (1997). *Scholarship assessed: Evaluation of the professoriate.* San Francisco, CA: Jossey-Bass.

Harper, S. R., Harris, F., III, & Mmeje, K. (2005). A theoretical model to explain the overrepresentation of college men among campus judicial offenders: Implications for campus administrators. *NASPA Journal, 42*(4), 565–588.

Harward, D. W. (2012). *Transforming undergraduate education: Theory that compels and practices that succeed.* Washington, DC: Rowman & Littlefield.

Harwood, D. (2012). *Personal communication.* Claremont, CA.: Pitzer College.

hooks, b. (2003). *Teaching community: A pedagogy of hope.* New York, NY: Routledge.

Jacoby, B. (Ed.). (2003). *Building partnerships for service-learning.* San Francisco: Wiley.

Jorge, E. (2003). Outcomes for community partners in an unmediated service-learning program. *Michigan Journal of Community Service Learning, 10,* 28–38.

Keyes, C. L. (2009). The black–white paradox in health: Flourishing in the face of social inequality and discrimination. *Journal of personality,* 1677–1706.

Kretzmann, J. P., & McKnight, J. (1993). *Building communities from the inside out.* Evanston, IL: Center for Urban Affairs and Policy Research, Neighborhood Innovations Network.

Machtmes, K., Johnson, E., Fox, J., Burke, M. S., Harper, J., Arcemont, L., Hebert, L., Tarifa, T., Brooks, R. C., Reynaud, A. L., Deggs, D., Matzke, B., & Arguirre, R. T. (2009). Teaching Qualitative Research Methods through Service-Learning. *The Qualitative Report, 14*(1), 155–164.

Marullo, S., & Edwards, B. (2000). From charity to justice the potential of university-community collaboration for social change. *American Behavioral Scientist, 43*(5), 895–912.

Miron, D., & Moely, B. E. (2006). Community agency voice and benefit in service-learning. *Michigan Journal of Community Service Learning, 12*(2), 27–37.

Palmer, P. J. (1992). Divided no more: A movement approach to educational reform. *Change: The Magazine of Higher Learning, 24*(2), 10–17.

Partnership Forum. (2008). *Findings from Portland State University's National Partnership Forum.* Portland, OR.: Portland State University.

Peterson, T. H., Dolan, T., & Hanft, S. (2010). Partnering with youth organizers to prevent violence: An analysis of relationships, power, and change. *Progress in Community Health Partnerships: Research, Education, and Action, 4*(3), 235–242.

Peterson, T. H. (2015). Reviving and revising the civic mission: A radical re-imagining of 'Civic Engagement' *Metropolitan Universities, 25*(3).

Ryff, C. D., & Keyes, C. L. M. (1995). The structure of psychological well-being revisited. *Journal of Personality and Social Psychology, 69*(4), 719.

Sandy, M. (2007). *Community voices: A California campus compact study on partnerships.* Hayward, CA: California Campus Compact.

Schmidt, A., & Robby, M. A. (2002). What's the Value of Service-Learning to the Community? *Michigan Journal of Community Service Learning, 9*(10), 27–33.

Simons, L., Fehr, L., Black, N., Hoogerwerff, F., Georganas, D., & Russell, B. (2011). The application of racial identity development in academic-based service learning. *International Journal of Teaching and Learning in Higher Education, 23*(1), 72–83.

Stoecker, R. (2005). *Research methods for community change: A project-based approach* (2nd ed.). Thousand Oaks, CA: Sage.

Strand, K. J., Cutforth, N., Stoecker, R., Marullo, S., & Donohue, P. (2003). *Community-based research and higher education: Principles and practices.* San Francisco, CA: Wiley.

Swaner, L. E. (2005). Educating for personal and social responsibility: A review of the literature. *Liberal Education, 91*(3), 14–21.

Vernon, A., & Ward, K. (1999). Campus and community partnerships: Assessing impacts and strengthening connections. *Michigan Journal of Community Service Learning, 6,* 30–37.

Villenas, S., Godinez, F., Delgado Bernal, D., & Elenes, A. (2006). *Chicana/Latina education in everyday life: Feminista perspectives on pedagogy and epistemology.* New York, NY: SUNY Press.

Westheimer, J., & Kahne, J. (2004). What kind of citizen? The politics of educating for democracy. *American Educational Research Journal, 41*(2), 237–269.

APPENDIX I: PITZER IN ONTARIO: LOCAL CULTURAL IMMERSION PROGRAM DESIGN AND SYLLABI

Pitzer in Ontario is a justice-oriented, interdisciplinary program in urban studies and community-based research. With theoretical foundations in the social sciences and a strong emphasis on experiential education, the program allows students to understand regional impacts of globalization and to engage in local social change efforts. These efforts are informed by long-standing relationships with community organizations, city agencies, and non-profits, and also by Ontario's community-organizing wing, which works with local organizers to identify and address pressing community issues.

Program students co-enroll in two core courses (totaling 3 credits), which take place at the Pitzer in Ontario Community Center, CASA (Community Advocacy, Social Action).

Core Courses

Critical Community Studies: The core course provides a transdisciplinary, theoretical, and contextual framework for the Pitzer in Ontario program. Through coursework, experiential learning, and reflective activities, students are asked to grapple with the issues that impact and shape communities in Southern California and the structural or systemic nature of urban crises such as the housing crisis, environmental racism and degradation, education, immigration policy, and the prison industrial

© The Editor(s) (if applicable) and The Author(s) 2018
T. Hicks Peterson, *Student Development and Social Justice*,
https://doi.org/10.1007/978-3-319-57457-8

complex. Students are also asked to explore and understand the dynamic and varied forces that define the nature of citizenship and community, and to consider the role they play in its production.

Research Methods for Community Change: This intensive research practicum experience provides students with a focused engagement with particular grassroots, social justice-oriented agencies in addressing a variety of issues in Ontario such as immigration, education, incarceration, environmental justice, community health, and labor rights. Fully executed project-based and community-based action research done through the course and in collaboration with community partners aim to directly inform community development and policy reforms currently underway through multiple partnerships in Ontario. In addition to the 150-hour research practicum, students learn about local and global strategies for creating social change—from grassroots organizing to transnational coalition building.

Sample syllabi: **Research Methods for Community Change, ONT 105**

Research Methods for Community Change, ONT 105, Syllabus

Pitzer in Ontario, Spring 2017

Professor Tessa Hicks Peterson

Class times: Tuesdays and Thursdays, 10:00 am–12:30 pm
Class location: CASA, Ontario

*

If you have come to help me, you are wasting your time. But if you have come because your liberation is bound up with mine, then let us work together...

—Aboriginal Activist group, Queensland 1970s

Course Purpose:

Research Methods for Community Change incorporates the study of diverse approaches of qualitative inquiry (i.e., ethnography, participatory action, project-based research) along with the praxis (theory+action+reflection) of community development and social change through a research practicum with community partnerships in Ontario. This class is centered around the intensive research internship and community immersion experience (150-hour commitment over the course of the semester) with grassroots organizations addressing a variety of issues in Ontario such as immigration, education, incarceration, environmental justice, community health, and labor rights. Fully executed project-based and community-based action research done through the course and in collaboration with community partners aims to directly inform community development and policy reforms currently underway through multiple partnerships in Ontario.

The course will explore the praxis of community-building and social change through interdisciplinary scholarship, in-class dialogues, critical reflection, interactive activities, fieldtrips, and community engagement. Through experiential learning (on-going participation in community-campus partnerships), students will engage in applications of community-based action research and community building and thusly will become aware of local knowledge, assets, challenges, and community-organizing projects. Examining literature on activist scholarship, this course will explore the complex intersections of charity, service, social justice, and community engagement practices as well as examine the underpinnings (current debates, ethical dilemmas, and theoretical approaches) of applied research. As such, students will investigate the roles and responsibilities of community engagement and the politics and history of conducting research in and with marginalized communities. Ethics will be rigorously explored and practiced in a weekly community engagement practicum, including how to negotiate issues of responsibility, respect, and reciprocity as they relate to collaborative projects and research. As a result of the course, students will gain a greater understanding of the principal concepts of social responsibility praxis and intercultural understanding, described in the below learning outcomes.

Teachers open the door. You enter by yourself

—Unknown

Student Learning Outcomes

Through course readings, films, lectures, individual and group exercises, and the internship partnership, students will achieve myriad student learning outcomes, which fulfill the Pitzer graduation requirements for Social Responsibility Praxis and Intercultural Understanding:

1. From the standpoint of their own and multiple cultural perspectives, students will be able to identify and describe social (in)justice issues

in the local community, such as environmental injustice, unequal quality of education, poor mental and physical health conditions and services, and their root causes (e.g., structural, political, social, economic, and/or environmental conditions) that have resulted in the need for community engagement.

2. Students will be able to engage with diverse groups of people through their 150-hour cultural immersion/community engagement internship in the community, developing common ground for interactions with those from other cultures while recognizing cultural and individual differences in interaction and communication and demonstrating the highest standards of professional and ethical conduct.

3. Students will be able to design and utilize strategies that attempt to address social justice/social responsibility issues through community engagement activities, such as community-organizing, community gardening, and community-based educational workshops on issues such as mental health, food justice, and immigration reform.

4. Students, in collaboration with community members, will be able to identify and describe different global and local manifestations of culture and discern cultural complexities, such as specific community assets and needs in the neighborhoods and partnerships related to their internships.

5. Students will be able to identify, describe, and critically analyze the benefits and potential pitfalls of community-campus partnerships through text, class discussions, and reflections with community partners.

6. Students will be able to describe how their community engagement alongside critical analysis of their own cultural norms, biases, and assumptions inform their understanding/worldview of social (in) justice issues and their awareness of power, privilege, and positionality and how this impacts their own life circumstances and those of people locally and globally.

7. Students will develop a working knowledge of the theory and principles of qualitative research and community change, as well as concrete research skills, such as how to conduct interviews, observations, and data analysis.

8. Students will examine the roles, responsibilities, and ethics of an applied researcher and community intern and the politics and history of doing research and engagement in marginalized communities.

Course Community Partners

Topic: Food Justice/Urban Farming

Huerta Del Valle (HDV) Community Garden in Ontario is a food justice project focused on providing healthy and affordable produce to the community. Through its collaboration with Pitzer College, the City of Ontario, and other health-focused organizations, Huerta del Valle aims to create substantial change in environmental policies and health practices at the local level.

Huerta del Valle provides students with internship opportunities in community organizing, outreach and promotion, urban farming, support and maintenance of community plots, food justice education workshops, event planning and coordination, documentation, childcare, and story-gathering. Basic Spanish conversational skills preferred.

Topic: Public Health/Social Determinants of Health

Partners for Better Health (PBH) is a not-for-profit 501(c)(3) public benefit corporation which works directly with existing agencies and community members to develop appropriate health services that meet both the health needs and preferences of local people through services and access solutions. In Ontario specifically, PBH has been a part of launching the Healthy Ontario Initiative through a HEAL Zone Grant that the city received. By working with various facets of the community, this initiative aims to reduce obesity in Ontario, improve access to healthy food options in schools and markets, and collect data on community health. Previously, students have been involved in The Zumba Project, providing access to Zumba exercise classes for youth and adults. However, there may also be opportunities to perform asset mapping or other new projects to benefit PBH.

The Community Health Promotoras Network is a statewide network of Spanish-speaking Community Health Workers which aims to improve the quality of care received by Latinxs in California. Promotoras are knowledgeable about and sensitive to the practical and cultural realities that increase health risks for Latinxs, and they are also aware of the health system barriers that limit access to preventive services. They use personal contacts, trust, and respect to address sensitive topics, counter misinformation, and advocate for quality healthcare. They serve as cultural, linguistic, and socioeconomic allies to individual members of the community and they have firsthand knowledge about community needs and resources. This is not a formal partner of PIO, but a project we started to develop Fall 2016 with Huerta del Valle and Lourdes Arguelles. A student intern, preferably from Huerta del Valle, could be placed with this project to help plan health workshops, chronicle its work, attend meetings, and conduct relevant research and evaluation.

Topic: Transportation Justice/Urban Planning

The Ontario Wheelhouse is a bicycle cooperative that promotes bicycling within the City of Ontario and its neighboring communities. During peak season, The Wheelhouse has served over 100 people per month and maintains several programs throughout the year. Some of these services include a build-a-bike program, bike safety, and maintenance education. The Wheelhouse offers an educational, safe, and substance-free workspace for cyclist from all rides of life to learn to use, service, and love bicycles. Unfortunately, the program has been on hiatus this past year, so interns should focus on helping the Wheelhouse reestablish itself in a new location. Basic Spanish conversational skills and bicycle mechanic experience preferred but not required.

Topic: Immigrant Justice, Youth and Adult

Inland Empire Immigrant Youth Coalition is an undocumented youth-led grassroots organization in the IE, committed to creating a safe space for immigrant youth, regardless of legal status, sexuality, or other intersections that are crucial to the undocumented identity. They aim to achieve equal access to higher education and justice for immigrant communities by empowering those who are most affected. Together, these organizations work on campaigns such as Free the People, Stop the Pol(ICE), The California TRUST Act, and an Undocuqueer Book Project. Previously, Pitzer students have conducted research on young people's experiences with DACA. This work may be continued, or students can explore new projects in collaboration with these organizations.

The Inland Coalition for Immigrant Justice is a pro-immigrant rights coalition advocating for just and humane immigration reform and respect. The members of this coalition include over 30 grassroots, community, faith-based, legal service, policy, and worker's rights organizations. The group has been involved in major victories which have limited cooperation between ICE and local law enforcement, supported immigrant youth in their fight for DACA, and broadened access to drivers' licenses and healthcare for immigrants. Their mission is to unite organizations to collectively advocate and work to improve the lives of immigrant communities and fight for a just and fair immigration system.

Topic: Anti-Incarceration/Anti-Discrimination for Housing and Employment

IE Fair Chance Coalition/RAOUON (Riverside All of Us or None) is a grassroots civil and human rights organization fighting for the rights of formerly and currently incarcerated people and families. Their goal is to strengthen the voices of people most affected by mass incarceration and the growth of the prison industrial complex. The Riverside Chapter operates under the umbrella of Starting Over Inc., a housing complex for formerly incarcerated people, and is led by a core team of organizers, 75% of whom are formerly incarcerated. RAOUON is also a member of The IE Fair Chance Coalition, which is a collaboration of various congregations, universities, and civil rights organizations all aiming to ensure that people with criminal convictions have a fair chance to gain employment, housing, and the support they need to thrive.

Some of the work these groups do include the "Ban the Box" Campaign, which calls for the elimination of the questions about past convictions on initial public employment applications, working to stop jail expansion in Riverside, becoming a part of statewide campaigns to end the practice of mass incarceration, and redefining "crime-free housing" so that eligibility is not based on past mistakes, but current behaviors. Students interning with this collective would be focused on researching and documenting the local Fair Chance Hiring campaign. Findings have the chance of becoming part of a project being done by The Formerly-Incarcerated and Convicted Peoples' and Families' Movement, a group made up of families and communities who have been directly impacted by the prison industrial complex.

The Youth Mentoring Action Network—A critical mentoring program dedicated to leveraging the power of mentoring relationships to increase access to opportunities and higher education for high school youth.

Course Assignments

The following assignments are designed to guide learning throughout this course:

1. Active Participation

Participation and co-learning are important concepts in community-based research, and thus it is necessary that you attend and actively participate in class. The sharing, exchanging, and appreciation of people's ideas and experiences are part of the process that builds critical thinking skills. Since a significant part of the class will be interactive (as opposed to one-way lectures), class engagement must include active, contemplative listening and proactive but mindful verbal engagement. You are expected to attend all class sessions or scheduled events. If you cannot attend a class session due to extenuating circumstances, please communicate with me prior to the missed session. You are also expected to read and reflect on all of the assigned readings prior to class on Thursday and to develop relevant discussion questions. Each student will be required to come to each class with at least one discussion question per reading, inspired by your analysis of the readings. These questions will be used as prompts at the start of each class for our collective review of the readings. Also, it is our aim to create a community feeling in the class, space, and Ontario program; please take care of each other like family and CASA like it was your own home (or better!) Cleaning the space each week is a critical part of this. Lastly, please no lap tops or phones out during class time.

2. Interaction with the Community

The purpose of the course is to explore ways to participate with communities in community development and research aims. Field notes are a venue for you to react to and integrate your thoughts and ideas related to your experience in the community. Your field notes should include your observations at your internship site, analysis and reflections on the social issues present, summary of your research progress there, and reflections on your role as researcher (including critical or challenging events, questions, feelings, etc.). The format and length of your field notes is not important; the content of your notes, however, is crucial. Please write them after each site visit (thus, research itself begins your first day on site, with your participation and observation). Bring notes to class where they will be sporadically reviewed so highlight for me particular field notes that provide a description of some interaction or observation with your analysis of it. There is no length requirement, but field notes should be kept regularly and crafted thoughtfully; they will be submitted in their raw form in your final paper. Please also keep up the program logs regarding hours and transportation.

3. Written Assignments

In addition to weekly readings, you will be required to complete a number of short written assignments throughout the semester. These assignments are designed to help you develop an understanding about community change in Ontario and key elements of your research project. There will be an autobiographical essay, IRB training, coding/analyzing themes that emerge from the data through the preparation of an integrative memo (which will serve as a first draft of the analysis section of your research paper), a section on methodology and setting, and the final paper itself. It is expected that you will complete and submit assignments online to the "assignments" section of Sakai the day of the assigned class session. *Grades for written assignments will be deducted ½ point for each day they are turned in late and are due on the day they are listed on the syllabus.* Below are instructions for each written assignment, with correlating due dates:

A. **Research Autobiography**

During the first weeks of class, you will write a 4-page research autobiography focusing on who you are and how your positionality, perspective, and past impact your work in terms of social change. What life experiences have shaped your values? What role did race, place, culture, gender, sexual orientation, socioeconomic status, religion, and family position have in shaping those values? What are your research interests? What motivates you to research these areas? What life experiences might bias your perspectives about the research participants or social phenomenon you engage this semester? This will form the first draft of your "positionality" statement for your final paper Bring a hard copy of your paper to class on the day it is due, 2/16

B. **Research Ethics Exercise/IRB Application**

Go to the following website and take the online training on research ethics: http://phrp.nihtraining.com/users/register.php?submit=Register.   The training takes 2 hours: make sure to upload to Sakai the final certificate to show you have completed the training. In addition to this training, read the

IRB application that exists for your site (on Sakai) and add to it by writing a brief description oof the project-based component of your work (what you plan to produce with the site through your research practicum) and some behind-the-scenes analyses of doing/gathering info for/implementing it. **Due 3/9**

C. Methodology and Setting

This 4-page paper will describe the setting where you are doing research (a good description of the site and its mission, values, and key players as well as local neighborhood), the type of research you are conducting (i.e., participatory action, community-based research, project-based, ethnographic), and the methods you are using for research (i.e. participatory observation, interviews, focus groups, archival research) as well as the theoretical approach that grounds your analysis. Stating your methodology (i.e., critical race theory, critical feminist theory) provides a larger academic context for the issue you are researching, connecting what you investigate with larger theoretical constructs and perhaps addresses structural and systemic issues that created the context and condition for the issues studied. **Due 3/23**

D. Data Coding and Thematic Analysis

Based on transcriptions of your interviews and focus groups, your field notes, documentation from your community partner, and literature review, you will code and analyze your data. You will create a list of codes (thematic areas) that develop in the coding process and an integrative memo that begins to analyze and link the significance of each theme. **Due 4/27**

E. Final Research Paper

Your final product for this class will be twofold—a product that is useful for your site (i.e., a grant proposal, a narrative history of the organization, a short documentary) as well as a final paper (approximately 20 pages double-spaced) based on research. Your paper will summarize the semester's work, including how you collaborated on the purpose and need for the research, the ethics and positionality of yourself as a researcher, a description of methods and methodology, a literature review, critical interpretations and analysis of the data, discussion of actions, outcomes, and results that emerged from your research, concluding remarks, recommendations and critiques, a bibliography, and an appendix (including your raw data/field notes). Papers must be submitted electronically via Sakai as well as in hard copy to my office. At the close of the semester, you will present the findings of your fieldwork to your fellow PIO students, site supervisors, and other interested Pitzer and local community members through a formal presentation. **Both final paper and final presentation due 5/9**

Evaluation Plan:

In-class participation, facilitation and discussion based on reading	10%
Written assignments: 4 total (10% each)	40%
Internship engagement: hours, achievements, fieldnotes and site's feedback	20%
Final research paper and final presentation	30%
Total grade	*100%*

Required Readings
All research articles are available for download on Sakai under Resources.

Expectations

Generous Reading/Generous Listening
While critical thinking, reading, and discussion involve exercising skepticism, useful and constructive ways of thinking, talking, and reading also call for a spirit of generosity. When we practice "generous" reading and listening, we look for the contributions and possibilities for learning and growth a piece of writing or comment can offer. Students are often told to be "critical" thinkers and readers; this is important, yet it does <u>not</u> mean that in order to be "critical," you should simply "rush to criticize." Instead, take a moment to ask yourself, "What new ideas or experiences does this reading bring into my life? How can another students' comment help me think and grow in new ways? Whether or not I agree with its argument, how can this author's work help me sharpen my own thinking, writing, and argumentation?" Of course, along with practicing generous reading and listening, assess the contribution honestly and thoughtfully. The main idea is this: you will not really like or really agree with everything you read or

hear in this or any course; instead of having a kneejerk reaction, or shutting down by refusing to engage, practice searching for the "kernel of truth" or discovering how the reading contributes to your thinking, discussion, and writing. Let us be both skeptical *and* generous.

Academic Integrity

Academic dishonesty will not be tolerated. In accordance with the College's Code of Student Conduct as stated in the *Pitzer College Student Handbook*, work produced through academic misconduct (e.g., plagiarism, cheating, etc.) will be dealt with according to the academic integrity guidelines. Students who violate the standards of academic integrity are subject to disciplinary sanctions.

Accommodations

If you require accommodations due to a documented disability, please come see me during office hours the first week of class to discuss your needs. Your right to accommodations will be kept confidential. To request academic accommodations, contact Office of Student Affairs.

Community Events

Several events outside of class will be required; some are already included in the syllabus but expect to attend others—we will provide dates and logistical plans as soon as possible. Attendance at these events is required and, if not occurring during class times, can count towards your overall community engagement hours.

Class Schedule

Week 1: Course Overview, Community Introductions

1/17: Orientation with Community Partners (Grove house)
1/19: Introductions, Syllabus Review, Icebreakers, Observations, Discuss readings.

Readings:

Sandy & Arguelles, Fusing Horizons pp. 21–29

Week 2: 1/24 (Tuesday, 10–12:30) Community Fieldtrip in Ontario

Fieldtrip to Graber House and Huerta del Valle—Agriculture and culture in the IE

Readings:

Emerson, Writing Ethnographic Fieldnotes, Chap. 1

Week 3: 2.2 Community Engagement and Social Justice

Readings:
Peterson, Student Development and Social Justice, Chaps. 2 and 4
(Write your response to critical reflection prompts)
This week only: Students must attend a CEC orientation

CEC Orientations @ GSCMPR	February 3	February 4	February 7
Mandatory for all student in terns	2–6 pm	10–2	2–6 pm

Week 4, 2/9: Student Development and Social Justice

Readings:

1. Peterson, Student Development and Social Justice, Chap. 3
   (*Write your response to critical reflection prompts*)
2. Vaccaro, Racial identity and service-learning

Week 5, 2/16: Social Service or Social Change?

Readings:

1. Kottler, J. (2001) "Bringing the Mystery Back Home." Psychotherapy Networker.
2. Powers, W. (2009) "Future Zarahs" The Sun Magazine.
3. Kivel, "Social Service or Social Change?" in INCITE! Women of Color Against Violence, (Eds) The Revolution will not be funded: Beyond the Non-profit Industrial Complex.
4. Rasmussen, "Cease to do Evil, Learn to do Good" in Bowers (Ed) Rethinking Friere.
5. We are Everywhere, ed. Notes from Nowhere, selected pages.

Due: Research Autobiography

Week 6, 2/23: Doing Research With, Not On or For the Community

1. Tellez, Doing Research at the Borderlands.
2. hooks, Teaching to Transgress, pp. 59–75.

3. Ward, Community-centered service-learning: Moving from doing for to doing with.
4. Tuhiwai Smith, Research Through Imperial Eyes, Decolonizing Methodologies.

Due: Bring in First Set of Field Notes

Week 7, 2/28: Engaged Scholarship

Readings:

1. Lipsitz, American Studies as Accompaniment.
2. Phillips. 2015. "Co-Conspiracy."
3. Jones, from Good to Ghetto.
4. Lather, Research as Praxis, pp. 257–277.

Week 8, 3/9 Applied Research in a Community Development Context

Readings:

1. Stoecker, Research Methods for Community Change, Chaps. 1 and 2.
2. Bickman and McNiff: Handbook of Applied Social Research, pp. ix–xix only.

IRB Training and review of current IRB Application
Due: IRB Training Certificate, submit a copy or screenshot to assignments

Week 9: Spring break

Week 10, 3/23 Research Approaches and Processes

Readings:

1. Stoecker, Research Methods for Community Change, Chap. 3.
2. Hesse-Biber & Leavy, Chap. 2 "Approaches to Qualitative Research" pp. 15–28.
3. Bickman and McNiff: Handbook of Applied Social Research, pp. 69–99 only.

Due: Methodology paper

Week 10, 3/30: Interviewing as Qualitative Research Method

1. Hesse-Biber & Leavy, Chap. 5 "In-Depth Interview" pp. 93–126.
2. Interview guideline example.
3. Collins, "When Sex Work isn't 'Work'" pp. 115–139.

In class: Create Interview Guide

Week 11, 4/6 Power/Ethics in Applied Qualitative Research

Readings:

1. Goffman, Alice, skim book and read appendix *On the Run.* 2014.
2. Teaching from the Storm http://cte.rice.edu/blogarchive/2015/07/16/teachingthestorm.
3. Muñiz, Ana, 2015 "We don't need no gang injunction! We just out here tryin' to function!" *Police, Power, and the Production of Racial Boundaries.*
4. Hesse-Biber & Leavy, Chap. 4, "The Ethics of Social Research."

Week 12, 4/13: Critical Ethnography

Readings:

1. Madison, "Introduction to Critical Ethnography" pp. 1–15.
2. Valenzuela, "Chapter 1: Introduction" Subtractive Schooling. pp. 3–32.
3. Vargas, "Chapter 1," Catching Hell in the City of Angels."

Film in class: "N!ai, The Story of a !Kung Woman," by John Marshall, 1980.

Conduct research in the field!

Week 13, 4/20: Analysis: Transcription, Sorting, Organizing, and Indexing

Readings:

1. Saldana, coding.
2. Emerson, Chap. 6 "Processing Fieldnotes: Coding and Memoing" pp. 142–168.

Bring in ALL Data for coding lecture and workshop

Week 14, 4/27: Research Progress Updates

Readings:

1. Stoecker, Chaps. 6–7.
2. Thomas, Critical Ethnography, pp. 61–72.

Due: Data coding and thematic analysis paper 4/27

Week 15, 5/04: Interpretation Through "Writing-Up"
Peer Review of final papers, Practice Presentations, Class overview and closure

Readings:

1. Emerson, Chap. 7 "Writing an Ethnography" and "Conclusion" pp. 169–216.

Week 16, 5/9: Community Research Symposium Presentations
5/9 Community Research Symposium—Final Presentations

Due 5/9, Final Paper

Appendix II: Healing Ourselves, Healing Our Communities: Local and Global Program Design and Syllabi

Healing Ourselves and Healing Our Communities—Local Course

ONT 110, Spring 2010 Professor Tessa Hicks Peterson

Monday and Wednesdays, 11:00 a.m.–12:30 p.m. Outdoor Classroom

In a world marked by violent ethnic, racial and religious conflict and deepening social and economic inequality, any possibility of social transformation also requires a spiritual revolution, one which transforms conventional understandings of power, identity and justice-understandings which are currently limited by a series of false distinctions between the spiritual and the material, the sacred and the secular, the human and the divine.

—Leela Fernandes

Course Purpose

The focus of the course is to explore theories, strategies, and practices of personal and collective healing for individual, social, and environmental ills. Diverse scholars and theories will be presented regarding knowledge generation and different ways of knowing, decolonization of the mind and cultural affirmation of devalued indigenous cultural traditions, biodiversity, and regeneration, practices of engaged mindfulness and compassionate activism, and the praxis of asset-based community development. Readings

© The Editor(s) (if applicable) and The Author(s) 2018   253
T. Hicks Peterson, *Student Development and Social Justice*,
https://doi.org/10.1007/978-3-319-57457-8

will include indigenous and Buddhist studies and community development scholars, such as Vandana Shiva, Joe Kincheloe, Linda Tuhiwai Smith, Thomas Hartmann, Thich Nhat Hanh, Leela Fernandes, John McKnight, Joanna Macey, and more. Students will learn indigenous, alternative, and ancient wisdom traditions that address the interwoven aims of healing ourselves and our communities and through text, guest speakers, experiential activities, and service they will learn, practice, and create strategies for healing. Research and service ethics will be rigorously explored and practiced in a weekly practicum, including how to negotiate issues of responsibility, respect, and reciprocity as they relate to participation with local community mentors and organizations. Through this community engagement, students will become more aware of local knowledge, assets, and cultures. As a result of the course, students should have an understanding of how healing ourselves, our communities, and our earth are understood and enacted differently depending on the cultural lens and local knowledge of the practitioner. Students will engage in a personal reflection on their own journey of healing as it relates to community engagement and social change. Lastly, they will grasp the principal concepts of social responsibility (intercultural effectiveness, self-knowledge, community knowledge, and interpersonal competency).

Course Structure

> *I have come to realize that once we strip radical social movements down to their bare essence and understand the collective desires of people in motion, freedom and love lay at the very heart of the matter. Indeed, I would go so far as to say that freedom and love constitute the foundation for spirituality, another elusive and intangible force with which few scholars of social movements have come to terms.*
>
> —Robin D.G. Kelley

There are various components of this course: reading, class discussions, experiential activities, writing, and community engagement (service and mentorship). Your total participation in each facet of the course is crucial to your individual success in this class (i.e., the grade you earn) and to the collective success of our efforts at healing in our local communities (and the commitments we have made to community partnerships). This class promises to challenge, inspire, invigorate, and teach you; your promise (by virtue of your enrollment and consistent participation) is to give back fully to the course content (readings, writings, and discussions as well as community engagement activities). Thus, expect a rigorous commitment of time and personal/mental energy and expect to receive much in return. Accordingly, your participation (in terms of being consistently present, well-read, and vocal at each class) is not only something expected in respect to your grade but out of respect for your peers. Similarly, your familiarity and compliance with Pitzer's Student Code of Conduct and academic honesty is to be assumed. It is also expected that you will complete all weekly readings and writing assignments (and attach assignments online to the "assignments" section of Sakai at least one hour before the following class meeting). It is up to you to become familiar with the Sakai class website and visit it between classes for announcements, returned assignments, and more. Assignments will be docked a 1/2 point for each day that they are turned in late. In order to ensure that you are keeping up with the readings, each student will be required to come to each class with at least one discussion question, inspired by your analysis of the readings. These questions will be used as prompts for our collective review of the readings and should be written down and brought to class. Note that fieldtrips have been scheduled into the semester, in addition to usual class sessions. If you feel you are faltering in your ability to keep up with the course content and community engagement obligations, please see me immediately.

Course Requirements

Teachers open the door. You enter by yourself.

—*Unknown*

Weekly: Each week you will complete a 2-page writing assignment, alternating weekly between a reading analysis and an experiential reflection. The first week you will write a two-page critical commentary on the theories presented and the conclusion you have drawn on at least two of the recently assigned readings. The second week you will reflect on either one of the experiential activities we have done or on one of our guest lecture presentations—how they impact you personally and how you relate them to the topics of the course, readings, and your community engagement. You will alternate these assignments weekly and post them to Sakai every Friday by 10:00 a.m.

Final Paper: Your final paper should reveal an in-depth personal and critical analysis on the topic of healing ourselves and our communities, using lessons from readings, guest lectures, experiential activities, service project, mentorship, and personal experience. Paper can be complemented by visual and/or ceremonial components. 10–15 pp. paper due 5/10.

Action: Service project, determined by you and your community partner, plus brief (4–5 pages) critical reflection on it. Due by the last week of class, 5/7.

Practicum: Service and Learning

> *If you have come to help me, you are wasting your time. But if you have come because your liberation is bound up with mine, then let us work together...*

—Aboriginal Activist group, Queensland 1970s

Students will engage in a partnership with one of three local community members/groups. The purpose of this is to learn from and give back to local, native communities. The learning and service should center around the themes of this course (healing ourselves and healing our communities) but will unfold uniquely within each partnership. Ideally, each student will meet with their community partner twice a week to learn from them about their culture, history, and practices of healing. On alternate weeks, the student will participate in a service project, which has been outlined by that community partner. Students should also participate in cultural events hosted by that community partner, as part of their learning. The students will work together in groups of five within the three different options listed below; each group should communicate with their community partner about scheduling and service project needs. Each student should garner 60 hours of service/learning over the semester; this can occur and however it works best for the needs of the service project, community partners' schedule, and the student groups' schedule. Open communication, accountability, respect, reciprocity, and dedication are key to the success of this partnership.

Community Partnership Options

Costanoan Rusmen Carmel Tribe Mentor: Tribal Chair: Tony Cerda (Office hours: 1–5 pm M-F) Service Options: Organic Farm (help create proposal to City and secure land/design farm) Computer Classes (conduct basic computer education sessions weekly) Wellness Center (weekly meetings, Tuesdays 11 am–1 pm). Documentary on Indian healthcare access (collaborate with Media Studies) Ohlone Sandwich (youth mentoring, life skills and college prep, Sundays, 5 pm) Drumming (open to public, Thursdays 6–9 pm)

Tongva Tribe Mentor: Julia Bogany (Cultural Affairs Director) Moniikanga Tongva Village and Educational Habitat/Science Center. Service Options:

Archival research on governmental contracts; attend and video events; recruit volunteers; Traditional Basket weaving and doll-making-gifts for hospice; Healing circles for women and elders; Domestic violence advocacy.

Seneca/Tubotolobal/Ohlone Mentor: Robert John Knapp. Service Options: Secure, design and create native plants/ceremonial foods farm at Pitzer (including creation of traditional tools from found, natural objects). Harvest plants and learn to cook traditional ceremonial foods through cooking class

Guest Lectures

> *'Radical' is from a Latin word that means 'root.' Radical means going to the roots of the matter, and the roots of the spirit. A radical person is a person who searches for meaning and affirms community.*

> —Ed Chambers

- Julia Bogany: Co-Founder/Vice President/Educational Advisor of "Keepers of Indigenous Ways"; Cultural Affairs Director for Tongva Tribe
- Tony Cerda: Tribal Chairman of the Costanoan Rumsen Carmel Tribal Council/Former Boxer and Boxing Coach/Anti-Gang Program Leader
- RobertJohn Knapp: Spiritual Leader and Sundancer, Talabalaba Sioux/Seneca/Ohlone
- Larry Ward: Ordained Minister and Dharma Teacher/Consultant on diversity education, organizational change and executive coaching
- Alane Daughtery: Professor of Kinesiology and Health Sciences at Cal Poly Pomona
- Cecelia Garcia: Chumash Healer and Spiritual Leader
- Hala Khouri: Somatic Psychology Therapist; Yoga Teacher; Co-Founder of Off the Mat!
- Vandana Shiva: Environmental activist and physician

Course Topics and Readings

What are we healing? Social, cultural, spiritual, political, and environmental issues

> *A human being is part of the whole, called by us 'universe,' a part limited in time and space. He experiences himself, his thoughts and feelings, as something separate from the rest—a kind of optical delusion of consciousness. This delusion*

is a kind of prison for us, restricting us to our personal desires and to affection for a few persons nearest to us. Our task must be to free ourselves from this prison by widening our circle of compassion to embrace all living creatures and the whole of nature in its beauty.

—Albert Einstein

January 20: Week 1
Coming Back to Life Blessed Unrest
Due Friday: Writing Assignment—Reading Analysis
January 25: Week 2
The Better World Handbook—pp. 1–55 only
Freedom Dreams: The Black Radical Imagination
Ideas for Action: Relevant Theory for Radical Change—Chap. 1 only
Due Friday: Writing Assignment—Experiential Reflection

Ancient Wisdom Traditions/Indigenous Approaches Regarding What To and How To Heal

Each one of us must make his own true way, and when we do, that way will express the universal way. This is the mystery. When you understand one thing through and through, you understand everything. When you try to understand everything, you will not understand anything. The best way is to understand yourself, and then you will understand everything.

—Suzuki Roshi

February 1: Week 3
Everyday is a Good Day
Eating Fire, Tasting Blood: An anthology of the American Indian Holocaust
Feb 3-Guest speaker: Julia
Due Friday: Writing Assignment—Reading Analysis
February 8: Week 4
Decolonizing Methodologies: Research and Indigenous Peoples
Due Friday: Writing Assignment—Experiential Reflection
Feb 10-Guest speaker: Robert John
February 13th (all day fieldtrip): Sweatlodge with Robert John in Riverside
February 15: Week 5
The Spirit of Regeneration: Andean Culture Confronting Western Notions of Development

Due Friday: Writing Assignment—Reading Analysis
February 22: Week 6
Cultural Affirmation and Affirmation of Cultural Diversity in the Andes
What is Indigenous Knowledge? Voices from the Academy (Chaps. 1 and 2 only)
February 24-Guest speaker: Tony
Due Friday: Writing Assignment—Experiential Reflection
March 1: Week 7
What is Indigenous Knowledge? Voices from the Academy (Chaps. 10, 14, 16)
Vandana Shiva guest lecture, TBD
March 3: 9–3 pm/Fieldtrip to Moniikanga Tongva Village: guided tour and service
Due Friday: Writing Assignment—Reading Analysis
March 8: Week 8
The Mindful Brain: Reflection and Attunement in the Cultivation of Well-being
Creating Peace—pages TBA
March 10-Guest speaker: Hala Due Friday: Writing Assignment—Experiential Reflection
March 15: Week 9 Spring Break!
March 22: Week 10
Zen Mind, Beginner's Mind: Informal Talks on Zen Meditation and Practice
Creating Peace—pages TBA
March 24-Guest speaker: Larry
Due Friday: Writing Assignment—Reading Analysis

Spiritualizing Politics

> *Spiritualism is the highest form of political consciousness.*

> —Haudenosaunee message to the world, Mankiller, p. 11

March 29: Week 11
Transforming Feminist Practice; Non-violence, Social Justice and the Possibilities of a Spiritualized Feminism.
Due Friday: Writing Assignment—Reading Analysis
April 5: Week 12
Transforming Feminist Practice; Non-violence, Social Justice and the Possibilities of a Spiritualized Feminism.

Due Friday: Writing Assignment—Experiential Reflection
April 12: Week 13
The essential writings and speeches of Martin Luther King, Jr.
The essential writings of Mahatma Gandhi.
April 13: Ethnobotanical tour, hours TBA
Due Friday: Writing Assignment—Reading Analysis
April 19: Week 14
Sing, Whisper, Shout, Pray! Feminist Visions for a Just World
Consciousness in Action: The Power of Beauty, Love and Courage in a
Violent Time
Ideas for Action: Relevant Theory for Radical Change, C. Kaufman (Chap. 11)
April 21-Guest speaker: Cecelia Garcia
Due Friday: Writing Assignment—Experiential Reflection

Diverse Strategies for Healing Ourselves and Communities

> *One of our problems today is that we are not well acquainted with the literature
> of the spirit. We're interested in the news of the day and the problems of the hour.
> It used to be that the university campus was a kind of hermetically sealed-off
> area where the news of the day did not impinge upon your attention to the inner
> life and to the magnificent human heritage we have in our great tradition—
> Plato, Confucius, the Buddha, Goethe, and others who speak of the eternal
> values that have to do with the centering of our lives. When you get to be older,
> and the concerns of the day have all been attended to, and you turn to the inner
> life—well, if you don't know where it is or what it is, you'll be sorry.*

—Joseph Campbell

April 26: Week 15
The Last Hours of Ancient Sunlight
May 5:
Joseph Campbell's The Hero's Journey
Due Friday: Writing Assignment—Reading Analysis
May 3: Week 16
Rethinking Freire: Cease to Do Evil, Then Learn to Do Good
Building Communities from the Inside Out: A Path Toward Finding and
Mobilizing a Community's Assets
Due Friday: Writing Assignment—Experiential Reflection, Final action
project due
May 10: Week 17

Roots for Radicals: Organizing for Power, Action, and Justice, E. Chambers, pp. 13–43
The Better World Handbook: 291–293; **Finals due, 5/10**

Summer Program: "Healing Ourselves and Healing Our Communities, Part II"
Location: Temixco, Morelos, Mexico
Pitzer Professor/Program Director: Tessa Hicks Peterson
Mexico Program Coordinator/Guest Lecturer: Estela Roman
1 credit course:
Native Mexican healing traditions for personal and social transformation within a local/global context
Class times: Monday and Wednesdays, 3 pm–6 pm and Fridays, 10 am–4 pm
Preparing and eating traditional meals, 1:00–2:30 pm Monday–Thursday
1 credit course:
Spanish language development and cultural immersion
Class times: Monday–Thursdays, 9 am–12 pm: Language classes
Tuesday and Thursday, 3 pm–6 pm: Internship hours
10 hours weekly: Language and cultural immersion with host family—
activities, meals, outings, household responsibilities, etc.

Program Overview

Organized by Pitzer College in collaboration with Estela Roman, this summer program takes place in Mexico over four weeks. Through intensive Spanish language courses, a seminar on indigenous knowledge and healing in Mexico, internships, fieldtrips, and family stays, you will explore native traditions for healing while furthering your Spanish language skills, gaining an understanding of the life and culture of Mexico, and linking local and global lessons of this paired course program.

This is a very structured, intensive program for students willing to work hard; the rewards will be great and commensurate with your efforts, however! You earn two course credits in only four weeks, but more importantly you will experience a very special opportunity to live with families, work in the community, travel in a beautiful country, and meet people you will never forget. You will also gain exposure to ancient healing practices of Mexico rarely shared with typical tourists.

Host Institution

Estela Roman is our host, program coordinator, and guest lecturer in Mexico. She helps in planning and teaching the curriculum, facilitates your host family stays, provides the meeting place and daily meals for all classes, arranges the internships, guest lectures, and fieldtrips, and works closely with you in all aspects of the program. As a leader in her community, an expert in her field and a coordinator opening her home to this program, please demonstrate your patience, gratitude, and respect to Ms. Roman throughout the course of this program.

Internships

The intensive internship of 6 hours per week for four weeks provides you with a focused exposure to the roles that particular agencies play in addressing healing, healthcare prevention and intervention, and education. You will gain firsthand experience with the models and assumptions on which an agency operates, the particular problem-solving strategies it utilizes, and the cultural traditions that underlie these things. A final reflective paper on your internship experience is a required part of the course.

Home Stays

Estela will arrange your family stay in a home that should be no more than 20-minute walk from Estela's house. Our policy is to have no more than one student in a home so that you can maximize your language learning and participate fully in family life. You and at least one other student in the program will generally be assigned homes close together so you will have someone with whom to share walks, taxi rides at night, and so forth. All homestays will be within the town of Temixco (pop. 20,000)

Study Trips
To deepen your understanding of topics covered in the core course, you will be offered several fieldtrips to local sites of historical healing properties throughout the state of Morelos including the pyramids of Tepoztlan, Las Crutas de Cacahuamilpa (one of the largest caverns in the world), El Jardin Ethnobotanico (the ethnobotanical garden in Cuernavaca), and the local farmer's markets and flea markets in the area.

Description of Courses:

I. Native Mexican healing traditions for personal and social transformation within a local/global context: theory seminars, guest lectures, group discussions, experiential activities, and cultural fieldtrips.
Continuing the study of native practices for healing that were begun in the local component of this program, this summer course will provide a brief, though intensive exploration into indigenous Mexican cosmologies and practices for healing. It will focus on the philosophies surrounding illness and wellness, the interconnection of mind–body–heart–spirit, and the spiritual knowledge that drives these energetic, botanic, and meditative practices of healing. Through an exploration of both theory and practice, students will gain exposure to Mexican cosmovisions of life, death, spirituality, indigenous knowledge, justice, and peacemaking. This course intends to guide students in their search for a deeper understanding of their relationship with nature, land, peoples and local environments. Students will review philosophical concepts that relate individual behavior and attitudes with key elements within the laws of nature. We explore how presuppositions of indigenous and non-indigenous philosophy, including epistemology (how/what we know), metaphysics (what is), science (methods), and ethics (practices), affect ecology, biodiversity, health, housing, food, employment, economic sustainability, peace negotiations, climate justice, and human/treaty rights. The understanding of local knowledge and culture will be situated in a global context, recognizing the effects of globalization in perpetuating both a valuing and a degradation of these practices. Diverse scholars and theories (situated in feminist theory, cultural studies, globalization studies, indigenous studies, and border studies) will shed light on the impact of global restructuring on indigenous

communities, indigenous knowledge, and social/cultural/ecological justice. Students will gain skills and knowledge to critically analyze and dialogue about the role, tensions, and praxis of indigenous healing practices within a global context, using appropriate philosophical vocabulary, concepts, and resources. Students will grasp the principal concepts of social responsibility (intercultural effectiveness, self-knowledge, community knowledge, and interpersonal competency) and connect their local and global understanding of the topics of this course as a result of their paired course learning.

Students will learn through other voices of the Earth not often heard or read: symbolic images, oral stories and beliefs, and guest lectures by spiritual leaders, as well as experiential activities (such as sweat lodges, energetic healing massage, herbal remedies, meditation, and song), fieldtrips, and the inclusion of conventional scholarly texts. Local traditional healers (curanderos/shamans) will do guest lectures and activities in the course. Fieldtrips to local sites within the state of Morelos (pyramids, caves, ethnobotanic gardens, waterfalls, natural springs, ancient ruins, etc.) will take place weekly. Lastly, students will engage in a personal reflection on their own journey of healing as it relates to community engagement and social change, as well as produce a scholarly analysis of their learning (full syllabus available upon request).

II. Language and Cultural Immersion: language classes, internships, and home-stay

Daily Spanish language instruction will provide an in-depth exposure to beginning and intermediate Spanish language development. Written, oral, and comprehension in Spanish will be sought through language lab, textual, and conversational activities. Intensive in-class and out-of-class study should be expected. Further (informal) language instruction and practice will occur with host stays, and daily hours spent with host families engaged in daily Mexican life (from cooking and cleaning to eating and playing to family outings and casual conversation). Host families will provide students breakfast and dinner daily; these shared meal times will provide further opportunities for understanding Mexican culture and engaging in familial dialogue. Cultural immersion and intercultural understanding will also occur through twice weekly internship hours at a local convivencia (orphanage) or traditional health clinic (students' choice). Spanish language communications with community members in these placements will further strengthen exposure to and use of the language. The open, kind, engaged, and flexible involvement of Pitzer students with their host families, neighbors, language instructors, and internship sites is expected in order to respect and maximize the study abroad experience.

A more detailed syllabus will be distributed the first day of class, though the reading list will be emailed to students ahead of time so that they will have time to order any books or Readers they will need to bring with them to Mexico. Any materials from the Spring semester "Healing Ourselves and Healing Our Communities" course that will be needed for the Mexico course will be specified ahead of time, as well. Some additional materials will be available in Mexico.

Appendix III: Community Engagement in Student Graduation Requirements—Policy

Social Justice Theory/Social Responsibility Praxis Educational Objective:
Graduation Guidelines, Student Learning Outcomes, and Course Criteria

Educational Objectives of Pitzer College
Social Justice, Social Responsibility, and the Ethical Implications of Knowledge and Action Educational Objective

Through the Social Justice Theory and Social Responsibility Praxis paired course sequence, students will acquire a concern with and commitment to social justice and social responsibility through both theory and practice courses that emphasize these themes. Students satisfy this objective by completing two courses:

a. Social Justice Theory (SJT)

The social justice theory course will emphasize diverse theoretical frameworks, movements, and histories of social justice.

b. Social Responsibility Praxis (SRP)

The social responsibility praxis course emphasizes the manifestation of social responsibility through community engagement, theoretical analysis, and critical reflection, or "praxis."

© The Editor(s) (if applicable) and The Author(s) 2018   267
T. Hicks Peterson, *Student Development and Social Justice*,
https://doi.org/10.1007/978-3-319-57457-8

I. Social Justice Theory: Student Learning Outcomes and Course Criteria

A. Social Justice Theory Student Learning Outcomes

1. Students will be able to identify and describe the ethical and political implications of injustice, such as social problems, social stratification, the interdependence and intersection of systems of oppression, interpersonal and structural discrimination, and unequal distribution and access to power and resources (including natural resources).
2. Students will be able to identify barriers to equality and/or inclusiveness and explore strategies to remove them.
3. Students will be able to identify and describe the hegemonic structures and practices that further social injustice and oppression as studied in their course.

B. Social Justice Theory Course Criteria

All of the following criteria must be met in order for courses to fulfill the guideline. Consider the criteria as they relate to your discipline or your field of study.

1. Courses should have assignments that can be used to assess the provided Social Justice Theory student learning outcomes.
2. Course topics should be about the theory, history, current events, and/or social movements surrounding social (in)justice issues pertinent to at least one of the following: race, ethnicity, class, sexual orientation, gender identity, immigration status, nationality, ability status, environmental justice, religion, and/or social stratification. For example, the course might explore the history and current status of social justice movements, such as Civil Rights, Women's Movements, Immigration Reform, Sexuality, and Labor.
3. Course topics should enable students to acquire knowledge and sensitivity to the ethical and political implications of at least one of the following: social problems, oppressive systems, interpersonal and structural discrimination, unequal distribution and access to power and resources (including natural resources), and the interdependence and intersection of systems of oppression.
4. Course readings and discussions should challenge hegemonic structures and practices that further social injustice and oppression,

and promote strategies to redress systemic barriers to equality and inclusiveness.

II. Social Responsibility Praxis: Student Learning Outcomes and Course Criteria

A. Social Responsibility Praxis Student Learning Outcomes

1. Students will be able to identify and describe social (in)justice issues and their root causes (e.g., structural, political, social, economic, and/or environmental conditions) that have resulted in the need for community engagement.
2. Students will be able to demonstrate the highest standards of professional and ethical conduct when negotiating engagement in the community.
3. Students will be able to design and utilize strategies that attempt to address social justice/social responsibility issues through community engagement activities.
4. Students, in collaboration with community members, will be able to recognize community assets and needs.
5. Students will be able to identify, describe, and critically analyze the benefits and potential pitfalls of community-campus partnerships.
6. Students will be able to describe how their community engagement alongside critical reflection on their own perceptions, biases, and assumptions inform their understanding of social (in)justice issues and their awareness of power, privilege, and positionality.

B. Social Responsibility Praxis Course Criteria

1. Community engagement may come in the form of service, research, community-based education, or another form of collaboration, conducted by faculty members in a way that is appropriate to their pedagogy, methodology, and personal approach, and operating from a framework that honors reciprocal, respectful, ethical partnership with the community members, agencies, or institutions with whom the faculty member and students are collaborating.
2. Community engagement fieldwork normally includes at least 40 hour in a single semester and is complemented by classroom discussions, lectures, and assignments (which correlate with stated Social Responsibility Praxis student learning outcomes) to engage critical

reflections and rigorous analysis that address the theories of social justice that are specific to the disciplinary and community context.

3. The agenda for the community engagement is made in collaboration between college partners (students, faculty, and/or staff) and the primary community partner contacts, attempting always to recognize and build on existing assets of the community.

4. Community engagement actions address the structural, political, social, economic, and/or environmental conditions (and any other root causes) that have resulted in the need for community engagement, and explore the benefits and potential pitfalls of community-campus partnerships.

5. (As applicable/If applicable) Community engagement courses that involve research must follow appropriate ethical standards, such as informed consent, mutual benefits, equal partnership in designing and conducting research, and sharing of end products.

Intercultural Understanding of Educational Objective

Graduation Guidelines, Student Learning Outcomes, and Course Criteria

Educational Objectives of Pitzer College: Intercultural Understanding

By learning about their own culture and placing it in comparative perspective, students appreciate their own and other cultures, and recognize how their own thoughts and actions are influenced by their culture and history. This understanding supports a set of cognitive, affective, and behavioral skills and characteristics that facilitate effective and appropriate interaction in a variety of cultural contexts. In order to meet the student learning outcomes (SLOs) for Intercultural Understanding and provide students with a well-rounded perspective on this educational objective, it is important that students demonstrate these SLOs regarding both global and local contexts. Students, working closely with their advisers, will select a set of courses and/or programs to demonstrate intercultural understanding from (A) a global or international perspective *and* (B) from a domestic (US) or local perspective.

A. Demonstration of an understanding of the intercultural from a global or international perspective.

Students will meet this objective by either

1. completing an approved study abroad program (a semester or, in extenuating circumstances,[1] a summer program) or

2. taking a course that discusses or addresses a culture (or cultures) outside of the US (including historical cultures and civilizations).

B. *Demonstration of an understanding of the intercultural from a domestic (US) or local perspective.*
Students will meet this objective by either

1. completing the Pitzer in Ontario Program or
2. taking a course that addresses historically marginalized cultures in the US including but not limited to current offerings in Ethnic Studies departments, Gender and Feminist Studies, American Studies, and courses on queer theory. See course criteria.

Student Learning
Student Learning Outcomes for Intercultural Understanding (global and/or local, international and/or domestic can be selected as appropriate for an IU-G or IU-L course)
Intercultural Understanding focuses on knowledge, empathy, and the application of learning. The Student Learning Outcomes associated with this perspective of Intercultural Understanding are as follows:

1. Students will be able to identify and describe different global and local manifestations of culture and discern cultural complexities.
2. Students will be able to critically analyze their own cultural norms and biases and describe how these affect their world-view.
3. Students will be able to draw upon personal experiences and class learning to develop common ground for interactions with those from other cultures.
4. Students will be able to identify, describe, and analyze important social issues from multiple cultural perspectives.
5. Students will be able to engage with diverse groups of people while recognizing cultural and individual differences in interaction and communication.
6. Students will be able to identify and describe how power, positionality, privilege, and other socio-structural factors impact their own life circumstances and those of people locally and globally.

Course/Program Criteria for the Intercultural Understanding
A. Program Criteria for meeting the intercultural understanding guideline on a study abroad program:

Study Abroad should entail a deep engagement with another culture and the learning that comes from that as a part of a four-year liberal arts education. Program components that normally best promote intercultural learning on study abroad are as follows:
intensive language instruction once you are there (where applicable);
homestays;
a core course on the culture and important issues of the area or region;
guided reflection on your experience through writing assignments; and
a directed independent study project.
*Students on exchanges will take a distance learning course, MLLC 110 *Portfolio Writing*, which helps students link their experiences abroad with the Intercultural Understand educational objective.

B. Course Criteria for meeting the intercultural understanding guideline in a course that discusses or addresses a culture (or cultures) outside of the US.

"Global/International" courses are not just courses that focus on the international or on other countries. For the intercultural requirement, there must be significant focus on non-US "cultures." The course will:

1. *examine a culture or cultures outside of the US* (to include historical cultures and civilizations) OR
2. provide a comparative perspective between the US and other culture (s), with at least half of the course focused on non-US cases.

C. Course Criteria for meeting the Intercultural Understanding guideline in a course that addresses different cultures in the US. While recognizing that some course criteria will not be applicable to courses in all fields, courses that meet the Intercultural Understanding guideline for different cultures in the US should

1. expose students to marginalized communities (via course materials, art work, readings, films, and/or internship/social responsibility sites) and ask students to reflect their upon understandings of specific issues via assignments, journal entries, and/or reflective essays;
2. directly discuss the role of individual privilege as it relates to the denied privileges of socially disadvantaged groups (e.g., role of social and cultural capital);

3. investigate the impact of and counter the ideas of ethnocentrism and Eurocentrism as these terms relate to how marginalized populations are characterized and caricatured;
4. encourage the development of cultural empathy, respect, and understanding for host/community/local perspectives within class discussion and oral/written assignments about social stratification, socio-structural barriers, and social inequality as systems of oppression;
5. ask students to investigate the intersections between racialized, gendered, and/or classed identities as they relate to how intersecting axes of oppression, such as heterosexism, racism, classism, and/or ableism, affect marginalized communities in the US and abroad;
6. push students to recognize how historical structures, individual agency, and the relations between the two are exhibited within the social circumstances of marginalized communities in the US and abroad; and
7. teach students how to use social theory to analyze and describe why social hierarchy persists and the ways in which it impacts the life chances of marginalized populations.

Faculty should articulate these criteria in ways that are appropriate for their discipline or field. For a Humanities course that meets the Intercultural Understanding guideline that addresses different cultures in the US, there are alternative course criteria that could be used in place of some of the criteria above. These courses could

1. examine unequal power relations embedded in the cultures and histories of the United States;
2. enable students to explore diverse cultural perspectives on the United States society and history by analyzing the production of art, literature, or philosophy; and
3. encourage the development of cultural empathy, respect, and understanding for ethnic studies.

NOTE

1. "Extenuating circumstances" might include a New Resources student or any student who has justifiable reasons for not studying abroad for a full semester.

Appendix IV: Community Engagement in Faculty Appointments, Promotion and Tenure Policy

A. Pitzer Criteria For Contract Renewal, Promotion, and Tenure

Pitzer College, first and foremost, values excellence in teaching. Pitzer aims to renew, promote, and tenure faculty members who are actively engaged as effective educators, mentors to students, scholars in their disciplines, intellectual resources for colleagues, students, and the community, and responsible participants in College governance. The scheduling of contract renewals, promotion, and tenure is outlined in Section 4.6 of the By-Laws. The criteria for contract renewal, promotion, and tenure are specified in Section 4.4 of the By-Laws. These criteria are organized into three major categories, which are listed below. Teaching and advising is the most important category. Scholarly and artistic activities and service to the college and other communities are equally important categories. Faculty are expected to make contributions to all three areas, with the understanding that expressions may vary by the disciplinary or interdisciplinary nature of a faculty member's work.

1. *Teaching and Academic Advising*

Pitzer College expects all faculty members to be effective teachers and advisors. Pitzer College recognizes that there are many different

© The Editor(s) (if applicable) and The Author(s) 2018
T. Hicks Peterson, *Student Development and Social Justice*,
https://doi.org/10.1007/978-3-319-57457-8

teaching and advising styles, and that effective teaching and advising encompasses a variety of approaches, methods, and activities. Although there are no precise guidelines for evaluating effectiveness in teaching and advising, these can be manifested in a number of ways, such as, but not limited to:

a. Teaching

- effectiveness inside and outside the classroom
- curricular contributions to the faculty member's field group
- curricular contributions to the educational objectives of the college
- curricular innovation and development
- non-traditional means of teaching and learning
- supervising student participation in research projects or internships
- teaching, mentoring, or overseeing students in the context of public, campus- or community-based courses or projects

b. Academic Advising

- effectiveness in orienting first year students to the Pitzer experience
- helping students design courses of study appropriate to their interests and needs
- assuring that advisees meet concentration requirements and the educational objectives of the college
- assisting students in establishing summer and post-graduation plans

2. *Scholarly and Artistic Activities*
Pitzer College greatly values the contributions of its faculty members to scholarship and the arts. Pitzer faculty are expected to show involvement in their field(s) by, for example:

- publication of books, articles, and reviews;
- performances and exhibitions where relevant;
- presentation of papers at professional meetings;
- editing of scholarly journals and publications;
- serving as panel chair or as a discussant at professional meetings;
- portfolios, products, reports, or artifacts of public, campus- or community-based scholarship, artistic activities, or other forms of engaged and applied scholarship;
- other evidence of ongoing professional activity.

The relative importance of particular forms of scholarly or artistic activities differs by field(s) of study. Through the annual review process, field groups, as well as the Dean of Faculty, are expected to provide early and ongoing guidance to colleagues regarding appropriate scholarly and artistic productivity (see Section V.L, below).

3. *Service to the College and Other Communities*
   As an institution committed to self-governance, Pitzer College places a high value on faculty members' contributions to the governance of the college. It also values the contributions its faculty makes to the intellectual life of the college and the services provided by faculty members to the community. These efforts can be exhibited in a number of ways, such as the following:

   - participation in the governance of the college (e.g., faculty meetings, college council);
   - service on college and intercollegiate committees and contributions to college and intercollegiate programs;
   - service to field group(s);
   - acting as an intellectual resource for colleagues, students, and the community;
   - serving as a mentor to other faculty members;
   - participating in the governance of professional associations;
   - public, campus- or community-based projects that advance the educational objectives of the college;

- facilitating public access to academic knowledge, art, and resources;
- participation in public or community-based initiatives.

BIBLIOGRAPHY

Ahmed, S. (2014, 25 August). Self care as warfare. *Feminist Killjoys*, Retrieved July 8, 2017, from https://feministkilljoys.com/2014/08/25/selfcare-as-warfare/.

Ahmad, A. (2015). A note on call-out culture. *Briarpatch Magazine*, 2 March. Retrieved February 2, 2017, from https://briarpatchmagazine.com/articles/view/a-note-on-call-out-culture.

Albelda, R., Badgett, M., & Gates, A. S. G. (2009). *Poverty in the lesbian, gay, and bisexual community, rapport déposé au*. Los Angeles: William Institute.

Alexander, M. J. (Ed.). (2003). *Sing, whisper, shout, pray! Feminist visions for a just world*. Edgework Books.

Alfred, T. (2005). *Wasáse: Indigenous pathways of action and freedom*. Peterborough, ON: Broadview Press.

Alfred, T., & Corntassel, J. (2005). Being indigenous: Resurgences against contemporary colonialism. *Government and Opposition, 40*, 597–614.

American Psychological Association. (2012). *Stress in America. Missing the healthcare connection*. Stress in America Survey.

American Psychological Association. (2016). *Stress in America: The impact of discrimination*. Stress in America Survey.

Angelou, M. (2006, November 30). *Interview with Dave Chappelle*. Iconoclasts, season 2, episode 6. http://www.imdb.com/title/tt0874578/.

Angelou, M. (2016). *Finding our families, finding ourselves*. Museum of tolerance, Los Angeles, CA (viewed 30 April 2016).

Anti-Defamation League. (2007). *Personal self-assessment of anti-bias behavior*. The Anti-Defamation League's Education Division, a World of Difference Institute. Retrieved March 1, 2017, from https://www.adl.org/sites/default/files/documents/assets/pdf/education-outreach/Personal-Self-Assessment-of-Anti-Bias-Behavior.pdf.

Anti-Defamation League. (2017). *Establishing a safe learning environment*. The Anti-Defamation League's Curricular Resources. Retrieved March 1, from, https://www.adl.org/education/resources/tools-and-strategies/establishing-a-safe-learning-environment.

Anzaldúa, G. (1987). *Borderlands: La frontera* (Vol. 3). San Francisco: Aunt Lute.

Anzaldua, G., & Moraga, C. (Eds.). (1981). *This bridge called my back: Writings by radical women of color*. London: Persephone Press.

Apffel-Marglin, F., & PRATEC, (1998). *The spirit of regeneration: Andean culture confronting western notions of development*. New York: Zed Books.

Armstrong, J. (2006). Community: Sharing one skin. In J. Mander & V. Tauli-Corpuz (Eds.), *Paradigm wars: Indigenous peoples' resistance to globalization*. San Francisco: Sierra Club Books.

Aronson, R. (2015). *We: Reviving social hope*. Chicago, IL: University of Chicago.

Ash, S. L., & Clayton, P. H. (2009). Generating, deepening, and documenting learning: The power of critical reflection in applied learning. *Journal of Applied Learning in Higher Education, 1*, 25–48.

Association of American Colleges and Universities. (2012). *Liberal education and America's promise. An introduction to LEAP*. Retrieved December 18, 2012, from http://www.aacu.org/LEAP/index.cfm.

Association of American Colleges and Universities. (2013). *It takes more than a major: Employer priorities for college learning and student success*. Washington, DC: Hart Research Associates. Retrieved March 3, 2017, from https://www.aacu.org/sites/default/files/files/LEAP/2013_EmployerSurvey.pdf.

Astin, A. W., & Sax, L. J. (1998). How undergraduates are affected by service Participation. *Journal of College Student Development, 39*, 251–263.

Astin, A. W., Vogelgesang, L. J., Ikeda, E. K. & Yee, J. A. (2000). How service learning affects students. Higher Education Research Institute. Los Angeles, CA: University of California.

Atkinson, D. R., Morten, G., & Sue, D. W. (Eds.). (1989). *Counseling American minorities: A cross-cultural perspective* (3rd ed.). Dubuque, IA: William C. Brown.

Bacon, N. (2002). Differences in faculty and community partners' theories of learning. *Michigan Journal of Community Service Learning, 9*(1).

Barnhardt, R., & Kawagley, A. O. (2005). Indigenous knowledge systems and Alaska Native ways of knowing. *Anthropology & Education Quarterly, 36*(1), 8–23.

Battistoni, R., & Hudson, W. (Eds.). (1997). *Practicing democracy: Concepts and models of service-learning in political science*. Washington, DC: American Association for Higher Education.

Baumeister, R. F., & Leary, M. R. (1995). The need to belong: Desire for interpersonal attachments as a fundamental human motivation. *Psychological Bulletin, 117*, 497.

Baxter, L. A., & Montgomery, B. M. (1996). *Relating: Dialogues and dialectics*. New York: Guilford Press.

Beath, A. (2005). *Consciousness in action: The power of beauty, love and courage in a violent time*. New York, NY: Lantern Books.

Bell, L. A. (2016). *Teaching for diversity and social justice.* New York, NY: Routledge.

Berila, B. (2016). *Integration mindfulness into anti-oppression pedagogy.* New York, NY: Routledge.

Bernal, D. D., Elenes, C. A., Godinez, F. E., & Villenas, S. (Eds.). (2006). *Chicana/Latina education in everyday life: Feminista perspectives on pedagogy and epistemology.* Albany: New York Press.

Bickman, L., & Rog, D. J. (Eds.). (2008). *The Sage handbook of applied social research methods.* Thousand Oaks, CA: Sage Publications.

Bisignani, D. (2014). Transgressing intellectual boundaries begins with transgressing physical ones: Feminist community engagement as activist-apprentice pedagogy. In S. Iverson & J. James (Eds.), *Feminist community engagement: Achieving praxis* (pp. 93–111). New York, NY: Palgrave Macmillan.

Blanchard, L. W., Hanssmann, C., Strauss, R. P., Belliard, J. C., Krichbaum, K., Waters, E., et al. (2009). Models for faculty development: What does it take to be a community-engaged scholar. *Metropolitan Universities, 20*(2), 47–65.

Boss, J. A. (1994). The effect of community service work on the moral development of college ethics students. *Journal of Moral Education, 23*(2), 183–198.

Blouin, D. D., & Perry, E. M. (2009). Whom does service learning really serve? Community-based organizations' perspectives on service learning. *Teaching Sociology, 37*(2), 120–135.

Bowman, N., Brandenberger, J., Lapsley, D., Hill, P., & Quaranto, J. (2010). Serving in college, flourishing in adulthood: Does community engagement during the college years predict—Adult well-being? *Applied Psychology: Health and Well Being, 2*(1), 14–34.

Bowers, C. A. (2004). *Re-thinking Freire: Globalization and the environmental crisis.* New York, NY: Routledge.

Boyte, H. D., & Farr, H. (1997). The work of citizenship and the problem of service-learning. In R. Battistoni & W. Hudson (Eds.), *Experiencing citizenship: Concepts and models of service-learning in political science* (pp. 35–48). Sterling, VA: Stylus.

Bringing Theory to Practice. (2013). *The well-being and flourishing of students: Considering well-being, and its connection to learning and civic engagement, as central to the mission of higher education.* Washington DC: AAC&U.

Brown, B. (2010). *The gifts of imperfection: Let go of who you think you're supposed to be and embrace who you are.* Center City: Hazelden.

Butin, D. (2010). *Service-learning in theory and practice: The future of community engagement in higher education.* New York, NY: Palgrave Macmillan.

Butin, D. W. (Ed.). (2014). *Teaching social foundations of education: Contexts, theories, and issues.* New York, NY: Routledge.

Butin, D. W. (2003). Of what use is it? Multiple conceptualizations of service-learning within education. *Teachers College Record, 105*(9), 1674–1692.

Cajete, G. (2000). *Native science: Natural laws of interdependence.* Santa Fe, NM: Clear Light Publishers.

Calderon, J. Z. (Ed.). (2007). *Race, poverty, and social justice: Multidisciplinary perspectives through service learning.* Sterling, VA: Stylus Publishing.

Calleson, D. C., Kauper-Brown, J., & Seifer, S. D. (2005). *Community-engaged scholarship toolkit.* Seattle, WA: Community-Campus Partnerships for Health.

Carr, W., & Kemmis, S. (1986). *Becoming critical: Education knowledge and action research.* London: Falmer Press.

Cavallaro, C.C. (2016). Recognizing engaged scholarship in faculty reward structures: Challenges and progress. *Metropolitan Universities Journal, 2.*

Chung, L. (2017, January 27). The whole student: Intersectionality and well-being. *Building public trust in the promise of liberal education and inclusive excellence.* Annual Conference of the American Association of Colleges and Universities. San Francisco, CA.

Chung, L., & Ting-Toomey, S. (2011). *Understanding intercultural communication* (2nd ed.). Oxford: Oxford University Press.

Clifford, J., & Marcus, G. E. (1986). *Writing culture: The poetics and politics of ethnography.* University of California Press.

Cochrane, A. (2007). *Understanding urban policy: A critical approach.* Malden, MA: Blackwell Publishing.

Collins, P. H., & Bilge, S. (Eds.). (2016). *Intersectionality.* Malden, MA: Polity Press.

Collins, P. H. (1990). *Black feminist thought: Knowledge.* Routledge, New York, NY: Consciousness and the politics of empowerment.

Combahee River Collective. (1977). *The Combahee river collective statement.* Retrieved March 1, 2017, from www.circuitous.org/scraps/combahee.html.

Conn, J. (2016). *Personal communication.* Sierra Madre, CA.

Cooks, L., Scharrer, E., & Castaneda Paredes, M. (2004). Toward a social approach to learning in community service learning. *Michigan Journal of Community Service Learning, 10*(2).

Corn, S. (2015, 5 February). *Tessa Hicks Peterson: Social justice, yoga and awareness of inequalities,* Interview with Tessa Hicks Peterson. *Yoga Journal.*

Costa, A. L., & Kallick, B. (2000). *Discovering and exploring habits of mind. A developmental series.* Alexandria, VA: Association for Supervision and Curriculum Development.

Center for Courage and Renewal. (2017). *The circle of trust approach.* Retrieved March 10, 2017, from http://www.couragerenewal.org.

Cotton, D., & Stanton, T. K. (1990). Joining campus and community through service learning. *New Directions for Student Services, 50,* 101–110.

Cox, W. (2015, 21 August). *California: Land of poverty.* NewGeography. Retrieved March 1, 2017, from http://www.newgeography.com/content/005026-california-land-poverty.

Cremin, L. A. (1970). *American education: the colonial experience, 1607–1783.* New York, NY: Harper & Row.

Crenshaw, K. (1987). Demarginalizing the intersection of race and sex: A black feminist critique of antidiscrimination doctrine, feminist theory, and antiracist politics. *University of Chicago Legal Forum,* 1989, pp. 139–167.

Creswell, J. W. (2013). *Qualitative inquiry and research design: Choosing among five approaches.* Thousand Oaks, CA: Sage.

Crimes Rates in Pomona, CA. (2017). *City-data.com.* Retrieved February 27, 2017, from http://www.city-data.com/crime/crime-Pomona-California.html.

Crisp, G., & Cruz, I. (2009). Mentoring college students: A critical review of the literature between 1990 and 2007. *Research in higher education, 50*(6), 525–545.

Cross, W. (1991). *Shades of black: Diversity in African American identity.* Philadelphia, PN: Temple University Press.

Cruz, N., & Giles. D. E. (2000). Where's the community in service-learning? *Michigan Journal of Community Service Learning,* 28–34.

Daugherty, A. (2014). *From mindfulness to heartfulness: A journey of transformation through the science of embodiment.* Bloomington, IN: Balboa Press.

Delgado, F., & Gomez, F. (2003). *Knowledge and belief systems in Latin America.* In B. Haverkort, K. V. Hooft & W. Hiemstra (Eds.), *Ancient roots, new shoots, endogenous development in practice.* London: Zed Books.

Delworth, U. (1989). Identity in the college years: Issues of gender and ethnicity. *NASPA Journal, 26*(3), 162–166.

Denson, N., Vogelgesang, L., & Saenz, V. (2005). *Can service learning and a college climate of service lead to increased political engagement after college.* Higher Education Research Institute, UCLA.

Denzin, N. K., & Lincoln, Y. S. (2005). *The Sage handbook of qualitative research* (3rd ed.). Thousand Oaks, CA: Sage.

Denzin, N. K., & Lincoln, Y. S. (2011). *The Sage handbook of qualitative research.* Sage.

Desy, P. L. (2016, 17 February). Dis-ease: Healing term. *ThoughtCo.* Retrieve 2 December 2016.

Dewey, J. (1938). *Experience and education.* The Kappa Delta Pi lecture series, no. 10.

DiAngelo, R., & Sensoy, O. (2012). *Is everyone really equal? An introduction to key concepts in social justice education.* New York, NY: Teachers College Press.

Dick, B. (2000). *A beginner's guide to action research.* Retrieved June 3, 2004, from http://www.scu.edu.au/schools/gcm/ar/arp/guide.html.

Dorado, S., & Giles, D. E. (2004). Service-learning partnerships: Paths of engagement. *Michigan Journal of Community Service Learning, 9*, 25–37.

Driscoll, A., Holland, B., Gelmon, S., & Kerrigan, S. (1996). An assessment model for service-learning: Comprehensive case studies of impact on faculty, students, community, and institution. *Michigan Journal of Community Service Learning, 3*, 66–71.

Dunlap, M., Scoggin, J., Green, P., & Davi, A. (2007). White students' experiences of privilege and socioeconomic disparities: Toward a theoretical model. *Michigan Journal of Community Service Learning, 13*(2).

Ehrlich, T. (2009). *Engagement in civic work as spiritual development: An interview with Thomas Ehrlich.* Spirituality in Higher Education Newsletter, pp. 1–5.

Ellison, J., & Eatman, T. (2008). *Scholarship in public: Knowledge creation and tenure policy in the engaged university.* Syracuse, NY: Imagining America.

Elo, A., Ervasti, J., Kuosma, E., & Mattila, P. (2008). Evaluation of an organizational stress management program in a municipal public works organization. *Journal of Occupational Health Psychology, 13*(1), 10–23.

Eyler, J., Giles, D. E., & Schmiede, A. (1996). *A practitioner's guide to reflection in service-learning: Student voices and reflections.* Nashville, TN: Vanderbilt University.

Eyler, J., Giles, D. E., Jr., & Braxton, J. (1997). The impact of service-learning on college students. *Michigan Journal of Community Service Learning, 4*, 5–15.

Eyler, J., & Giles, D. E., Jr. (1999). *Where's the learning in service-learning?.* San Francisco, CA: Jossey-Bass.

Eyler, J. S. (2000). What do we most need to know about the impact of service-learning on student learning? *Michigan Journal of Community Service Learning* 11–17.

Eyler, J., Giles, D. E., Jr., Stenson, C. M., & Gray, C. J. (2001). *At a glance: What we know about the effects of service-learning on college students, faculty, institutions and communities, 1993–2000* (3rd ed.). Nashville, TN: Vanderbilt University.

Fernandes, L. (2003). *Transforming feminist practice; non-violence, social justice and the possibilities of a spiritualized feminism.* San Francisco: Aunt Lute Books.

Ferrari, J. R., & Worrall, L. (2000). Assessments by community agencies: How 'the other side sees service-learning. *Michigan Journal of Community Service Learning, 7*(1).

Finley, A. (2012a). *Making progress? What we know about the achievement of liberal education outcomes.* Washington, DC: AA&U.

Finley, A. (2012b). The joy of learning: The impact of civic engagement on psychosocial well-being. *Diversity and Democracy, 3*, 8–10.

Finley, A. (2013). Assessing well-being as a function of learning well. In Bringing theory to practice, *The well-being and flourishing of students: Considering well-being, and its connection to learning and civic engagement, as central to the mission of higher education* (p. 7). Washington, DC: AAC&U.

Finley, A., & McNair, T. (2013). *Assessing underserved students' engagement in high impact practices.* Washington, DC: AAC&U.

Flanagan, C., & Bundick, M. (2011). Civic engagement and psychosocial well-being in college students. *Liberal Education, Spring, 97*(2), 20–27.

Freeman, D., & Richards, J. C. (1996). *Teacher learning in language teaching.* Cambridge, MA: Cambridge University Press.

Freire, P. (1970). *Pedagogy of the Oppressed* (Myra Bergman Ramos, Trans.). New York, NY: Continuum Publishing.

Freire, P. (2006). *Pedagogy of the oppressed.* 30th anniversary edition. New York, NY: Continuum Publishing.

Freire Institute. (2015, 27 June). *Concepts used by Paulo Freire.* Retrieved May 28, 2016, from http://www.freire.org/paulo-freire/concepts-used-by-paulo-freire.

Freire, P., & Shor, I. (1987). *A pedagogy for liberation: Dialogues on transforming education.* Westport, CT: Bergin & Garvey.

Frenzel, F., & Koens, K. (2012). Slum tourism: Developments in a young field of interdisciplinary tourism research. *Tourism Geographies, 14*(2), 195–212.

Gaiafield Project. (2017). What is subtle activism? *Gaiafield Project: Subtle Activism for Global Transformation, para. 1.* Retrieved March 7, 2017, from http://gaiafield.net/what-is-subtle-activism/.

Galura, J., Pasque, P. A., Schoem, D., & Howard, J. (2004). *Engaging the whole of service-learning, diversity, and learning communities.* Ann Arbor, MI: OCSL Press.

Gallup Healthways *WellBeing Index.* (2017). Retrieved February 12, 2017, from http://www.gallup.com/poll/106756/galluphealthways-wellbeing-index.aspx.

Gannon, B., & Davies, S. (2012). Collective biography and the entangled enlivening of being. *International Review of Qualitative Research, 5,* 357–376.

Gartner, A., Greer, C., & Riessman, F. (Eds.). (1973). *After deschooling, what?.* New York, NY: Harper & Row.

Gelmon, S. B., Holland, B. A., Seifer, S. D., Shinnamon, A., & Connors, K. (1998). Community-university partnerships for mutual learning. *Michigan Journal of Community Service Learning, 5,* 97–107.

Gelmon, S. B., Holland, B., Driscoll, A., Spring, A., & Kerrigan, S. (2001). *Assessing service-learning and civic engagement: Principles and techniques.* Boston, MA: Campus Compact.

Gelmon, S. B., Jordan, C., & Seifer, S. D. (2013). Community-engaged scholarship in the academy: An action agenda. *Change: The Magazine of Higher Learning, 45*(4), 58–66.

Giles, D. E., Honnet, E., & Migliore, S. (1991). *Setting the agenda for effective research in combining service and learning in the 1990's.* Raleigh, NC: National Society of Experiential Education.

Giles, D. E., & Eyler, J. (1994). The impact of a college community service laboratory on students' personal, social, and cognitive outcomes. *Journal of adolescence, 17*(4), 327.

Ginwright, S. (2011). Hope, healing, and care: Pushing the boundaries of civic engagement for african american youth. *Liberal Education, 97*(2), 34–39.

Ginwright, S. (2015). *Hope and healing in urban education: How urban activists and teachers are reclaiming matters of the heart.* New York, NY: Routledge.

Glass, C. R., Doberneck, D. M., & Schweitzer, J. H. (2011). Unpacking faculty engagement: The types of activities faculty members report as publicly engaged scholarship during promotion and tenure. *Journal of Higher Education Outreach and Engagement, 15*(1), 7–30.

Glassick, C. E., Huber, M. T., & Maeroff, G. I. (1997). *Scholarship assessed: Evaluation of the professoriate.* San Francisco, CA: Jossey-Bass.

Gómez-Quintero, J. D. (2015). La colonialidad del ser y del saber: la mitologización del desarrollo en América Latina. *El Ágora USB, 10*(1), 87–105.

Gramsci, A. (1971). *Selections from the prison notebooks.* New York, NY: International Publishers.

Gray, M. J., Ondaatje, E. H., & Zakaras, L. (1999). *Combining service and learning in higher education: Learn and serve America, higher education.* Santa Monica, CA: RAND.

Greene, D., & Diehm, G. (1995). Educational and service outcomes of a service integration effort. *Michigan Journal of Community Service Learning, 2,* 54–62.

Hale, C. R. (2008). *Engaging contradictions: Theory, politics, and methods of activist scholarship.* Oakland, CA: University of California Press.

Hall, N. (1997). Creativity and Incarceration: The purpose of art in a prison culture. In D. Gussak & E. Virshup (Eds.), *Drawing time: Art therapy in prisons and other correctional settings* (pp. 25–41). Chicago, IL: Magnolia Street Publishers.

Hall, S. (1997). *Representation: Cultural representations and signifying practices* (Vol. 2). Thousand Oaks, CA: Sage.

Hanh, T. N. (2003). *Creating true peace: Ending violence in yourself, your family, your community, and the world.* New York: Free Press.

Hanson, R. (2009). *Buddha's brain: The practical neuroscience of happiness, love, and wisdom.* Oakland, CA: New Harbinger Publications.

Haraway, D. J. (2001). "Gender" for a Marxist dictionary: The sexual politics of a word. *Women, gender, religion: A reader* (pp. 49–75). New York, NY: Palgrave Macmillan.

Harding, S. G. (1987). *Feminism and methodology: Social science issues.* Bloomington, IN: Indiana University Press.

Harper, S. R. (2009). Race-conscious student engagement practices and the equitable distribution of enriching educational experiences. *Liberal Education, 95*(4), 38–45.

Harper, S. R., Harris, F., III, & Mmeje, K. (2005). A theoretical model to explain the overrepresentation of college men among campus judicial offenders: Implications for campus administrators. *NASPA Journal, 42*(4), 565–588.

Harvey, A. (2017). What is sacred activism. *Andrew Harvey Institute for Sacred Activism.* Retrieved March 7, 2017, from http://www.andrewharvey.net/sacred-activism/

Harward, D. W. (2012). *Civic provocations.* Washington, DC: Bringing Theory to Practice.

Harward, D. W. (Ed.). (2016). *Well-being and higher education: A strategy for change and the realization of education's greater purposes.* Washington, DC: Bringing Theory to Practice.

Helms, J. (1990). *Black and white identity development: Theory, Research and Practice.* Westport, CT: Greenwood.

Hess, D. J., Lanig, H., & Vaughan, W. (2007). Educating for equity and social justice: A conceptual model for cultural engagement. *Multicultural Perspectives, 9*(1), 32–39.

Hesse-Biber, S. N. & Piatelli, D. (2012). The feminist practice of holistic reflexivity. In S. N. Hesse-Biber (Ed.), *Handbook of feminist research: Theory and praxis* (2nd ed., p. 2). Thousand Oaks, CA: Sage.

Hicks, T. (2005). *The interconnected community: Lessons from the Andes on ecological regeneration and interculturalism.* Unpublished thesis. Claremont, CA: Claremont Graduate University.

Hicks, T. (2009). *Engaged scholarship and education: A case study on the pedagogy of social change.* Unpublished Dissertation. Claremont, CA: Claremont Claremont Graduate University.

Honnet, E. P., & Poulsen, S. J. (1989). *A wingspread special report.* Racine, WI: The Johnson Foundation.

hooks, b. (1989). Choosing the margin as space of radical openness. *Framework: Journal of Cinema and Media, 36*, 15.

hooks, b. (1994). *Teaching to transgress: Education as the practice of freedom.* New York, NY: Routledge.

hooks, b. (2000). *All about love: New visions.* New York, NY: William Morrow.

hooks, b. (2003). *Teaching community: A pedagogy of hope* New York, NY: Routledge.

hooks, b. (2014). *Black looks: Race and representation.* New York, NY: Routledge.

hooks, b. (2016, 20 April). *Dialogue featuring bell hooks and Parker J. Palmer.* De Pere, WI: St. Norbert College.

Hoy, W. (2012). School characteristics that make a difference for the achievement of all students: A 40-year odyssey. *Journal of Educational Administration, 50*(1), 76–97.

Hoy, W. K., & Tschannen-Moran, M. (1999). Five faces of trust: An empirical confirmation in urban elementary schools. *Journal of school leadership, 9*, 184–208.

Hurtado, S., Ruiz, A., & Whang, H. (2012). Advancing and assessing civic learning: New results from the diverse learning environments survey. *Diversity & Democracy, 15*, 10–12.

Illich, I. (1971). *Deschooling society*. New York, NY: Harper and Row.

Inside-Out Prison Exchange Program. 2017. *Inside-out prison exchange program: Social change through transformative education*. Retrieved March 10, 2017, from http://www.insideoutcenter.org/.

Ishizawa, J. (2006). *From Andean cultural affirmation to Andean affirmation of cultural diversity—Learning with the communities in the Central Andes*. Dag Hammarskjold Foundation.

ITK and NRI. (2006). *Negotiating research relationships with inuit communities: A guide for researchers*. In S. Nickels, J. Shirley & G. Laidler (Eds.), *Inuit Tapiriit Kanatami*. Ottawa and Iqaluit: Nunavut Research Institute.

Iverson, S. V. D., & James, J. H. (2014). *Feminism and community engagement: An overview*. In *Feminist community engagement: Achieving praxis* (pp. 9–27). Palgrave Macmillan US.

Iyer, R. N. (1991). *The essential writings of Mahatma Gandhi*. USA: Oxford University Press.

Jacoby, B. (Ed.). (2003). *Building partnerships for service-learning*. San Francisco: John Wiley & Sons.

James, J. H. (2014). *Conclusions: Re-visioning community engagement as feminist praxis*. In S. V. D. Iverson & J. H. James (Eds.), *Feminism and community engagement: An overview. In Feminist Community Engagement: Achieving Praxis* (pp. 193–203). Palgrave Macmillan US.

Jorge, E. (2003). Outcomes for community partners in an unmediated service-learning program. *Michigan Journal of Community Service Learning, 10*, 28–38.

Keith, N. Z. (2005). Community service learning in the face of globalization: Rethinking theory and practice. *Michigan Journal of Community Service Learning, 11*(2), 5–24.

Keith, N. Z. (1998). Community service for community building: The school-based service corps as border crossers. *Michigan Journal of Community Service Learning, 4*, 86–96.

Keith, M. (1985). The irony of service: Charity, project, and social change in service-learning. *Michigan Journal of Community Serivce Learning, 2*, 19–32.

Kelley, R. D. G. (2002). *Freedom dreams: The black radical imagination*. Boston, MA: Beacon Press.

Kemmis, S., McTaggart, R., & Nixon, R. (2014). *Doing critical participatory action research* (6th ed.). New York, NY: Springer.

Kendrick, J. R., Jr. (1996). Outcomes of service-learning in an introduction to sociology course. *Michigan Journal of Community Service Learning*, 72–81.

Keyes, C. L. (2002). The mental health continuum: From languishing to flourishing in life. *Journal of Health and Social Behavior*, 207–222.

Keyes, C. L. (2009). The Black–White paradox in health: Flourishing in the face of social inequality and discrimination. *Journal of Personality*, 1677–1706.

Keyes, C. L., & Haidt, J. (Eds.). (2003). *Flourishing: Positive psychology and the life well-lived*. Washington, DC: American Psychological Association.

Kezar, A., & Rhoads, R. (2001). The dynamic tensions of service-learning in higher education: A philosophical perspective. *The Journal of Higher Education, 72*, 148–171.

Khanmalek, T. (2013). Outro: A healing justice retrospective. *Nineteen Sixty Nine: An Ethnic Studies Journal, 2*(1).

Khouri, H. (2010, April 6). Guest lecture: "Conscious activism". In *Healing ourselves in healing our communities course*. Claremont, CA: Pitzer College.

Khouri, H. (2016, April 27). Guest lecture: "Trauma and justice". In *Healing arts and social change course*. Norco, CA: California Rehabilitation Center.

Kiely, R. (2005). A transformative learning model for service-learning: A longitudinal case study. *Michigan Journal of Community Service Learning, 12* (1).

King, M. L., Jr., & West, C. (2016). *The radical king*. Boston, MA: Beacon Press.

Kinzie, J. (2012). High-impact practices: Promoting participation for all students. *Diversity Democracy, 15*(3), 13–14.

Kirkness, V. J., & Barnhardt, R. (1991). First nations and higher education: The four R's-respect, relevance, reciprocity, responsibility. *Journal of American Indian Education* 1–15.

Kivel, P. (2007). Social service or social change. In Incite (Eds.), *The revolution will not be funded: Beyond the non-profit industrial complex* (pp. 129–149). Cambridge, MA: South End Press.

Klassen, R. M., Perry, N. E., & Frenzel, A. C. (2012). Teachers' relatedness with students: An underemphasized component of teachers' basic psychological needs. *Journal of Educational Psychology, 104*(1), 150.

Klein, N. (2016, 9 November). It was the democrats embrace of neoliberalism that won it for Trump. *The Guardian*. Retrieved February 12, 2017, from https://www.theguardian.com/commentisfree/2016/nov/09/rise-of-the-davos-class-sealed-americas-fate.

Kretzmann, J. P., & McKnight, J. (1993). *Building communities from the inside out*. Evanston, IL: Center for Urban Affairs and Policy Research, Neighborhood Innovations Network.

Kuh, G. D. (2008). *Excerpt from high-impact educational practices: What they are, who has access to them, and why they matter*. Washington DC: Association of American Colleges and Universities.

Kuh, G. D., Jankowski, N., Ikenberry, S. O., & Kinzie, J. (2014). *Knowing what students know and can do: The current state of student learning outcomes assessment in US colleges and universities.* Urbana, IL: University of Illinois and Indiana University, National Institute for Learning Outcomes Assessment (NILOA).

Ladislaus, M. S., & Kincheloe, J. L. (1999). *What is indigenous knowledge? Voices from the academy.* New York, NY: Routledge.

Lather, P. (1986). Research as praxis. *Harvard Educational Review, 56*(3), 257–278.

Lave, J., & Wenger, E. (1991). *Situated learning: Legitimate peripheral participation.* Boston, MA: Cambridge University Press.

Lewis, T. L. (2004). Service learning for social change? Lessons from a liberal arts college. *Teaching Sociology, 32*(1), 94–108.

Levine, P. A. (1997). *Waking the tiger: Healing trauma.* Berkeley, CA: North Atlantic Books.

Levine, P. A. (2010). *Healing trauma: A pioneering program for restoring the wisdom of your body.* Boulder, CO: Sounds True Publishing.

Little, D. (2007). False consciousness. *Understanding Society: Innovative thinking about a global world.* Retrieved February 12, 2017, from http://www-personal.umd.umich.edu.

Lipsitz, G. (2006). *The possessive investment in whiteness: How white people profit from identity politics.* Philadelphia, PA: Temple University Press.

Longley, M. J., Driscoll, A., Gelmon, S. B., Holland, B., Kerrigan, S., Spring, A., et al. (1998). *Assessing the impact of service learning: A workbook of strategies and methods.* Center for Academic Excellence. Portland, OR: Portland State University.

Lorde, A. (1988). *Burst of light: Essays by Audre Lorde.* Ithaca, NY: Firebrand Books.

Lorde, A. (1984). *Sister outsider: Essays and speeches by Audre Lorde.* Berkeley, CA: Crossing Press.

Mabry, J. B. (1998). Pedagogical variations in service—Learning and student outcomes: How time, contact, and reflection matter. *Michigan Journal of Community Service Learning, 5,* 32–47.

Mabry, L. (1999). *Portfolios plus: A critical guide to alternative assessment.* Corwin Press, Inc.

Macy, J., & Brown, M. Y. (1998). *Coming back to life: Practices to reconnect our lives, our world.* Gabriola Island, BC: New Society Publishers.

Madison, D. S. (2011). *Critical ethnography: Method, ethics, and performance.* Thousand Oaks: Sage.

Mamidipudi, A., & Gajjala, R. (2008). Juxtaposing handloom weaving and modernity: Building theory through praxis. *Development in Practice, 18*(2), 235–244.

Mander, J., & Tauli-Corpuz, V. (eds.). (2006). *Paradigm wars: Indigenous peoples' resistance to globalization.* Sierra Club Books.

Mankiller, W. (2004). *Every day is a good day: Reflections by contemporary indigenous women.* Golden, CO: Fulcrum Publishing.

Manuel, Z. J. (2015). *The way of tenderness: Awakening through race, sexuality, and gender.* Somerville, MA: Wisdom Publications.

Markus, G. B., Howard, J. P., & King, D. C. (1993). Integrating community service and classroom instruction enhances learning: Results from an experiment. *Educational evaluation and policy analysis, 15*(4), 410–419.

Martin, C. E. (2010). *Do it anyway: The new generation of activists.* Beacon Press.

Marullo, S., & Edwards, B. (2000). From charity to justice the potential of university-community collaboration for social change. *American Behavioral Scientist, 43*(5), 895–912.

McIntosh, P. (1989). *'White privilege: Unpacking the invisible knapsack' peace and freedom magazine,* (pp. 10–12). Philadelphia, PN, July/August.

McIntosh, P. (2009). *White privilege: An account to spend.* Minnesota: The Saint Paul Foundation.

McKnight, J. (1995). *The careless society: Community and its counterfeits.* New York, NY: Basic Books.

Miron, D., & Moely, B. E. (2006). Community agency voice and benefit in service-learning. *Michigan Journal of Community Service Learning, 12*(2).

Mexico Solidarity Network. (2017). "Zapatismo" *Autonomous University of Social Movements.* Retrieved January 27, 2017, from http://www.mexicosolidarity. org.

Minh-ha, T. T. (1989). *Woman, native, other: Writing postcoloniality and feminism.* Bloomington, IN: Indiana University Press.

Miron, D., & Moely, B. E. (2006). Community agency voice and benefit in service-learning. *Michigan Journal of Community Service Learning,* 27–37.

Mitchell, T. D. (2008). Traditional vs. critical service-learning: Engaging the literature to differentiate two models. *Michigan Journal of Community Service Learning, 14*(2).

Moely, B. E., Furco, A., & Reed, J. (2008). Charity and social change: The impact of individual preferences on service-learning outcomes. *Michigan Journal of Community Service Learning, 15*(1), 37–48.

Moore, M. (Ed.). (2006). *Eating fire, tasting blood: Anthology of the American Indian holocaust.* New York: Thunder Mouth Press.

Moraga, C., & Anzaldúa, G. (Eds.). (2015). *This bridge called my back: Writings by radical women of color* (4th ed.). New York, NY: Suny Press.

Morton, K. (1995). The irony of service: Charity, project and social change in service-learning. *Michigan Journal of Community Service Learning, 2*(1), 19–32.

Mosha, R. S. (1999). The inseparable link between intellectual and spiritual formation in indigenous knowledge and education: A case study in Tanzania. In M. S. Ladislaus & J. L. Kincheloe (Eds.), *What is indigenous knowledge? Voices from the academy* (pp. 209–223). New York, NY: Routledge.

Myers-Lipton, S. J. (1998). Effect of a comprehensive service-learning program on college students' civic responsibility. *Teaching Sociology*, 243–258.

National Survey on Student Engagement. (2008). *Promoting engagement for all students: The imperative to look within, 2008 results.* Retrieved December 20, 2012, from http://nsse.iub.edu/NSSE_2008_Results/docs/withhold/NSSE2008_Results_revised_11-14-2008.pdf.

Nickels, S., Shirley, J., & Laidler, G. (eds.). (2006). *Negotiating research relationships with inuit communities: A guide for researchers.* Inuit Tapiriit Kanatami and Nunavut Research Institute: Ottawa and Iqaluit.

Nicotera, N., Brewer, S., & Veeh, C. (2015). Civic activity and well-being among first-year college students. *The International Journal of Research on Service-Learning and Community Engagement*, 3(1).

Noel, J. (2014). *Developing sustainable community engagement by repositioning programs into communities.* In S. V. D. Iverson & J. H. James (Eds.), *Feminist community engagement: Achieving Praxis* (pp. 175–191). Palgrave Macmillan US.

Nussbaum, M. (2004). Liberal education and global community. *Liberal Education, 90*(1), 42–47.

Obama, B. (2004). *Keynote address.* 2004 Democratic National Convention, FleetCenter, Boston, MA. Retrieved March 1, 2017.

Oden, R. S., & Casey, T. A. (2007). Advancing service learning as a transformative method for social justice work. In J. Z. Calderon (Ed.), *Race, poverty, and social justice: Multidisciplinary perspectives through service learning* (pp. 3–22). Sterling, VA: Stylus Publishing.

OEHHA. (2017). *CalEnviroScreen.* OEHHA Science for a better California. Retrieved November 3, 2016, from https://oehha.ca.gov/calenviroscreen.

On Being with Krista Tippett. (2015a). radio podcast. *The Inner Landscape of Beauty.* Interview with John O'Donahue, Minneapolis. Retrieved 1 September, 2016.

On Being with Krista Tippett. (2015b). radio podcast. *Opening the Question of Race to the Question of Belonging.* Interview with John Powell, Minneapolis. Retrieved 22 April, 2016.

On Being with Krista Tippett. (2016a, 18 February). radio podcast. *The Resilient World We're Rebuilding Now.* Interview with Patrisse Cullors and Robert Ross. Minneapolis. Retrieved February 23, 2016.

On Being with Krista Tippett, (2016b, 10 November). radio podcast. *Is America Possible?* Interview with Vincent Harding, Minneapolis. Retrieved November 17, 2016.

Outterson, K., Selinger, E., & Whyte, K. (2011). Poverty tourism, justice, and policy: Can ethical ideals form the basis of new regulation. *Public Integrity*, Winter, 12, *14*(1), 39–50.

Overbaugh, R. C., & Schultz, L. (2012). *Bloom's taxonomy*. Retrieved August 7, 2016, from http://www.odu.edu/educ/roverbau/Bloom/blooms_taxonomy.htm.

Page, C. (2010, 5 August). Transforming wellness & wholeness. *INCITE blog reflections from detroit: Transforming wellness and wholeness*, web log post. Retrieved March 1, 2017, from https://inciteblog.wordpress.com/2010/08/05/reflections-from-detroit-transforming-wellness-wholeness/.

Palmer, P. J. (1992). Divided no more: A movement approach to educational reform. *Change: The Magazine of Higher Learning*, *24*(2), 10–17.

Palmer, P. J. (2000). *Let your life speak: Listening for the voice of vocation*. San Francisco, CA: Jossey-Bass.

Palmer, P. J. (2009). *A hidden wholeness: The journey toward an undivided life*. San Francisco, CA: John Wiley & Sons.

Pancer, S. M., & Pratt, M. W. (1999). Social and family determinants of community service involvement in Canadian youth. In M. Yates & J. Youniss (Eds.), *Roots of civic identity: International perspectives on community service and activism in youth* (pp. 32–55). New York, NY: Cambridge University Press.

Partners for Better Health. (2017). *Build health challenge*. Retrieved November 3, 2017, from http://p4bhealth.org/build-health-challenge/.

Pasque, P. A. (2008). *Bridging civic engagement and mental health*. Proceedings from the National Symposium for Civic Engagement and Mental Health.

Peterson, T. H. (2009). Engaged scholarship: Reflections and research on the pedagogy of social change. *Teaching in Higher Education*, *14*(5), 541–552.

Peterson, T. H., Dolan, T., & Hanft, S. (2010). Partnering with youth organizers to prevent violence: An analysis of relationships, power, and change. *Progress in Community Health Partnerships: Research, Education, and Action*, *4*(3), 235–242.

Peterson, T. H. (2015). Reviving and revising the civic mission: A radical re-imagining of 'civic engagement'. *Metropolitan Universities*, *25*(3).

Peterson, T. H. & Khouri, H. (2015). *The trauma of injustice*. Online Course, Off the Mat and Into the World.

Phillips, S. (2015). Prison ethnography and activism. *Anthropology and mass incarceration*. Annual Meetings of the American Anthropological Association, Denver, CO.

Pitzer College. (2010). Educational effectiveness review. *Pitzer College Report for Western Association of Schools and Colleges (WASC)*. Retrieved March 7, 2016, from http://pitweb.pitzer.edu/institutional-research/wasc-accreditation/.

Pitzer College. (2013). *History and mission*. Retrieved March 19, 2013, from http://www.pitzer.edu/about/index.asp.

Pitzer College. (2016a). *Graduation requirements: Social responsibility praxis student learning outcomes and course criteria.* Claremont, CA: Pitzer College.

Pitzer College. (2016b). *Graduation requirements: Social justice theory student learning outcomes and course criteria.* Claremont, CA: Pitzer College.

Pitzer College. (2016c). *Graduation requirements: Local-global intercultural understanding student learning outcomes and course criteria.* Claremont, CA: Pitzer College.

Pitzer College. (2016d). *Faculty handbook amendment to tenure and rewards policy.* Claremont, CA: Pitzer College.

Polin, D. K., & Keene, A. S. (2010). Bringing an ethnographic sensibility to service-learning assessment. *Michigan Journal of Community Service Learning, 16*(2), 22–37.

Pompa, L., & Crabbe, M. (2004). *The inside-out prison exchange program: Exploring issues of crime and justice behind the walls.* Instructor's Manual. Rev. ed. Philadelphia: Temple University. http://www.insideoutcenter.org.

powell, j. a. (2015). *Racing to justice: Transforming our conceptions of self and other to build an inclusive society.* Bloomington, IN: Indiana University Press.

Prakash, M. S. (1999). Indigenous knowledge systems—Ecological literacy through initiation into people's science. In L. M. Semali & J. L. Kincheloe (Eds.), *What is indigenous knowledge? Voices from the academy* (pp. 157–178). New York and London: Falmer Press.

Prilleltensky, I., & Prilleltensky, O. (2006). *Promoting well-being: Linking personal, organizational, and community change.* New Jersey: John Wiley & Sons.

Razack, S. (1998). *Looking white people in the eye: Gender, race, and culture in courtrooms and classrooms.* University of Toronto Press.

Reich, J. (2013). *The well-being and flourishing of students: Considering well-being, and its connection to learning and civic engagement, as central to the mission of higher education.* Washington DC: Bringing Theory to Practice.

Rendón, L. (2014). *Sentipensante (sensing/thinking): Educating for wholeness, social justice, and liberation.* Sterling, VA: Stylus.

Reynolds, A. L., & Pope, R. L. (1991). The complexities of diversity: Exploring multiple oppressions. *Journal of Counseling and development, 70*(1), 174–180.

Riessman, C. K. (2005). Exporting ethics: A narrative about narrative research in South India. *Health, 9*(4), 473–490.

Richards, K. C. (1997). Views on globalization. In H. L. Vivaldi (Ed.), *Australia in a global world.* North Ryde, NSW: Century.

Rilke, R. M. (1903). *Letters to a young poet.* London: Norton and Company.

Roberts, P. (1998). Extending literate horizons: Paulo Freire and the multidimensional word. *Educational Review, 50*(2), 105–114.

Roessingh, H., & Elgie, S. (2014). From thought, to words, to print: Early literacy development in grade 2. *Alberta Journal of Educational Research, 60*(3).

Ryff, C. D., & Keyes, C. L. M. (1995). The structure of psychological well-being revisited. *Journal of personality and social psychology, 69*(4), 719.

San Bernardino County. (2015). *Community Indicators Report.* Retrieved February 1, 2017, from http://cms.sbcounty.gov/Portals/21/Resources% 20Documents/CIR_2015_Report.pdf.

Sandy, M. (2007). *Community voices: A California campus compact study on partnerships.* Hayward, CA: California Campus Compact.

Sax, L. J., Astin, A. W., & Avalos, J. (1999). Long-term effects of volunteerism during the undergraduate years. *The review of higher education, 22*(2), 187–202.

Sax, L. (1997). The benefits of service: Evidence from undergraduates. *Educational record* 25.

Schreiner, A. L. (2010). The "thriving quotient": A new vision for student success. *American College Personnel Association* and Wiley Periodicals.

Schutz, A., & Gere, A. R. (1998). Service learning and English studies: Rethinking 'public' service. *College English, 60*(2), 129–149.

Semali, L., & Kincheloe, J. L. (1999). *What is indigenous knowledge? Voices from the academy.* New York, NY: Routledge.

Schmidt, A., & Robby, M. A. (2002). What's the value of service-learning to the community? *Michigan Journal of Community Service Learning, 9*(1), 27–33.

Shabazz, R. (2014, 11 October). 12 *major corporations benefiting from the prison industrial complex.* Elementary Genocide. Retrieved March 14, 2017, from http://elementarygenocide.com/12-major-corporations-benefiting-from-the-prison-industrial-complex.

Shapiro, D. F. (2012). Collaborative faculty assessment of service-learning student work to improve student and faculty learning and course design. *Michigan Journal of Community Service Learning, 19*(1), 44–58.

Shavelson, R. J., Schneider, C. G. & Shulman, L. S. (2007). *A brief history of student learning assessment: How we got where we are and a proposal for where to go next.* Association of American Colleges and Universities.

Shiva, V. (1993). *Monocultures of the mind: Perspectives on biodiversity and biotechonology.* London: Zed.

Shor, I. (1992). *Culture wars: School and society in the conservative restoration.* Chicago, IL: University of Chicago Press.

Shor, I. (2012). *Empowering education: Critical teaching for social change.* Chicago, IL: University of Chicago Press.

Siegel, D. J. (2007). *The mindful brain: The Neurobiology of well-being.* New York, NY: WW Norton & Co.

Singhal, A. (2004). *Entertainment-education through participatory theater: Freirean strategies for empowering the oppressed.* Entertainment-education and social change: History, research, and practice, pp. 377–398.

Simons. (2017, 6 March). Happiness minister takes job seriously. *Los Angeles Times* 1.

Simons, L., Fehr, L., Black, N., Hoogerwerff, F., Georganas, D., & Russell, B. (2011). The application of racial identity development in academic-based service learning. *International Journal of Teaching and Learning in Higher Education*, *23*(1), 72–83.

Smith, L. T. (1999). *Decolonizing methodologies: Research and indigenous peoples.* London: Zed books.

Stanton, T. K. (1987, 18 October). *Liberal arts, experiential learning and public service: Necessary ingredients for socially responsible undergraduate education.* Annual Conference of the National Society for Internships and Experiential Education.

Stanton, T. K., Giles, D. E., & Cruz, N. I. (1998). *Service learning: A movement's pioneers reflect on its origins, practice, and future.* San Francisco: Jossey Bass.

Steinberg, S. R., & Kincheloe, J. L. (1998). *Students as researchers: Creating classrooms that matter.* London: Falmer Press.

Steinman, E. (2011). "Making space": Lessons from collaborations with tribal nations. *Michigan Journal of Community Service Learning, 18*(1), 5–19.

Strage, A. (2004). Long-term academic benefits of service-learning: When and where do they manifest themselves? *College Student Journal, 38*(2), 257.

Strand, K. J., Cutforth, N., Stoecker, R., Marullo, S., & Donohue, P. (2003). *Community-based research and higher education: Principles and practices.* San Francisco, CA: Wiley.

Stevenson, B. (2016, 29 March). American injustice: Mercy, humanity and making a difference. *Criminal justice symposium.* Claremont, CA: Pomona College.

Stoecker, R. (2005). *Research methods for community change: A project-based approach* (2nd Ed.). Thousand Oaks, CA: Sage.

Sudbury, J., & Okazawa-Rey, M. (2015). *Activist scholarship: Antiracism, feminism, and social change.* New York, NY: Routledge.

Swaner, L. E. (2005). Educating for personal and social responsibility: A review of the literature. *Liberal Education, 91*(3), 14–21.

Swaner, L. E. (2007). Linking engaged learning, student mental health and well-being, and civic development: A review of the literature. *Liberal Education, 93*(1), 16–25.

Sweitzer, H. K., & King, M. A. (2009). *The successful internship: Personal, professional, and civic development.* Australia: Thomson Brooks.

Sweitzer, H. K., & King, M. A. (2014). *The successful internship: Personal, professional, and civic development in experiential learning* (4th ed.). Belmont, CA: Brooks/Cole Cengage.

Tatum, B. D. (1992). Talking about race, learning about racism: The application of racial identity development theory in the classroom. *Harvard Educational Review, 62*(1).

Téllez, M. (2005). Doing research at the borderlands: Notes from a Chicana feminist ethnographer. *Chicana/Latina Studies 46–70.*

The National Task Force on Civic Learning and Democratic Engagement. (2012). *A crucible moment: College learning and democracy's future.* Washington, DC: Association of American Colleges and Universities.

Theatre of the Oppressed. (2017). *International theatre of the oppressed website.* Jana Sanskriti Internatoinal Research and Resource Institute. Retrieved June, 6, 2016, from http://jsirri.org.

Thoits, P. A., & Hewitt, L. N. (2001). Volunteer work and well-being. *Journal of health and social behavior,* pp.115-131.

Ting-Toomey, S. (2015). *Identity negotiation theory.* The International Encyclopedia of Interpersonal Communication, 1–10.

Thom, K. C. (2016). *8 steps towards building indispensability (instead of disposability) culture.* Retrieved February 10, 2017, from http://everydayfeminism.com.

Tisdell, E. J. (1998). Poststructural feminist pedagogies: The possibilities and limitations of feminist emancipatory adult learning theory and practice. *Adult Education Quarterly, 48*(3), 139–156.

Tomlinson, B., & Lipsitz, G. (2013). American studies as accompaniment. *American Quarterly, 65,* 1–30.

Tufts College, Medford, MA .(2012). *Tisch college of citizenship and public service. Student civic learning outcomes.* Received December 18, 2012, from http://activecitizen.tufts.edu/wp-content/uploads/learning_outcomes_13.pdf.

University of Michigan. (2014). *LARA/LARI and empathy.* Ann Arbor, MI: The Program on Intergroup Relations.

University of Michigan. (2016). *Deepening dialogue through "affirming inquiry".* Ann Arbor, MI: The Program on Intergroup Relations.

Unnecessary Evils. (2008, 3 November). Attributing words. Retrieved March 7, 2017, from http://unnecessaryevils.blogspot.com/2008/11/attributing-words.html#links.

Vaccaro, A. (2009). Racial identity and the ethics of service learning as pedagogy. In S. Evans, C. Taylor, M. Dunlap, & D. Miller (Eds.), *African Americans and community engagement in higher education* (pp. 119–134). Albany, NY: SUNY Press.

Valenzuela, A. (1999). *Subtractive schooling: U.S.-Mexican youth and the politics of caring.* New York, NY: State University of New York Press.

Van Der Kolk, B. (2014). *The body keeps the score.* New York, NY: Viking.

Van Gelder, S. (2016). *The radical work of healing: Fania and Angela Davis on a new kind of civil rights activism.* Yes! Magazine. Spring. Retrieved March 1, 2017, from http://www.yesmagazine.org/issues/life-after-oil/the-radical-work-of-healing-fania-and-angela-davis-on-a-new-kind-of-civil-rights-activism-20160218.

Vasquez, G. R. (1998). Education in the modern west and the Andean culture. In F. Apffel-Marglin & PRATEC (Eds.), *The spirit of regeneration: Andean culture confronting western notions of development* (pp. 172–192). New York: Zed Books.

Verba, S., Schlozman, K. L. & Brady, H. E. (1995). *Voice and equality: Civic voluntarism in American politics*. Harvard University Press.

Verjee, B., & Butterwick, S. (2014). Conversations from within: Critical race feminism and the roots/routes of change. In S. Iverson & J. James (Eds.), *Feminist community engagement: Achieving praxis* (pp. 31–51). New York, NY: Palgrave Macmillan.

Vernon, A., & Ward, K. (1999). Campus and community partnerships: Assessing impacts and strengthening connections. *Michigan Journal of Community Service Learning, 6,* 30–37.

Villenas, S., Godinez, F., Delgado Bernal, D., & Elenes, A. (2006). *Chicana/Latina education in everyday life: Feminista perspectives on pedagogy and epistemology*. New York, NY: SUNY Press.

Walker, A. (2014). Activism is my price for living on the planet. *Alice Walker: Beauty in truth.* Documentary film, written and directed by Pratibha Parmar, Kali Films. Aired 7 February, PBS.

Ward, K., & Wolf-Wendel, L. (2000). Community-centered service learning moving from doing for to doing with. *American Behavioral Scientist, 43*(5), 767–780.

Washington, J. M. (Ed.). (1986). *A testament of hope: The essential writings and speeches of Martin Luther King, Jr.*. New York, NY: Harper Collins.

Watkins, M., & Shulman, H. (2008). *Towards psychologies of liberation*. New York, NY: Palgrave Macmillan.

West, C. (1999). *The cornel west reader*. New York: Basic Civitas.

Westheimer, J., & Kahne, J. (2004). What kind of citizen? The politics of educating for democracy. *American Educational Research Journal, 41*(2), 237–269.

Whitney, B. C., & Clayton, P. H. (2011). *Research on and through reflection in international service learning* (pp. 145–187). International Service Learning: Conceptual frameworks and research.

Wilson, S. (2008). *Research is ceremony: Indigenous research methods*. Black Point, Nova Scotia: Fernwood Publishing.

Wolf, M. (1992). *A thrice-told tale: Feminism, postmodernism, and ethnographic responsibility*. San Jose, CA: Stanford University Press.

Youniss, J., & Yates, M. (1997). *Community service and social responsibility in youth*. Chicago, IL: University of Chicago Press.

Złotkowski, E. (1998). A service learning approach to faculty development. *New Directions for Teaching and Learning* 81–89.

Zimmerman, K., Pathikonda, N., Salgado, B., & James, T. (2010). *Out of the spiritual closet: Organizers transforming the practice of social justice*. Oakland, CA: Movement Strategy Center.

INDEX

CPSIA information can be obtained
at www.ICGtesting.com
Printed in the USA
LVHW080903300619
622769LV00013B/348/P